WALTER BENJAMIN'S
ANTIFASCIST EDUCATION

WALTER BENJAMIN'S ANTIFASCIST EDUCATION

From Riddles to Radio

Tyson E. Lewis

Published by State University of New York Press, Albany

© 2020 State University of New York

All rights reserved

No part of this book may be used or reproduced in any manner whatsoever without written permission. No part of this book may be stored in a retrieval system or transmitted in any form or by any means including electronic, electrostatic, magnetic tape, mechanical, photocopying, recording, or otherwise without the prior permission in writing of the publisher.

For information, contact State University of New York Press, Albany, NY
www.sunypress.edu

Library of Congress Cataloging-in-Publication Data

Names: Lewis, Tyson E., author.
Title: Walter Benjamin's antifascist education : from riddles to radio / Tyson E. Lewis.
Description: Albany : State University of New York Press, 2020. | Includes bibliographical references and index.
Identifiers: LCCN 2019036255 | ISBN 9781438477510 (hardcover : alk. paper) | ISBN 9781438477534 (ebook)
Subjects: LCSH: Benjamin, Walter, 1892–1940. | Education—Philosophy. | Educational sociology. | Fascism and education. | Democracy and education.
Classification: LCC LB775.B322 L48 2020 | DDC 370.1—dc23
LC record available at https://lccn.loc.gov/2019036255

10 9 8 7 6 5 4 3 2 1

Contents

Acknowledgments	vii
Introduction	1

Part I

Instruction	31
Radio Broadcasts	63
Children's Theater	93

Part II

Collections	113
Cityscapes	133
Cinema	155
Riddles	179
Conclusion	201
Notes	211
Bibliography	235
Index	245

Acknowledgments

I would like to thank Matthew Charles for his careful reading of an early version of this book and his copious suggestions. The result is, without a doubt, indebted to his interest and expertise in the educational potentialities of Benjamin's work. Igor Jasinski was generous enough to help ensure the accuracy of German translations and give feedback on the form and content of the book throughout its evolution.

INTRODUCTION

A Constellation of Educational Forms

In the summer of 2018 amid mounting scandals in the Donald Trump presidency, the disturbing separation of undocumented families at the United States–Mexico border, and a rather pathetic yet highly visible "Unite the Right 2" rally in Washington, DC, organized by neo-Nazi activists, a book chapter I had recently written on the topic of white privilege and education suddenly and for a brief and intense moment became a lightning rod of controversy. It started with a request for an interview from the online "journal" Campus Reform (CR). The website was founded by the Leadership Institute, which has an explicit agenda to increase the number of conservatives in government and the media. According to Media Bias/Fact Check, CR rates as "strongly biased" toward conservative views, is prone to using loaded words to characterize liberal or leftist professors, and publishes misleading reports. CR actively polices higher education, openly shaming and mocking individual professors deemed liberal or leftist (and thereby a threat to "American" values). In my own case, a staff writer contacted me via email, perhaps to discuss the chapter with me, or to obtain a comment, or at the very least, to be able to say (at the end of the eleventh-hour window she had given me to reply) that "the author could not be reached for comment" before going live; I declined to participate (by not responding). Giving CR and its "reporter" any response seemed to me to merely legitimate the source as a serious new outlet, and while they went through the motions of reaching out to me, this was an exchange in which I did not want any part. Without my response, CR published a critique of my chapter that was absolutely ridiculous. They clearly did not understand its discipline-specific content, and rather than researching further, they doubled-down on their misreading. The interpretation CR settled on was so far from the actual argument of the text that at first I laughed it off; I never could have imagined what happened next. Within hours, the CR story had gone viral, appearing in alt-right twitter feeds, blogs, and a host of other fake news sites across the internet that cater to extremist, fringe elements associated to various degrees with white nationalism and/or right-wing reactionaries. I started receiving dozens and dozens of hate emails, each clearly using CR's initial misreading as a jumping off point for their own wildly imaginative interpretations.

Still in its first days on CR's website, activity surrounding the essay did not abate, and kept amplifying to the point that by that afternoon, my chapter (or, at least, what my chapter had been interpreted as symbolizing for the alt-right in this moment) was featured on Rush Limbaugh's radio program. Like CR, Limbaugh had no idea what my essay was actually about, and his staff never reached out to do any fact-checking. Limbaugh himself was simply scrolling through a feed of whichever alt-right posts were getting lots of action in that moment, and there was the mention of my article, trending near the top, stirring up lots of angry responses that he simply magnified by bashing the article, my own education, my looks, my purported intellectual elitism, and so on, all the while using the air time as an opportunity to repeat my name and current university position as many times as possible. This caused another round of hate mail, which flooded into my university email account and escalated to alt-right "watchdog" groups that called the dean of my college demanding that I be fired. My Academia.edu page received over 500 hits within a matter of hours, and became another outlet for people to post derogatory messages (I ended up shutting down my site, as the flow of hate mail became absolutely overwhelming). While I had read the first few hate messages in a state of bemused detachment, I was increasingly appalled and distressed by the threats, intimidation, and bigotry. As the escalation continued, university leadership published a statement in support of independent scholarship and, in the end, campus police had been brought in to investigate those messages that threatened bodily harm and made me fear for my and my family's personal safety.

The tone and focus of these hate emails varied: some were nearly unintelligible verbally—simply strings of curses all piling up to produce a very clear affective message of hate; others critiqued me as both product and perpetuator of the liberal university; and a large number were overtly racist and, at times, homophobic. As a white, heteronormative, male professor, the emails I received from (white) hate groups simultaneously wanted to identify with my whiteness while distancing themselves from me as a race traitor. Here is one verbatim quote out of dozens I received: "Why don't you move down here to New Orleans and enjoy the diversity of black savage behavior. A little cock sucker like you would really enjoy these thick lipped savages on a daily basis and they like commie philosophy, you know-taking from the productive and giving it to them. But I know you snowflake fags stay inside your college walls with the rest of you clowns." The implication of such assaultive speech is that the United States is predominantly white, and that blacks, homosexuals, and communists are unwanted invaders who threaten to destabilize the real America. Here is another verbatim version of this theme: "Why dont you turn your illegitimate white degree in. Step down from your illegitimate white job and make room for a minority. You leave this white created world, turn off your white created electricity, get in your white invented car and drive down one of those white engineered roads. Maybe come to georgia and let stick my white foot up your ass. I would recommend Africa, yea go there, very few white people." In this email, the world and all technical achievements are deemed the result of whites. Blacks are effectively written out of the history of the United States in one fell swoop. Because only whiteness is associated with technical progress and "civilization," any critical reflection on whiteness as privilege or power is equated with becoming a race traitor, and transitively, a traitor to the United States, which is a *white* country. The strange irony here is that while whiteness is deemed to be so powerful, noble, and strong, it also appears utterly fragile, vulnerable, and constantly under siege. As a race traitor, I am subsequently instructed to deport myself to Africa. In short, nationalism is mixed with vitriolic racism and xenophobia toward difference, which is inherently viewed with suspicion as a harbinger of potential intellectual degeneration.

Other emails attempted to appeal to me on intellectual grounds, recommending readings that could help my classes become more "fair and balanced." Take for instance one email that suggested I read the works of Comte Joseph Arthur de Gobineau, a nineteenth-century French aristocrat who is infamous for his attempts to legitimize racism through scientific means. The concerned citizen conveniently photocopied and scanned several pages of texts by de Gobineau and even underlined passages, including the following excerpt concerning the Aryan race: "Everything great, noble, or fruitful in the works of man on this planet, in science, art, and civilization, derives from a single starting point, is the development of a single germ; . . . it belongs to one family alone, the different branches of which have reigned in all the civilized countries of the universe . . . History shows that all civilization derives from the white race. . . ." It would appear that contemporary research in the social and physical sciences denouncing this perspective as nothing less than racist superstition might be dismissed by supporters of Gobineau's thesis on a priori grounds because of the perceived liberal bias in universities today. The rather unusual upshot of this thesis is that only "research" conducted by white men without the danger of blowback from colleagues of color (or, even worse, female colleagues of color!) and the censorship of political correctness can be trusted as "objective"—hence, the turn to nineteenth-century pseudoscience. The appearance of scientific rigor, objectivity, and legitimacy thus transforms into its opposite: a deeply disturbing retreat from intellectual investigation into a dogmatic, pseudoscientific past immune to all revision or scrutiny.

While much of this rhetoric in these emails can be explained using conceptual tools inherited from critical race theory,[1] I also began to feel that the unique blending of populism, nationalism, racism, armored masculinity, and anti-intellectualism expressed in these emails was, in some way, connected to historical forms of twentieth-century fascism. Considering the increasing influence of far-right political parties across Europe (including, but not limited to, France, Germany, Austria, and Italy), not to mention the 2014 election of India's Prime Minister Narendra Modi and the 2018 election of Brazilian president Jair Bolsonaro, fascism is no longer an out-of-date term relegated to the distant past. In the United States, discussions of fascism might seem particularly foreign, yet, as will be discussed below, Trumpian-style politics bear an uncanny resemblance to authoritarian precursors.

There are essentially two questions here. First, is there a connection between current manifestations of far-right extremism, pushback against diversity work and civil liberties, and fascist predecessors? And second, if so, what might be the best resources for combating the toxicity of fascist politics? It is my contention in this book that Walter Benjamin's work contains within it a strong antifascist potentiality for democratic education, broadly conceptualized. This does not mean that Benjamin himself was aware of this potentiality.[2] Instead, it means that we who have inherited his work have to read it anew, given the current historical moment, in order to discover the outlines of a new kind of educational practice.

Fascism Then and Now

Fascism is a notoriously difficult concept to define. There are some who suggest it is a term that only applies to Italian *fascismo* at a specific historical moment in the twentieth century, while others attempt to generalize fascism in order to take into account a variety of political movements that do not clearly fall into democratic or Marxist paradigms (e.g., Nazism). Generic theories of fascism draw interpretive inspiration from a wide variety of theoretical traditions, including Max Weber's theory of ideal types, Ludwig Wittgenstein's theory of family resemblances, and Deleuzian affect theory.[3] In this section, I will narrow my focus to theories of fascism that emerged from within the Institute for Social Research, also known as the Frankfurt School, especially during the late thirties and forties in the United States. I do so for two reasons. First, while Benjamin was never an official member of the Frankfurt School, he was certainly affiliated with it, and his work influenced various members (in particular Theodor W. Adorno). As such, the Frankfurt School's engagement with fascism is within the general orbit of Benjamin's own reflections on the topic and provides a useful benchmark for highlighting Benjamin's unique insights into both fascism and antifascist education. Second, as I will illustrate, the Frankfurt School's general approach to fascism as *both* a historico-political reality and a psychosocial potentiality is highly influential to this day, both in terms of diagnosing fascism and in offering up solutions (especially in terms of education). In particular, I will highlight the ongoing relevancy of Adorno's depiction of the protofascist personality type while also pointing toward a complex array of political and economic triggers, then and now, responsible for creating fascist political movements. I will then pivot toward Benjamin, who, on my reading, offers a more embodied interpretation of fascism that is particularly appropriate for understanding and ultimately combating today's fascist revival. The goal is not to give the impression that Nazism is alive and well in the United States, but rather to chart the unique features of the fascist personality still operative (although somewhat modified) within a society prepared to vote figures like Donald Trump into the presidency; in turn, I suggest that Adorno's groundwork in this area ought to be supplemented with Benjamin's more embodied, innervative, and mimetic understanding of education.

Perhaps the most comprehensive place to start thinking about historical fascism is the work of Franz Neumann. As Neumann argued in his classic work *Behemoth: The Structure and Practice of National*

Socialism, Nazism emerged as a "solution" to the catastrophic political, economic, and social crises facing Germany in the year 1932. In response, the Nazi party rose to power by promoting autocratic and charismatic leadership, total military mobilization, a totalitarian form of capitalism, control of mass media, suppression of labor power, resurgent imperialist expansionism, a collapse of democratic systems, vicious attacks against "liberal" institutions and conventions, and populist, race-based fanaticism. The ideology underlying National Socialism was, as Neumann describes it, incoherent and constantly shifting. It was fueled largely by a set of nonrational concepts such as blood, community, and the folk that were loosely strung together through various propaganda campaigns to appeal to the disenchanted masses. While incoherent, this ideology was nevertheless ballasted by two clear "magical beliefs" in "leadership adoration" and the "supremacy of the master race."[4] Together, these formed the epicenter of National Socialist thought. The former led to the eventual eclipse of the German constitution and the investment of power in the figure of the Führer as the unity of the party, the people, and the state. Under the charismatic leadership of the Führer, the economic structure of Germany also shifted, producing a blend of command and monopolistic economies that did not fully resolve the contradictions in capitalism (as in socialism) so much as minimize conflict between cartels, military leaders, and bureaucrats through imperialist and ideological means. With the resulting cult surrounding Hitler, we see how "charisma has become absolute, calling for obedience to the leader not because of his useful functions, but because of his alleged superhuman gifts."[5] The second magical belief in racial superiority was closely linked to the first. The absolute authority of the leader did not rest on political or economic or even cultural grounds so much as on the *racial* superiority of the Germanic people. Neumann summarizes the centrality of racialized thinking as follows: "Long before Hitler, the political bond among free men tended to give way to the natural bond among racial Germans."[6] The position of Germans at the pinnacle of the racial hierarchy, in turn, justified and activated the imperial project of National Socialism while downplaying internal conflicts. For instance, unifying the German people against "external" degeneration served to incorporate the working classes into a larger, national project, and thus prevented class warfare from breaking out. The concurrent rise in antisemitism only helped bolster the Aryan identity by providing a convenient scapegoat for many of Germany's ills. The result, for Neumann, was a political system that lacked any equivalent in history, except perhaps Hobbes's concept of the stateless and lawless behemoth.

Eric Fromm, another Frankfurt School member, turned toward social psychology in order to understand the complex relationship between individual libidinal structures and larger social and political structures that led to Nazism. While Neumann's Marxist reading of fascism focused on social determinates (fascism as an ideological smokescreen to prevent class struggle), Fromm's methodology was more subtle, rejecting the exclusivity of either economic or psychological approaches. As Fromm summarizes, "Nazism is a psychological problem, but the psychological factors themselves have to be understood as being molded by socio-economic factors; Nazism is an economic and political problem, but the hold it has over the whole people has to be understood on psychological grounds."[7] Instead of individual pathologies, Fromm was interested in "social character" or the "essential nucleus of the character structure of most members of a group which has developed as the result of the basic experiences and mode of life common to that group."[8] Hence the need for a social psychology of fascism—a dynamic understanding of character as poised between social forces and individual libidinal forces. For instance, post–World War I Germans were seized by feelings of profound individual insignificance and powerlessness. While these feelings were not the causes of Nazism, they were the psychological predispositions which enabled Nazism to develop and take hold of the populous with such force. Stated simply, for Fromm, retreat into Nazi fascism was one way of escaping from the burden of subjective insecurity and aloneness emerging out of financial and political uncertainties plaguing Germany in the interwar period. As compensation for these ills, fascism offered the allure of sadistic and masochistic power over others and a narrative of strength, security, and glory.

Although many of the major fascist regimes were ultimately defeated at the end of World War II, members of the Frankfurt School nevertheless worried that the psychological predisposition for fascism might outlive its institutional forms and policies and return in liberal democracies. At the end of *Escape from Freedom*, Fromm ominously warns, ". . . there is no greater mistake and no graver danger than not to see that in our own society [the United States] we are faced with the same phenomenon that is fertile soil for the rise of Fascism anywhere. . . ."[9] Several years before Fromm's prediction, in an article from the *New York Times* dated September 12, 1938, Professor Halford E. Luccock of the Divinity School of Yale University was quoted as issuing a similar concern regarding the possibility of the spread of fascism in the United States. Luccock wrote, "When and if fascism comes to America it will not be labeled 'made in Germany'; it will not be marked with a swastika; it will not even be called fascism; it will be called, of course, 'Americanism.'"[10] Luccock found the seeds of fascism within a preexisting, highly authoritative strain of home-grown nationalism. The very same nationalism that had already fueled the genocide of indigenous peoples across North America, justified slavery through highly questionable pseudoscience, and encouraged numerous imperialist projects throughout the Western hemisphere. In the 1940s, the American Jewish Committee's antisemitism project funded important Frankfurt School empirical studies conducted in the United States, including *Prophets of Deceit: A Study of the Techniques of the American Agitator* (1949) by Leo Lowenthal and Norbert Guterman and *The Authoritarian Personality* (1950) by Theodor W. Adorno, Else Frenkel-Brunswik, Daniel J. Levinson, and R. Nevitt Sanford. Together, we can read these empirical studies as concrete analyses of the relationship between certain sadomasochistic personality traits and magical beliefs defining fascism within an American context. The first study focused on leadership adoration of the American agitator while the second focused on the psychological precursors necessary to invest in such leadership and in the belief in a master race. Together the studies outlined the dangerous crossover between liberal democracy and fascism in the industrialized West.

For instance, Adorno's groundbreaking social psychology of the authoritarian personality was a concentrated attempt to understand the constitutive dimensions of the fascist personality responsive to and triggered by a mobile set of economic, social, and political factors underlying what Luccock referred to as Americanism. While there are certainly differences between Adorno's work in this area and Fromm's, it is important to note a clear continuity or shared methodological interest in the dynamics existing between individual psychology and the social totality. For Adorno, like Fromm, the fascist personality type was not merely an individual problem. Instead, it could be "regarded as a product of interaction between the cultural climate of prejudice and the 'psychological' responses to this climate."[11] In this sense, the fascist "type" was not an abstraction of personality from a given historical context. Instead, the two were mutually reinforcing, emerging out of a dynamic process. Stated differently, the psychological structure that made the individual susceptible to fascism was not merely a problem with ego development but was itself already reflective of broader political, social, and economic factors. In fact, there is a feedback loop between self and society that makes fascism particularly daunting as a political and educational issue. Adorno summarizes, "It may well be the secret of fascist propaganda that it simply takes men [sic] for what they are: the true children of today's standardized mass culture, largely robbed of autonomy and spontaneity. . . . Fascist propaganda has only to *reproduce* the existent mentality for its own purposes;—it need not introduce a change—and the compulsive repetition which is one of tits foremost characteristics will be at one with the necessity for its continuous reproduction."[12] Fascism adds nothing new, it merely taps into and channels existing, unconscious tendencies found in mass culture. This makes it particularly effective but also efficient, and thus potentially threatening.

As Adorno and colleagues summarize in the introduction to *The Authoritarian Personality*, "The major concern was with the *potentially fascistic* individual, one whose structure is such as to render him particularly susceptible to anti-democratic propaganda [and who would] readily accept fascism if it should become a strong or respectable social movement."[13] To measure unconscious, fascist potentials, Adorno and his research team developed questionnaires that were distributed to participants in California, Oregon, and Washington, DC. The responses received were then ranked in terms of four scales that measured antisemitism, ethnocentrism, conservative ideological commitment, and fascistic indicators (including conventionalism, submissiveness, aggression, anti-intraception, superstition/stereotypical thinking, hardness and coldness, destructiveness, projectivity, and sexual repression). *The Authoritarian Personality* did not make any claims concerning the general prevalence of the protofascistic personality type throughout American society. Instead, it offered up a detailed typology of authoritarian and antiauthoritarian traits found within a specific population of white, native-born, gentile, middle-class Americans. Yet, the research, as a whole, did sound a cautionary note that hints of a fascistic potential found in the limited population studied that could become a mass phenomenon given the right social, political, and economic factors.

With the risk of being overly reductive, I argue that Adorno's description of the protofascist personality can be distilled down to three interlocking and mutually reinforcing dimensions: manipulativeness, hardness, and coldness. Briefly summarized, manipulativeness is equal parts (1) instrumentalization and (2) reification. Instrumentalization is the seduction of efficiency for doing things with little regard for social or political consequences (a rage for organization and standardization as ends in themselves, even if there are exceptional human or environmental costs). Spontaneous relations between individuals, in turn, take on the character of "mechanical rigidity."[14] In this way, relations become increasingly impersonal to the point where people can be reified into things, stereotypes, and/or data points (all of which can be easily manipulated without having to contemplate possible effects on *actual* lives). The ideal of being hard is an "indifference toward pain"[15] that enables cruelty to take hold and become a common occurrence. Hardness constructs boundaries, both between self and others and between the self and its own senses. The body becomes immunized against shock, becoming numb to the outside world. These boundaries are essential for repelling feelings of attachment to anything that might, if threatened, cause pain or remorse in the psyche. Indeed, Hitler himself described the ideal fascist education as "a harsh one," where "weakness must be stamped out" in order to produce a "violent, masterful, dauntless, cruel younger generation" with "nothing weak and tender about it."[16] The heroic ideal here is one in which students are prepared for eternal war, struggle, and domination without mercy. The resulting cruelty induces coldness or a freezing over of libidinal investments into self and others. For those who have become cold, "whatever of the ability to love somehow survives in them they must expend on devices."[17] These devices include technological gadgets but also devices of manipulation such as empty catchphrases and rabble-rousing slogans. Adorno points out that love, in such situations, is no longer invested in individual relationships or in ethical ideals. Instead, love is rerouted into abstract notions such as the "nation." And when this happens, there is no longer empathy toward the suffering, only a will to dominate and exert power and influence over those who are considered part of the out-group, and therefore inferior. To cite Hitler again, a child's "entire education and development has to be directed at giving him the conviction of being absolutely superior to the others."[18] "Freezing" also refers to the inability to think through the contradictions or the nonidentical within concepts. The result is a normalization of "stereotypical thinking"[19] about the world, reducing complexity to simple, one-dimensional formulae or conspiracy theories. Together, manipulativeness, hardness, and coldness speak to a condition Adorno refers to as the "inaccessibility to experience" differences that might contradict one's preexisting beliefs.[20] Appeals to experience (now rendered inaccessible) cannot help but fall short of dislodging stereotypes once they have rigidified and frozen over. The result is a disposition toward aggressive nationalism, leadership adoration, and belief in a master race.

Importantly, in the introduction to *The Authoritarian Personality*, Adorno and his colleagues point out that "The major influences upon personality development arise in the course of child training" both in formal and informal settings.[21] In "Education after Auschwitz," Adorno offers a further justification for focusing on education in antifascist efforts. In a rather pragmatic move, Adorno argues that while fascism is a social phenomenon, immediate attention must be given to its "subjective dimension,"[22] especially as manipulativeness, hardness, and coldness take root in early childhood. Education, on this reading, is the dialectical hinge that connects the subjective and objective dimensions of lived experience, and as such is an important terrain in the battle against the development of fascistic personality types. In sum, Adorno places an enormous amount of pressure on the school for promoting antifascist and prodemocratic forms of thinking. "The pathos of the school today, its moral import, is that in the midst of the status quo it alone has the ability, if it is conscious of it, to work directly toward the debarbarization of humanity."[23]

Schools can either promote or prevent the consolidation of protofascist, authoritarian personality types. But to fulfill the latter, teachers have to struggle against the rather barbaric history of the school, still latent within its structure, rules, and taboos. For instance, through his examination of the educational unconscious, Adorno reveals that the notion of the teacher emerges alongside the image of the "flogger." In the novel *The Trial*, Franz Kafka "presents the teacher as the physically stronger who beats the weaker."[24] Beyond naming a mere literary trope, this observation actually reveals the obscene underside of schooling, connecting teaching and learning to the kind of hardness and coldness easily susceptible to fascist proclivities. In Adorno's analysis, pervasive taboos against the profession of teaching have ancient roots in the fear of the manipulativeness and hardness of corporal punishment. As Adorno ominously warned, "The image of the teacher repeats, no matter how dimly, the extremely affect-laden image of the executioner."[25] If schools are the last bastion for hope against the rising tide of barbarism, they also contain within themselves the very same barbaric potentials they have to fight against. This barbaric potential also manifests itself in the various competitive relations between children in school, including rampant bullying. Drawing on his own childhood, Adorno recalls, "The outbreak of the Third Reich did, it is true, surprise my political judgment, but not my unconscious fear. . . . The five patriots who set upon a single schoolfellow, thrashed him and, when he complained to the teacher, defamed him a traitor to the class—are they not the same as those who tortured prisoners to refute claims by foreigners that prisoners were tortured?"[26] The seeds of fascism have been sown in the brutal relations between schoolchildren, and merely await the right social, political, and economic triggers to grow to maturity. The teacher has to overcome these barbaric remnants linking school life to violence by advocating for the cultivation of critical self-reflection and, subsequently, self-determination in children. Self-reflection is essential to break down the manipulativeness, hardness, and coldness that cause violent lashing out. Adorno summarizes, "One must labor against this lack of reflection, must dissuade people from striking outward without reflecting upon themselves. The only education that has any sense at all is an education toward critical self-reflection."[27] The autonomy of a critically aware individual is the minimal subjective condition for resisting fascism. Once critical self-reflection is taken out of the equation, protofascist psychology becomes a self-fulfilling prophesy where social forces produce the psychological infrastructure (manipulativeness, hardness, and coldness) that is necessary to further perpetuate reification and standardization. Without the ability to critically reflect on one's self in relation to broader social, political, and economic trends, self-determination becomes an impossibility and democracy itself is put at risk. For Adorno, the lesson is clear: "The single genuine power standing against the principle of Auschwitz is autonomy, if I might use the Kantian expression: the power of reflection, of self-determination, and not cooperating."[28] The individual, relying only on his or her own reason, is, for Adorno, the last remaining image of the educated citizen capable of raising a single, solitary voice against fascism. The power of reason to overcome manipulativeness, hardness, and coldness is perhaps nowhere more apparent than when Adorno speculates that "If they [fascists] would stop to reason for a second, the whole performance would go to pieces, and they would be left to panic [at the loss of their irrational fantasy structure]."[29] It is up to education for and through critical self-reflection to end the innervation of libidinal energies into destructive social movements and authoritarian personalities.

In the end, Adorno calls on teachers to become aware of subjective potentialities for fascism and to take measures in early childhood education to prevent the students' potentialities from hardening into the authoritarian personality structure. As cited above, Adorno sounds distinctly Kantian in these moments. Indeed, Adorno approvingly cited Kant's famous essay "What Is Enlightenment?," arguing for an education that produces "maturity and responsibility" in the use of critical reason to combat the irrational barbarism of fascism.[30] Maturity combats fascist tendencies by promoting "self-reflection," whereby "racial problems . . . are viewed within historical and sociological perspective and thus seen to be open to rational insight and change, instead of being hypostatized in a rigidly irrational manner."[31] Preventing reification of otherness and difference culminates in a rejection of antiminority stereotypes and an opening up of the cold and hardened heart to sympathy. Importantly, maturity thus combines reason with feeling. The link that unites the two in the mature individual is a profound sense of justice. Instead of reverence for authority as an end in itself or the fetishization of things over people, the mature, reasonable individual instead pursues justice, even if this means criticizing authority or questioning the order of things. Here, a new educational ideal emerges: the mature, rational, and sympathetic individual as opposed to the manipulative, hard, and cold fascist.

In his survey of German educational reform after World War II, Adorno was struck by the lack of interest in the concept of maturity.[32] Instead, he found an emphasis on authority and tutelage, where commitment to authority was demanded regardless of justification or lack thereof. In this model, the student becomes habituated into systematic manipulation as a social norm, internalizing the forces that expect submission at all costs, echoing of school's own barbaric past. When responsibility toward authority as an end in itself dominates schooling practices, passivity and adaptability to conditions beyond one's understanding and one's control are elevated to the level of educational goods. Such relations then play themselves out in miniature between schoolchildren, who reproduce hierarchical relations of power. Maturity, on the other hand, employs reason to achieve autonomy from the overdependence on authority. This does not imply that authority ought to be rejected outright in antifascist educational practice. Adorno was keen to point out that certain forms of authority based on expert knowledge are important for developing autonomy in children, as autonomy can only manifest itself through an act of (critical) detachment. Stated differently, one can only experience the emergence of self in relation to and (in some sense) against an authority figure. The point here is that fascist education overreaches the reasonable bounds of authority in education, triggering the potentiality for authoritarian excesses in young children. Only education for maturity can combat the full actualization of an authoritarian personality. While certain assumptions made by Adorno might strike the reader as somewhat lagging behind developments in social theory, Adorno nevertheless provides a solid foundation for democratic education through his twin emphases on diagnostic critique (beginning with the dialectics of social psychology) and emancipation (through critical self-reflection and self-determination). In fact, many contemporary educational theorists on the left have returned to Adorno for inspiration in continuing the struggle for self-determination and democracy against ongoing strands of fascism.[33]

Likewise, there has been a resurgence of interest in reevaluating Adorno's social psychology in light of growing fears of a neofascist, global revival. Peter E. Gordon has argued that while it might be too simplistic to return to Adorno's psychological profile of the authoritarian personality (for methodological and historical reasons), nevertheless, Adorno's general insight into fascism as a social symptom (rather than a mere personal pathology) helps us locate emergent forms of quasi- or neofascism in the most crass impulses circulating throughout a neoliberal culture industry—an industry that revels in self-promotion, the performance of libidinal release (even if it only serves to produce new blockages), stereotyping, sensationalism, hyperbolic outrage, fake news, mediatized consumerism, and thoughtless, one-dimensional branding.[34] Gordon warns that Trumpism, for instance, is not isolated to particular groups (on the right or the left), but is indicative of broader cultural, political, social, economic, and psychological trends that are pervasive throughout American culture and might very well act as stimuli for triggering a resurgence of the authoritarian personality. I agree in full with Gordon's analysis, and would only add that his tempered appraisal of Adorno's original insights do not discount the continued relevance of manipulativeness, hardness, and coldness outlined above but rather prompt us to ask how these manifest themselves given current technological, social, political, and economic changes.[35]

William E. Connolly also draws connections between Adorno's work and what he refers to as "aspirational fascism" under Trumpism.[36] For Connolly, it is important to sketch out connections between Hitler's and Trump's rhetorical styles, notions of charismatic, authoritarian leadership, and deployment of racist beliefs and affects through a genealogical approach to fascism without collapsing one into the other. Connolly's analysis grounds fascist tendencies in current American cultural, political, and economic shifts, including the mobilization of the disenfranchised white working-class with false promises; the increase of paranoia over the Islamic faith in particular and immigrants in general; the rise of a white evangelical/capitalist machine; the singling out of the media as *the* enemy of the people; and the emboldening of the alt-right by normalizing their agenda and spreading rigid, hateful stereotypes, armored masculinity, and appeals to loyalty through narcissistic and charismatic leadership. I would add that we should not downplay the ongoing roll of anti-Semitism within this new breed of fascism. Globally, antisemitic sentiments coupled with hate crimes have been on the rise in countries such as France and Germany.[37] The United States is no exception. In 2017, the Anti-Defamation League reported a 57 percent rise in antisemitic incidents in the United States (the largest single-year increase on record),[38] culminating in the massacre of eleven people in the Tree of Life synagogue in Pittsburgh. There is little doubt that while Trump might not be directly responsible for such attacks against Jewish citizens, his rhetoric has emboldened and mainstreamed the views of extremists. For instance, Trump's use of the term *globalist* to refer to enemies such as Gary Cohn (former director of Trump's National Economic Council) is easily interpreted by his neofascist supporters as a dog whistle for a Jew loyal to international Zionism.[39] Certainly Adorno and his notion of the authoritarian personality is important in formulating this up-to-date diagnosis of aspirational fascism, yet Connolly is also critical of Adorno, arguing that more attention ought to be paid to the embodied dimensions of fascism (old and new). For instance, in his response to the challenges of aspirational fascism, Connolly moves beyond Adorno's emphasis on individuated, critical self-reflection, suggesting instead a new form of "affective communication" or "affective contagion" that is horizontal, pluralistic, and economically egalitarian.[40] The pluralism Connolly promotes taps into and takes advantage of the plasticity of instincts, drives, and desires against the libidinal machinery of fascism, fostering new, resistant habits and forms of collective embodiment. Also moving decisively away from Adorno's idealization of the autonomous, mature thinker, Lia Haro and Romand Coles add to the comparison between classical and contemporary fascisms by arguing that there are shared characteristics, but that Trumpism has taken on new features, including an intensification and normalization of shock politics, authoritarian leadership without ideological commitments, amplification of threats and violence via social media, hyperprerogative power, and so on. In response, Haro and Coles—not unlike Connolly—call for a series of insurgent actions including (but not limited to) a new "full-bodied politics" that heightens and expands receptive senses as well as new practices that generate "alter-shocks"[41] to an already shocking system. Thus, changes in fascist politics demand a counterinsurgency located within, not against, the forms of affective communication fueling this social pathology. In this sense, Adorno might have successfully diagnosed the problem of the protofascist psychology, but he lacked a solution that would address the ways in which such psychology affects and is affected by embodied sensations and preconscious, habituated comportments arising from within new modes of social media. At this point, I would like to pivot to Benjamin, who might very well act as a new foundational figure in the fight against neofascism, especially in relation to a full-bodied *educational* response to manipulativeness, coldness, and hardness.

A Turn toward Benjamin's Constellational Curriculum

Although antifascist social and educational discussions have revolved around Adorno's work in this area, Benjamin also has invaluable lessons for contemporary audiences concerned with educational interventions into current, quasi- or neofascist tendencies. If Adorno emphasized the social psychology of fascism and the need for critical, self-reflexive maturity as an educational ideal to combat these potentialities, Benjamin offers a rather different approach, one much more focused on the body, bodily practices, perception, and a new notion of a diasporic connectivity to others (human and nonhuman) as they emerge within yet against the barbarism of fascism. Stated simply, given fascism's grip on the body and its affective pull (as Connolly, and Haro and Coles argue), we might not be able to *think* our way out of it (as Adorno had hoped).

Although it is certainly true that Benjamin's theory of fascism is not as robust as Adorno's, we can see convergences and divergences between their analyses by looking at Benjamin's review of the book *War and Warriors* edited by Ernst Jüger, a leading voice on the German Right during the Weimar Republic. Here Benjamin pinpoints certain characteristics that define an emerging "dependable fascist class warrior."[42] First, technology becomes a "fetish of doom,"[43] an instrument of mass murder through which war takes on the "countenance of recordsetting."[44] War becomes a statistical science of tallying total losses and predicting possible casualties—a cold and cynical process where technology effaces nature, replacing it with the most destructive and abstract qualities of German idealistic thought. War itself becomes endless, cultic, and eternal, a "manifestation of the German nation,"[45] and is accompanied by an inability to face loss. The character of the fascist class that emerges out of these conditions is equal parts "hardness, reserve, and implacability."[46] Thus far, Benjamin's analysis sounds like a precursor to Adorno's assessment. Both agree on the broad strokes of the fascist psychology, or authoritarian personality. Yet it is in the solution that Benjamin shows a distinct difference from his colleague. He writes, "Until Germany has exploded the entanglement of such Medusa-like beliefs that confront it in these essays, it cannot hope for a future. Perhaps the word 'loosened' would be better than exploded,' but this is not to say it should be done with kindly encouragement or with love, both of which out of place here; nor should the way be smoothed for argumentation, for that wantonly persuasive rhetoric of debate. Instead, all the light that language and reason still afford should be focused upon that 'primal experience' from whose barren gloom this mysticism of the death of the world crawls forth on its thousand unsightly conceptual feet."[47] Emphasis here should be placed on the limits of love and/or the reasoned argumentation for addressing the problem, and the subsequent turn to the *primal experience* that forges fascist manipulation, hardness, and coldness. This deep level of experience cannot be disrupted or dislodged through critical reasoning alone.

In this book, I will discuss various educational forms from within Benjamin's variegated corpus of writings, each offering up unique pedagogical potentialities for cultivating an antifascist educational life. What unites these forms is an interest in unsettling the hardness, coldness, and manipulative tendencies of fascist social psychology as they exist in preconscious perceptual norms, bodily habits, relations to self and others, and perceptual relations toward media, technology, and even language. As Alison Ross has argued,[48] Benjamin had a consistent yet leery interest in various aesthetic forms throughout his work. Ross highlights his suspicion of the totalizing function of mythic forms in his early essay on Goethe's *Elective Affinities* and his attempts to redeem the notion of form through his reflections on allegory, mimesis, and ultimately dialectical images. I use the term *form* to mean any sensuous or nonsensuous shape or configuration that has the potential to make something knowable, visible, audible, recognizable, or legible. As such, educational forms point toward an ability (potentiality) within something that would otherwise be unknowable, invisible, silent, and so forth. In this case, "educational form" ought to be conceptualized broadly. It includes Benjamin's reflections on instruction, but also on an increasingly dispersed array of activities, media, and performances. They are to be found in unlikely places such as in radio broadcasts, children's theatrical productions, collections of odd bits of flotsam, cityscapes, public cinemas, and silly word games. It is my goal to redeem these forms and arrange them in such a way as to enable us to grasp anew an educational potentiality within Benjamin's work.

Each educational form offers a moment of *alchemical* (rather than developmental) potential for change in the partitioning of thought, bodies, and sensations and how they relate to one another. If the fascist shock to the system concerns the numbing of the senses and the freezing of critical capacities, then an educational alter-shock would be a confrontation between a subject and an excess that *innervates* the body, causing a disorganization of fascist perceptual-cognitive relay points. The resulting defamiliarization of self and world might open the body up to difference rather than partitioning it out (as enemy, other, or alien). The decomposition of existing partitions has certain features that exist across the various forms Benjamin experiments with. First, many of the educational forms explored throughout this book express a modality of distraction—distraction as alertness coupled with horizontal, nondiscriminating openness. As opposed to mere diversion, distraction for Benjamin has a certain educational value. It is the special mode of attunement that is both necessitated by modern living (e.g., in cities), while at the same time capable of rerouting its effects in less alienating and more emancipatory directions. Throughout the book, I will emphasize how distraction is radically disruptive of the present organization of things, actions, and relations, yet immanent to this very same present. It scrambles the present in order to make individuals open and alert to a potentiality outside of fascist hardness and coldness.

Distraction is not simply a mentalistic or conceptual interruption; it first and foremost concerns *perceptual innervation*. Innervation, in the context of Benjamin's work, implies the intensification and extension of psychic and physiological energies.[49] For Miriam Bratu Hansen, innervation is a "*two-way* process or transfer, that is, not only a conversion of mental, affective energy into somatic, motoric form but also the possibility of reconverting, and recovering, split-off psychic energy through motoric stimulation"[50] in order to produce an empowering and active rather than adaptive and negative relation to the world. As I will argue, distraction is an innervation of attention, or a special kind of perceptual swelling of the faculties to their point of dispersion in and through external stimulation. As it spreads the sensorium outward, distraction loosens up habituated partitions and fixed modes of sensing the self and the world. The field of sensation expands, intensifies, and extends itself via distraction, inducing a swerve effect on the overall perceptual field. The perceptual rules dividing what can from what cannot be seen are suspended, allowing a radical moment where (1) something new can appear, and (2) through this appearance, can alter the cognitive-perceptual relation, which itself now incorporates difference and alterity. This difference can threaten to dissolve the subject (or at least the apperceptive ability to unify the self under a stable "I" by unhinging faculties from their common sense alignment), but it can also propose a new, dispersed, intensive form of life that is open to diasporic collective formations.

More often than not, perceptual interruption of habits (distraction) happens through mimesis, wherein the child or adult suddenly takes on sensuous or nonsensuous forms of similarity with the nonidentical other, radically altering what a body can do. As we will see, for Benjamin, mimesis is not the reproduction of the same or the affirmation of identity, but rather the production of similarity or affinity (*Verwandschaft*) in a nondestructive, noncoercive manner through embodied performance. Mimesis simultaneously (1) displaces actors and actions into new domains that might otherwise be deemed disparate or inappropriate and (2) through this displacement, opens up to the potentiality for new habits and new forms of life to emerge from within the plastic nature of play. Thus, a preindividual affinity for otherness is expressed in the child's mimetic entanglement with a variety of objects, places, practices, technologies, and creatures that awakens the body to alternative, indeterminate gestures without predetermined destinations or use.

When placed together, these educational forms can be organized into a larger constellational curriculum, or a temporally and contextually specific configuration of forms that lights up a historical moment by bringing into relation elements that have no necessary, preexisting connections. Benjamin describes a constellation as a composition of "phenomena [that] are subdivided and at the same time redeemed so that those elements which it is the function of the concept to elicit from phenomena are most clearly evident at the extremes."[51] On my reading, the phenomena, which are subdivided yet redeemed, are forms that have different locations, materials, pedagogies, practices, and affective sensations; yet, when brought together, they support a new kind of educational life full of potentiality beyond fascist hardness, coldness, and manipulativeness. This potentiality is found at the extreme points in each of the forms, where *extreme* refers to the most vivid, clear, and swollen manifestation of a phenomena. The constellation is a shifting array of swelling points taken out of the flow of everyday life in order to punctuate this everyday experience of the world with a certain amount of educational shock. Constructing such a constellation is a highly tactical maneuver; Benjamin's work testifies to the struggle to continually shift the parameters of the constellation in relation to unfolding historical trends. Drawing inspiration from Benjamin, this book is also an attempt to map a curricular constellation composed of a variety of rather minor yet intense educational forms that together intervene in the present, historical moment of neofascism.

Over the course of the next few chapters, we will move from instruction to theatrical directing, to radio broadcasting, to collecting, to wandering the city, to collectively laughing in a cinema, and ultimately to children's riddles. With each turn, the teacher (often perceived in human-centric terms) fades more and more into the background and the educational moments become increasingly unintentional and incidental. In this sense, the book enacts a dispersal of education through wider and wider concentric circles, or waves of potentiality that swell up throughout social, political, economic, and cultural contexts until the dialectic between learning and teaching gives way to what Benjamin refers to as study. This diasporic spreading out of educational potentiality is an exploration of Benjamin's idea that ". . . everyone is an educator and everyone needs to be educated and everything is education."[52] For instance, in an early letter to Gerhard Scholem dated from 1917, a young Benjamin argues that the role of educational instruction is to make tradition "visible and *free*"[53] Over the course of Benjamin's writings, the function of the instructor as described here returns in the form of the dialectical image. Dialectical images—such as the nineteenth-century Parisian arcades but also a host of other strange objects and buildings in various states of decay—are described in similar fashion: as infused with historical "legibility" and "recognizability"[54] now made free in the moment of a flash. As such, everything becomes (given the right contextual factors) infused with the potentiality to make history recognizable (visible) and free. My constellation of educational forms is a map of this movement and this trajectory of education outward into collections, cities, cinematic experiences, and language itself.

The resulting antifascist constellation represents a form of educational life that stands in contrast to Adorno's endorsement of the "strength of the ego" necessary for the reasonable maturity of "the model of the middle-class individual"[55] or the "genuine liberal"[56] to save society from itself. In fact, if Haro and Coles are correct in their diagnosis of the new dimensions of fascism, then I argue that Benjamin is more important than Adorno for thinking through a *full-bodied* education capable of inducing *alter-shocks* to the fascist system through distraction, mimetic performance, and perceptual innervation that are distributed across the masses (rather than located within the individual ego of the middle-class liberal) and found in multiple, unexpected activities and places (outside and beyond the control of the schoolhouse). In fact, Benjamin bluntly states, "Persuasion is fruitless."[57] Learning does not primarily happen through reasoned argument or critical self-reflection on beliefs. Instead, it is through a repartitioning of what can and cannot be sensed that learning suddenly arrives to destabilize one's sense of self and world. "Truth," writes Benjamin, "wants to be startled abruptly, at one stroke, from her self-immersion, whether by uproar, music, or cries for help."[58] Here Truth is awakened by a *sonic* alter-shock. It emerges when the faculties are distracted, thrown off track, and disoriented by sonic waves coursing through the body in "one stroke." The content is not as important as the sensation of being abruptly halted. This is the moment in which the *potentiality* for a new habit, a new thought, a new critical reflection presents itself as the impetus for learning or studying. In a famous aphorism, Benjamin positively proclaims: "No imagination without innervation."[59] In other words, alternation of the body's energetic exchange with its environment is *educationally primary*, emerging from within the visceral and intuitive entanglement we have with lived experience. Educational experience is not antithetical to the modern world and its cacophony of sounds and other shocking stimuli. Instead, we must sift through this cacophony in order to find opportunities for perceptual learning, teaching, and studying to emerge.

When viewed together, Benjamin's educational forms intervene into the preconscious structures of deep experience that are deemed to be responsible for neofascist versions of manipulativeness, hardness, and coldness—such as a distracted lack of attentive discernment, hollow mimicry over autonomous individuality, and hyperindulgence in media stimulation and spectacle. Benjamin allows us to enter into the dream of neofascism *from the inside* and ready ourselves to take advantage of its phantasmagoria in such a way as to interrupt the calcification of the authoritarian personality. And in this sense, Benjamin's educational forms, as we read them today, make the nascent alter-(post)modernity found within neofascism available for a new use. In the short essay titled "Experience and Poverty," Benjamin accepts the poverty of experience in the modern world. Technological advancements coupled with the horrors of the First World War resulted in two seemingly opposed social and political tendencies. On the one hand, Benjamin points toward the "completely new poverty" that descended on the Western world. On the other hand, he correctly emphasizes how the reverse side of this poverty "is the oppressive wealth of ideas" now spreading through mass media.[60] Even before the rise of social media, Benjamin recognized a paradox at the heart of such technological revolutions, and how this paradox produced "a new kind of barbarism"[61] that was making the transmission of inheritance between generations increasingly difficult if not impossible. But importantly, Benjamin did not retreat from this barbarism. Instead, he remained immanent to it in order to produce what he refers to as "a positive concept of barbarism."[62] This approach stands in contrast to Adorno's lamentation of the autonomous individual whose intellectual capacity for critical self-reflection was the only possible bulwark against the barbarism of the times. Of course, I am not suggesting that critical self-reflection is not important. Rather, I want to highlight how Benjamin stays within the symptoms (within the dreamwork of barbarism) in order to redeem an unfulfilled potentiality lurking within as an alter-shock that surges through the body and its habits. If there is an affective dimension to Adorno's work on the antifascist personality (above and beyond his rather brief comments on sympathy yoked to reason, for instance), for Benjamin, the affective takes center stage along with perceptual and gestural redistributions of what can and cannot be sensed. Unlike Adorno, Benjamin's antifascist education finds its starting point in and through precarious, dangerous, innervating, bodily entanglements with the cultural detritus of barbarism.

Today, Benjamin's notion of education can be read as an embodied, perceptual, and affective response to the heightened forms of manipulativeness, hardness, and coldness we see emerging from within contemporary Trump-era shock politics, social media phantasmagoria, and racial and ethnic intolerance. For instance, distraction, mimetic displacements, and perceptual innervation are all threshold conditions that undermine the firm boundaries created by and through hardness that is supposed to protect or immunize the self against the damage induced via exposure to shock. In this sense, boundaries and walls give way to points of dissolve where self exposes itself to the potentiality for transformation beyond itself at the most vulnerable moments of awakening. Distraction is a maximal state of flexibility, openness, and alertness that breaks down rigidified borders that prevent or prohibit straying and wayfaring into the unknown, unanticipated, and unexpected. Against authoritarianism, distraction leads the subject astray, diffracting attention enough to expose alternative routes or detours but also new forms of massive collectivity without a center. Mimesis stands opposed to coldness in that it opens the self up to contamination and alterity. It is a performative entanglement with the nonidentical rather than a detachment of the self from intimate (albeit strange) relationships with otherness. As will be explored in later chapters of this book, mimesis is not simply imitation or mimicry but rather creative experimentation within a zone of gestural swellings. And finally, innervation expands the sensorium beyond the limits of the isolated individual or the lonely crowd, creating new kinds of preconscious connectivity that cannot be reified or instrumentalized into clearly delineated in-groups and out-groups. Altogether, distraction, mimetic performance, and perceptual innervation open the subject back up to experiences, to difference, to alterity in ways fascist rigidification denies. These examples of Benjamin's educational "extremism" are thus decisively different from fascistic variants. And in this sense, Benjamin offers a timely supplement to Adorno's educational prescriptions for school reform, anchoring antifascist education firmly within a wide variety of novel forms that work through the swollen and innervated subject that Adorno saw as already too compromised to be an agent of resistance. If fascism, at its base, is an attempt to keep asleep, lost in a dream, then Benjamin's antifascist education concerns bodily and affective awakenings to potentialities for other forms of life from within yet against this very dreamscape.

There is yet another key difference between Adorno and Benjamin's educational approach. Despite Adorno's careful, dialectical analysis of the differences and similarities between the rigidification of personality within the fascist type and his typology of this personality, he seems to be caught in the negative dialectic of his own construction wherein the only solution to the massification of personality in the modern era is typological symptomology and prescriptive corrective. As a methodological clarification, Adorno argues, "Not all typologies are devices for dividing the world into sheep and buck [as in the fascist personality type], but some of them reflect certain experiences which, though hard to systematize, have, to put it as loosely as possible, hit upon something."[63] Typologies produced by reasonable scientific inquiry need not be arbitrary, but rather can be important diagnostic tools for overcoming the very rigidity they might superficially seem to embody. Stated differently, the only way to accurately diagnose hardness is through a type that itself might appear to be "hard." More troubling is that while a reified typology might be useful for describing reified personality, Adorno also appears to have used typology to describe authentic, anti-authoritarian subjectivity, or a subjectivity purportedly outside of reification (the tolerant and reasonable "genuine liberal"). A reified typology (justified as a diagnostic tool) becomes a *reifying* prescription, determined in advance. Benjamin's alternative to fascism, on my reading, does not rest on replacing one type with another. Instead, he turns to *indeterminate* moments or thresholds/swellings that undo the determinants of personality, opening up a gap between what is and what ought to be that retains something of the unknown and unanticipated within it. These are precisely when and where educational awakenings make a latent potentiality beyond any predetermined typology visible and free. This claim does not deny Benjamin's penchant for producing types (such as the gambler or the flaneur). Rather, I want to highlight the importance of the indeterminacy of types in relation to educational experience for Benjamin. Education, as an extreme experience, exaggerates a type to the point of its own dissolution into otherness, and in this sense is beyond capture. In short, education might be the point at which the type is most vivid but also most precarious, toppling over into an indeterminate alterity that is unstable and full of potentiality for being otherwise.

At the heart of Benjamin's alternative educational operation is an innervating swell of potentiality that violently disrupts hardness, coldness, and manipulativeness (without necessarily replacing these traits with another personality type such as Adorno's "genuine liberal"). Each chapter of the present volume can be seen as exploring the indeterminating potentialities that disrupt boundaries that make experience inaccessible, freezing the dynamic qualities of life into rigid types. These potentialities are located in threshold states and include the following:

Introduction 25

Learning and Teaching

1. Instruction: transmissibility
2. Children's Theatre: collectivizability
3. Radio Broadcasts: historicity

Studying

4. Collections: traceability
5. Cityscapes: distractability
6. Cinema: mechanizability
7. Riddles: communicability and noncommunicability

In each case, the potentiality that rests in the gap separating and conjoining opposites is opened up at certain pressure points of swelling, agitation, and wave-like intensity that are the preconditions for transformation beyond fascistic subjective limitations. Each form produces its own full-bodied alter-shock to the system, promoting disjunctive sensibilities, wayfaring disorientations, and exaggerated intensifications and extensions that take the self to the absolute limit of awakening to that which is radically other. Whereas the dimensions of the fascist personality type resist such educational awakenings, Benjamin's educational forms, now set within a curricular constellation, shutter the slumbering halls of fascism (both subjectively and institutionally) with a powerful, barbaric, full-bodied alter-shock. In moments of extreme swelling, the plasticity of affective innervation, bodily comportments, and perceptual distributions disrupts the hardness and coldness of fascist personality types, exposing a vulnerable yet radical potentiality waiting to be reconfigured into as-of-yet indeterminate forms of collective life. While Winfried Menninghaus[64] has argued that Benjamin's works are organized around thresholds (such as awakenings), threshold-acts (including critiquing and rescuing mythology), and threshold-figures (such as Proust and Kafka), I emphasize the centrality of thresholds for thinking through *education* in Benjaminian terms. Education, on my reading, is antifascist because it is a composition of threshold-acts (awakenings as particular kinds of educational swellings) and threshold-figures (learners, studiers, and teachers) that break up rigid forms of hardness and coldness, repotentializing the present.

Of course, there are elements within Benjamin's writings that can be appropriated for fascist ends. As Jane O. Newman has pointed out, Benjamin's celebration of the *Trauerspiel* in his habilitation project as a particularly German tradition as well as the methodology employed to reveal the "aesthetic will" underlying the mourning plays were endorsed and taken up by certain scholars affiliated with National Socialism.[65] Despite this, I redeem those resources that Benjamin offers for combating fascism today by building up a constellation of educational forms that collectively contain (and mutually reinforce) a distinctly antifascist potentiality. This does not mean that any of these forms are "safe" or a "sure bet." But this is always the case, as educational forms have their own, autonomous lineages that can be selectively appropriated and reworked for a variety of political ends. My point is simply that historical precedence does not preclude a redemptive curricular strategy that focuses on lighting up and putting into circulation missed potentialities.

I also do not want to argue that *all* of Benjamin's educational forms are equally valid in the same ways at the same times. Certain elements within the educational constellation developed in the pages that follow will appear brighter at certain historical junctures. Or, better, certain educational wave-forms will rise and fall according to the sea conditions at any given moment. Either way, there is a flexibility to a constellational curriculum that enables it to adjust to specific conditions. For instance, Jack Zipes once wrote of Benjamin's children's theater that its role was "exaggerated"[66] since the rise of film and television. In this sense, the theatrical element of the constellation appears dim when compared to the brightness of film and perhaps radio. At the same time, Zipes also highlights how Benjamin's notion of children's theater was really meant for communists in a communist state. In this sense, it is not only temporally but spatially isolated from the other more or less "Western" elements in Benjamin's educational constellation.

What is most important to note is that the constellation, *as a whole*, illuminates a certain outline of antifascist education, offering various entry points for encountering an educational notion of self that neither abandons itself to fascist propaganda and behaviors nor retreats back into a now extinct form of autonomous subjectivity (as lamented by Adorno). No single educational form is adequate to the task of an antifascist education. Instead, they must be aligned or triangulated in order for the potentiality within each to swell up and become an alchemical agent. But there is no recipe for which forms will work best together, and the "timeliness" of any given form might not guarantee its effectiveness. In fact, if we take Benjamin's own method of critical theory seriously, then an understanding of the contemporaneity of his educational constellation would, in part, be predicated on its mixture of timely and untimely elements contingently stitched together. For, as Benjamin's "On the Concept of History" argues, the present can only be grasped in terms that are not its own.[67] One foot must be in the present and the other planted outside it in order for history to be made legible or knowable. As such, the appearance of being "out of touch" or "out of date" might be the key to providing resources for an antifascist education in the twenty-first century—an education dedicated to an ongoing and indeterminate experimentation with the ambiguous thresholds and swelling points found in mimetic displacements, perceptual disorientation, and absentminded distractions that are ignited while we rub our eyes and begin to stretch our slumbering bones in moments of awakening.

PART I

INSTRUCTION

As argued in the Introduction, I am concerned with creating a constellation of Benjamin's educational forms. Perhaps the most obvious of these forms is instruction—a central topic for Benjamin during his participation in the German Youth Movement and his educational activism as a university student.[1] And yet, what Benjamin has to say about instruction is far from obvious. In this chapter, I wish to draw on Benjamin's thoughts on instruction articulated in some of his earliest writings in order to focus more particularly on the origins of teaching and the persona of the teacher as they relate to learning. It is important to note at the outset that my interpretation of these early essays is itself an imaginative (de)formation. Instead of summary, it attempts to cite Benjamin in such a way as to expose new potentialities within his work for making the very notion of instruction visible and free for the present moment as an antifascist educational practice. This means analytically separating out teaching and learning as the two basic features of education: making visible and then free the potentiality of tradition. Stated differently, I want to make Benjamin's formulation more precise and argue that learning is the making visible of tradition (in its knowability) and teaching is making this visible tradition free (in its transmissibility) for new use by future generations. Teaching frees up tradition by making it citable via recordings, transcripts, lectures, and so forth. The research of the learner becomes a text that turns outward into a teaching. In this sense, the activities are interconnected and deal with the swelling up of a potentiality into the present moment. To be sensitive and responsive to such swelling points, a teacher must adopt a particular view of tradition, one that is absent-minded, imaginative, radically passive, violent, and comedic. Certainly, this outlook challenges many taken-for-granted assumptions about teachers and teaching as they are currently conceptualized as a competency-driven, skills-based, performance-oriented profession.[2] But more to the point, I argue that Benjamin is also offering us the outline of a particular kind of full-bodied, antifascist instructional practice.

The relation between instruction and tradition has been broached in the secondary literature on Benjamin in terms of inheritance. For instance, Gerhard Richter emphasizes the need to think through the concept of inheritance when dealing with Benjamin's thought. Importantly, Richter connects inheritance directly with education. He writes, "[I]nheritance, far from being an appropriable possession, *is* precisely this mournful process of reading and interpreting."[3] Inheritance is never a possession of the past as if we can control it or grasp it fully. Unlike the economic notion of inheritance, Richter is proposing an *educational* notion of inheritance. Indeed, he argues that the most valuable educational lesson from Benjamin concerns "learning how to inherit."[4]

Susan Buck-Morss makes a similar observation, connecting Benjamin's "materialist pedagogy" with a "nonauthoritarian system of inheritance, which compares less to the bourgeois mode of passing down cultural treasures as the spoils of conquering forces, than to the utopian tradition of fairy tales, which instruct without dominating. . . ."[5] In both cases, inheritance and education cross paths, forming a tight nexus around the question of the transmissibility of tradition. Which treasures and traditions ought to be transmitted and how, especially if the new barbarism of the present makes such transmission increasingly difficult? What is the responsibility of the teacher to the inheritance of tradition, especially given the present poverty of experience? As paradoxical as it might at first appear, this inheritance is only possible through the peculiar mixture of absentmindedness and (de)forming imagination that seize on the violence of barbarism but in a nondestructive way.

Learning as Awakening through Swelling

According to Howard Eiland, Benjamin's notion of learning is akin to a kind of perceptual awakening from inside a dream.[6] Concerning the relationship between dreaming and awakening, Benjamin writes, "The dream waits secretly for the awakening."[7] He also observes, "The realization of dream elements in the course of waking up is the canon of dialectics."[8] Education in this sense would be about a dream coming to know itself, or being able to reflect on its own dreamwork through dialectics. It is crucial that Benjamin frequently talks about *awakening* rather than being awake. For instance, Benjamin argues, "the Now of recognizability is the moment of awakening (Jung would like to distance awakening from the dream)."[9] The now of recognizability enables the dreamer to be distracted from the immanence of the dream. Such distraction induces a weakening of the powers of the enchantment of the dreamscape without leaving the dream behind (Benjamin's criticism of Jung is precisely his undialectical understanding of awakening and dreaming). Said differently, the state of awakening is *of* the dream but not *in* the dream. Awakening makes it possible for the dream to become *visible* as a dream (while still dreaming), and through a displacement of rapt attention to the content of the dream as it unfolds, the dream can become *free* to be otherwise than a simple tool for maintaining sleep. As Margaret Cohen usefully summarizes, Benjamin understands awakening in a post-Enlightenment way: he refuses the binary between waking and sleeping.[10] This is why Benjamin can argue that "The realization of dream elements, in the course of waking up, is the paradigm of dialectical thinking. Thus, dialectical thinking is the organ of historical awakening."[11] On my reading, awakening is neither the abandonment of the dream nor its negation, but rather the realization or the *making visible* of the elements of the dream for new use (dialectical thinking). Notice that in this case, the primary educational moment is in the perceptual and affective reorientation toward the dream (and away from it) via awakening. Learning is first and foremost a sensorial-phenomenal shift in what is visible rather than a detached, reflective, analytic analysis of the meaning of a dream from the perspective of being fully awake. Emphasizing awakening also has a messianic dimension to it. For Benjamin, messianic redemption is the slightest of shifts within the present condition that nevertheless changes everything. He summarizes, "Everything will be the same as here—only a little bit different . . . nothing remains and nothing disappears."[12] Education as awakening is situated within this messianic space and time.

Benjamin calls awakening a threshold experience. He comments, "We have grown very poor in threshold experiences. Falling asleep is perhaps the only such experience that remains to us. (But together with this, there is also waking up)."[13] A threshold, counter to what we might think, is not a linear passage from one state to another so much as a "swell"[14] within a given state. Benjamin writes, "The threshold must be carefully distinguished from the boundary. A *Schwelle* [threshold] is a zone. Transformation, passage, wave action are in the word *schwellen*. . . ."[15] A swelling is the outermost, extreme contour of something where it becomes most *visible*. Yet, at the same time, this exaggerated intensification and extension of something presses it beyond itself. Thus, there is a strange tension in the notion of swelling. It is a state that exposes something in its most acute form, yet in this acute form its recognizability almost becomes unrecognizable. In short, swelling thrusts the identical or self-same into a relationship with its own difference and alterity. This is why Benjamin states that a swell is *not* a boundary that separates and divides. Rather, it is a zone of experimental becoming. On my reading, we can think of *awakening as the swelling of a dream to its most extreme point*—or the point in the dream where the dream becomes visible, but in that visibility begins to pass beyond itself without leaving itself behind. Awakening, in this sense, is an innervation of the dream to such a degree that its internal logic begins to falter or stutter, revealing itself as an image. The innervation might come from the inside of the dream—provoked by a dream element—or might be the result of an external stimulus that is momentarily folded into the dreamwork only to dislodge it. In either case, the psychical energies enchanted by the dream are suddenly exposed to a surge that produces a swelling capable of pressing the dream to its maximal point of overflow in a state of awakening.

To summarize, awakening as a swelling is Benjamin's definition of learning.[16] On the shoreline between sleeping and being awake *is the place of educational now time*—a time that deactivates the dream world just enough so that something (tradition, for instance) can become visible and thus knowable through a learning process. As Benjamin summarizes, awakening is a "synthesis of dream consciousness (as thesis) and waking consciousness (as antithesis)" in such a way that the "now of recognizability"[17] reveals itself. Recognizability of the dream as a dream swells to the surface during awakenings, making itself available for learning. Here it is important to connect the notion of "-abilities" in Benjamin's workup with the theme of learning. In the book *Benjamin's -abilities*,[18] Samuel Weber argues that an ability, for Benjamin, is a virtual potentiality that always ensures that what is actual is unfinished. Awakening is a swelling up of a dream with its ability to be known, or its *knowability* (*Erkennbarkeit*). As such, knowability is the swelling from within the enchantment of the dream that marks a threshold between being inside the dream and outside the dream. Before cognitive reflection on what is known, there is a more basic, affective, and perceptual sense of knowability that swells to the surface in moments of learning that is never exhausted in any fully awakened state of knowing.

Already in Benjamin's earliest writings, he defined education in terms of tradition becoming "visible and free," like a wave that swells and then crashes because "it is full of life."[19] A wave is the swelling of the sea. It emerges from an abundance within the sea itself and is therefore a part of that which it separates itself from. The wave, as a swelling, makes visible the sea, but also opens the sea up to a dynamic state of crashing. Waves that do not quite break are referred to as swells. In this sense, a swell is like an awakening: it is not sleeping or being awake so much as a point of intensification and extension that indicates the arrival of a threshold. Such a state is undecided and indeterminate as the swelling contains in itself both a capacity to crest and break or to subside into calmness.

Illustrating the diffuse knowability that swells throughout the abundance of life, Benjamin aptly titled a series of anecdotes about children found in the book *One-Way Street* "Enlargements." On the one hand, the title could speak to the act of enlarging or magnifying small, seemingly insignificant events and activities of children. On the other hand, the title also speaks to the inherent connections between children and dynamic zones wherein life touches its potentiality for change through a swelling up of knowability. In each of the thought images, Benjamin highlights a particular threshold moment, or enlargement. Childhood is, on this reading, a dynamic movement that constantly expands itself through various educational encounters. Thus, the reading child is "unspeakably touched by the deeds, the words that are exchanged; and, when he gets up, he is covered over and over by the snow of his reading."[20] Or, the hiding child folds into the material world around him: ". . . behind a door, he himself *is* the door. . . ."[21] And the pilfering child, who "advances like a lover through the night"[22] by invading the larder, suddenly discovers a budding sexuality swelling up through fondling fingers. In all cases, the activities of childhood are swollen with a potentiality for knowability that constantly transforms childhood itself.

Perhaps we can push this even further and suggest that *youth* is the category of childhood swollen to the point of its dissolve. It is the most exaggerated crest of childhood as it both rises toward and withdraws from adulthood (and is therefore an indeterminate state of being). In an early piece titled "Romanticism: An Undelivered Address to Students," Benjamin describes youth as follows: "Youth is surrounded by hope, love, and admiration—coming from those who are not yet young, from the children, and from those who are no longer able to be young because they have lost their faith in something better."[23] In this quotation, youth are no longer children and not yet adults. They are not not-children, and as such, occupy a kind of liminal zone of indistinction between the binary couple of child and adult. Because of this precarious, exaggerated position, they are *most susceptible* to educational now time, or the time when abilities (collectivizability, historicizability, traceability, distractability, and so forth) express themselves most acutely and thus become knowable. Adults, as Benjamin continually emphasized, devalue youth. "The adult," as Benjamin sarcastically writes, "had already experienced everything . . ." and as such "devalues" the experience of youth.[24] Teachers, in particular, miss the unique opportunities of youth, opting instead to "push" youth directly into life's drudgery with "serious and grim" resolve.[25] The dream of youth is a swelling of childhood to the point of historical awakening. For Benjamin, the particular, exaggerated state that defines the threshold separating and conjoining adulthood to childhood is a youthful "struggle of the very possibility of values"[26]—a struggle for the potentiality to recognize new values in their knowability. Hence the repeated emphasis Benjamin places on youth, not only in his early, school reform essays, but throughout his many writings, as we will see.

The Origins of Instruction

Instruction begins with the question of tradition, of making tradition "visible and free,"[27] as Benjamin suggests. But how does this happen? How does tradition become visible and free in the form of teaching? To answer these questions, we have to begin to reconsider the relationship between one's teaching and one's learning. This is not to enslave teaching to learning outputs,[28] but rather to enable our understanding of teaching in relation to its learning-inputs (or what I will describe below as teaching's origins). Drawing on the notion of awakening as a kind of wave that swells, a teaching emerges through the internal swelling of learning to a point where a certain potential for transmissibility within what is knowable starts to manifest itself. Benjamin observes, a teacher's "learning has evolved into teaching, in part gradually but wholly from within."[29] Stated differently, teaching is the *awakening of learning to its potentiality for transmission* (its *transmissibility*). One becomes a teacher when transmissibility becomes thematized as a constitutive feature of one's learning. Teachers are those who are swollen with this transmissibility to the point where their learning reaches a maximal point of dispersal, becoming visible *and* free. The teacher abandons him- or herself to the swell (to what has been made visible through learning) "in such a way that it grows up to its crest and crashes down in a foam"[30] becoming free in its dispersal. The wave of education swells through learning into the crash of teaching, which sends the wave outward in a million directions.

In a strange sense, teaching is actually the making visible and free its own *origin*. The word *origin* is important in this context. For Benjamin, an origin is not a point in the chronological past but rather a dynamic rhythm within the present. He writes, "The term origin is not intended to describe the process by which the existent came into being, but rather to describe that which emerges from the process of becoming and disappearance."[31] Origin is neither an empirically verifiable point nor a specific, discrete moment that one can recount from the vantage of detached reflection (as if it were a completed event). Rather, origin is alive in the present as an acute swelling of knowability exerting pressure on contemporary conditions. As an active participant in what is unfolding, origin contributes to the rhythm of the present as a process of becoming and disappearing, of rising and falling, of swelling and crashing. As Benjamin says in the quote above, it *emerges*. Applied to the dynamic relation between learning and teaching, we might say that learning is not merely a progressive series of events leading from the past to the present, from ignorance to intelligence, from personal reflection to public demonstration. Teaching, on this account, would merely be the *outcome* of learning processes—an outcome that transcends what has been previously learned. Yet if we think of teaching as making visible and free its origins, then a different understanding of the dynamic is possible. On this alternative account, learning is not simply an inert background out of which teaching emerges but is an active force operating within teaching as teaching's truth. This truth is knowability as it swells to such a point that it transmits itself in the form of a teaching. Indeed, we can go so far as to say that teaching is the maximally enlivened *expression* of learning. *Expression* (e.g., pressing out) is not a metaphor for the activity of teaching but an ontological indicator of a swollen point of heightened tensions within learning that is suddenly gathered up and activated in the present (as a teaching), in order to give away (transmit) a certain knowability.

Importantly, the learner might have acquired real knowledge about tradition, but this is not what is transmitted in the moment of teaching. Instead, teaching transmits a certain knowability of tradition (tradition's ability to be known . . . its truth). Knowability rises to the point of becoming not only visible but also free through outward-facing forms of lectures, notes, transcribed dialogues, outlines, and so forth.[32] These various pedagogical forms are visible expressions of knowability as it crashes and disperses outward. There is thus an intermingling of roles between learning, researching, and teaching. They cannot be separated definitively one from the others (as if they existed in a simple, linear chronology), but rather are swept up together in the rhythm of education that oscillates between swelling, cresting, crashing, and swelling up again. Simply put, the teacher is the learner who is most swollen, and his or her notes are the exaggeration or enlargement of learning to the point where it expresses the transmissibility of learning's truth.

It might at first appear that this process is highly directional: waves lead to crashes as learning leads to teaching. Such linear determinacy would undo the plastic indeterminacy of the truth of learning at the moment when it becomes most visible and gives itself away. At the same time, there is a lack of directionality. Benjamin writes: "it [the wave as an image of education] all depends on the wave abandoning itself [literally giving itself over] to its movement [*sich seiner Bewegung so hinzugeben*]."[33] On my reading, learning is only possible when the directionality toward teaching is forgotten, and the learner gives him- or herself over to the movement/rhythm of that which makes it possible to have something to teach. Stated differently, the individual has to be *completely innervated by learning*. Abandoning the self to the rhythmic movement of the wave means that there is nothing in the wave that guarantees its culmination in the form of a crashing (a teaching). Teaching, in its most ontological sense, is never a chosen profession but rather an expression of an origin. It arrives when this origin is so full of potentiality (knowability) that it literally breaks open (crashes). Such a crash can only happen through yielding to the force that is not within the teacher's control. Because of this, there is no guarantee that learning will lead to teaching in any teleological way. Learning that lacks the necessary duration to build up a sense of knowability until it becomes transmissible is, as we will see in part 2 of this book, study.

This notion of teaching as immanent to learning (and vice versa) complicates the way we normally think of teaching. While there might be a tendency to think of education as *first and foremost* a relationship with students,[34] Benjamin highlights how teaching is latent *within* learning. Students are neither a necessary nor sufficient condition to define teaching. When students are present, the resulting teaching cannot be thought of as exemplary. The teacher's words, lectures, notes, or outlines are not definitive conclusions, nor are his or her actions models to be emulated. Indeed, Benjamin writes, "The concept of example (to say nothing of that of 'influence') should be totally excluded from the theory of education."[35] Professional teachers (or professors) often ground their pedagogy in examples. Yet, this approach makes teaching *impossible* precisely because examples do not make visible and free the active, dynamic origins in learning as they exist and exert force over the teacher. In short, there are three problems with teaching examples (or teaching as an example). First, the academy, for Benjamin, hides behind examples, which are merely facades of stability, permanence, self-assuredness, competency, completeness, and excellence. The teacher is *in control of presenting examples* that can be chosen *at will*. They are thus dead and inert things to be willfully pointed at rather than forces willing to be yielded to. Second, examples are more often than not intended to be used as models for how to think, act, and so forth. They are normative. While there might be pedagogical and sociological reasons for utilizing examples as models, such usage exchanges knowability for knowing, turning teaching into a conveyance of information rather than a crashing and dispersal of truth. Third, examples are oriented toward students' needs and interests. They are for student consumption and thus do not necessarily swell up from within the teacher's learning process as it exerts pressure to externalize itself. Rather than *presenting* examples as models for students, teaching—in its most radical form—ought to *express* its origins in learning, making this learning visible and free in whatever shape and size it *must* take given the nature of the swelling.[36] These expressions are free, but this does not mean that they are intentionally guided by student-centered concerns. In the end, this lack of concern for *who* the students are makes the teaching even *more* free and unbound, allowing it to spill outward in multiple, unintended directions (like a wave crashing and dispersing).

An example of the dynamism of a teaching that makes its own origins knowable can be found in Goethe's *Elective Affinities*. As Benjamin describes it, this book expresses Goethe's unresolved struggle with the mythic and tyrannical powers of nature to destroy human freedom.

Goethe's final writings "teach" this struggle "in detail, to the extent that a struggle which was kept secret in life emerges in the last of them."[37] *Elective Affinities*, in particular, "testif[ies] not only, and not at the deepest level, to the mythic world in [his] experience. For there is in him a struggle to free himself from its clutches, and this struggle, no less than the essence of that world, is attested to in Goethe's novel. In the tremendous ultimate experience of the mythic powers . . . Goethe revolted against them."[38] Goethe, as a learner, struggled with the forces within him subverting his freedom of decision (natural passions, death, etc.). At a certain point, this struggle swelled up and turned outward, expressing itself in the form of the novel, *Elective Affinities*. The novel did not resolve the crisis of freedom so much as made it visible and knowable at its "tremendous ultimate experience" (peak swelling point) that was, in turn, given away (made free) to its readership (whomever they might be). The reader inherits the tradition of this struggle now made visible and free, thus beginning another round of swelling, crashing, and dispersing. The indeterminateness of this process is coupled with a continual appeal to witness the struggle and the potentiality for freedom that it contains. In this sense, Goethe was an excellent teacher, even if his novels did not offer up viable "solutions" to the problems he transmitted to the next generation. What is inherited in this novel is the active origin of the struggle itself as it exerts pressure on Goethe as a truth. No message is transmitted (as an example); rather, the very transmissibility of the struggle as something knowable is at stake in this teaching.

The Poverty of the Teacher

It is important to situate this generic theory of teaching and learning within the larger, historical framework of the poverty of experience I introduced in the Introduction. While Sami Khatib highlights this poverty as a particularly pressing cultural and political problem concerning inheritance (and its impossibility),[39] I would add that it poses an *educational* problem as well. For instance, early on, Benjamin wrote in 1917 that "Instruction [*Unterricht*] is the only point of a free union [*Vereinigung*] of the older and the younger generation(s), like waves that create whitecaps [*Schaumkronen*] by flowing into each other [*im Ineinandergehen*]."[40] Through education, there is a union/communion of the generations that flow into each other like waves. Education is the "free union" of the generations through the mechanism of transmission of inheritance of what has been learned. As the teacher grows out of the swell of learning, so too does this essential rhythm act as the condition of possibility for communication across the generations. Yet, after the devastation of World War I, Benjamin highlighted a growing loss of experience and a concurrent inability to communicate across generations. In "The Storyteller" dated from 1936, he pointed to the end of storytelling as symptomatic of this trend. Benjamin's observation is important for historicizing his overall theory of education because a storyteller was one of the few to be able to join the "ranks of the teachers and sages."[41] In short, the new barbarism of the twentieth century put a strain on the "free union" of the generations. Teaching, in this new world, found itself impoverished and thus in crisis. Expanding on Benjamin's observations, we can refer to this condition as the poverty of the teacher. The teacher cannot depend on the pedagogical practices of the past to guarantee that his or her learning will swell and crash into the next generation.

It would be easy to lament this condition. For Benjamin, this would be a mistake. Instead, he might urge us to theorize a *positive* concept of the poverty of the teacher in order to discover new resources within the destruction of experience. The poverty of the teacher, as Benjamin might describe it, cannot rest on the great traditions of wisdom or virtues[42]—all of which attempt to overcome poverty by returning to the past in order to hold it up against the rising tide of fascism. Instead, we have to remember Benjamin's clarion call to "begin with a little and build up further."[43] Stated differently, what has been inherited is inoperative and cannot be retooled to solve contemporary educational problems concerning transmission. Yet this is precisely what we have to work with. Here, we might think of Benjamin's commentary on Brecht's positive redemption of poverty. According to Benjamin, Brecht was a teacher who recognized poverty as an asset. Indeed, Brecht's maxim is "Stick closely to the bare reality," without any frills, which allowed him to "come closer to reality than any rich man." In Brecht, we can see "how the thinker must make do with the few applicable ideas that exist; the writer, with the few valid formulations we have,"[44] and the teacher, with the few resources available to make a constellational curriculum out of the detritus of history. What will emerge below is a rather unusual description of a "poor teacher" that might very well be considered incompetent or unprofessional by the common and good sense of educators today or irresponsible by the high standards of wisdom of the ancients. Nevertheless, we can use Benjamin to redeem teaching at the precise moment when it seems to disappear. The outcome will not be the erasure of teaching, but rather the sudden appearance of its essential quality, which becomes clear only when the inheritance of tradition across the generations is put most at risk: transmissibility of potentiality as such.

To begin, a poor teacher is an *absentminded* or *distracted examiner* of the world. The phrase "absent-minded examiner" is taken from Benjamin's famous essay "The Work of Art in the Age of Mechanical Reproduction," where he uses it in reference to the film audience. Suggesting that absentmindedness is an educational virtue might seem rather unusual given Benjamin's seemingly positive comments on attentiveness. For instance, in his essay on Goethe's *Elective Affinities*, cited above, Benjamin argues that "When they [Goethe's characters] turn their attention away from the human and succumb to the power of nature, then natural life, which in man [sic] preserves its innocence only so long as natural life binds itself to something higher, drags the human down."[45] In this quotation, it would appear that a loss of attention is the harbinger of doom. Furthermore, we could argue that Goethe himself is the embodiment of attentiveness to the question of the human and its relationship to nature. It was only through his acute grasp of the human condition that critical reflection could open up a space for freedom to emerge. In his essay commemorating the ten-year anniversary of the death of Franz Kafka, Benjamin wrote, "Even if Kafka did not pray—and this we do not know—he still possessed in the highest degree what Malebranche called 'the natural prayer of the soul': attentiveness. And in this attentiveness he included all creatures, as saints include them in their prayers."[46] Like Goethe, Kafka is praised for his attentiveness, especially in relation to "all creatures." Yet, it is my contention that these comments on attention ought to be rethought in light of Benjamin's later turn toward distraction and its purported poverty.

Eiland points out different variants or inflections in Benjamin's writings between what he calls "productive distraction" as "a spur to new ways of perceiving" and "*mere* distraction" as diversion.[47] The German word *Zerstreuung*, for instance, refers to a state of being scattered, strewn, or dispersed, and corresponds to the productive notion of distraction. This could be contrasted to the more common word for distraction *Ablenkung*, which means to be steered away from (as in diversion or deflection). The former is nonexclusionary and connective, whereas the latter is exclusionary, separating the self from something or someone. Distraction as dispersion is nondirective and maximally flexible—the self is exposed to otherness without a particular, predetermined aim guiding the encounter or predetermined criteria to judge the encounter. On the other hand, distraction as diversion is directive, steering the self toward something (and thus away from something else). It constitutes boundaries that bind the self to a particular destination through the act of steering (as opposed to diasporic wandering). Adding to Eiland's subtle distinction, Carolin Duttlinger refers to the productive, positive valence of distraction as "alertness coupled with non-discriminatory openness."[48] A far cry from formal attentiveness (exemplified by a focused, narrowing of mental attunement toward this or that thing), distraction nevertheless contains within it the ability to be alert to potentiality on a much wider, more decentralized level beyond willful attentiveness and intentional directionality. I would add to Duttlinger's analysis that alertness is the *swelling* of attention to the point where it disperses itself, giving itself away. This means that distraction is not so much a deviation from attention as it is attention's maximally swollen openness toward the plenitude of a world as a whole.

Stated differently, we can (reductively) argue that one is alert in general and attentive in particular. This observation is similar to Heidegger's comparison between fear and anxiety.[49] Fear is highly directed *at* something causing the fear. Anxiety, on the other hand, is more diffuse, lacking a specific object cause, and because of this, the structure of "worldhood" as such suddenly lights up. When one is on "high alert," one is not looking for particular things or actions to pay attention to. Rather, one is sensitive and open in a general or distributed sense. This is a dispersive swelling up of attention in a nondiscriminatory way.

But perhaps more importantly, this open, nondiscriminatory alertness is not simply a modification in *mental* attunement. On my reading, alertness is less concerned with mental processes and more with a diffusion of attentiveness across the body and its sensorium. Productive distraction is the swelling of the body's preconscious receptivity to what the world offers below or above the parameters of the conscious, attentive subject. Evidence for this is found in Benjamin's reflections on the embodied dimension of mastery. That is, "mastery" for Benjamin is not a willful achievement, nor is it something that can be mentally planned out (premeditated) and set into practice. Instead, it concerns "success conjured up by luck" that can only happen when the mind lets go and abdicates its powers so that one's "body and each of [one's] limbs can act in accordance with their own rationality."[50] Mastery, in this sense, is a question of developing certain habits spread throughout the body as it engages with the world through subtle, gestural maneuvers. In a beautiful illustration of this kind of mastery, Benjamin writes, "This is why you can look for something for days, until you finally forget it; then, one day, when you are looking for something else, you suddenly find the first object. Your hand has, so to speak, taken the matter in hand and has joined forces with the object which had successfully resisted the dogged efforts of the will."[51] While the mind wanders off, the body remains on high alert to all the subtle variables of an experience that exceed conscious oversight and attentiveness, producing results as if by magic. In short, alertness as productive distraction does not first and foremost concern new ways of thinking so much as exaggerated and extended ways of *perceiving* the world. Stated differently, mastery is only possible precisely because of a poverty of mental attentiveness.

Absentminded examiners are perpetually alert to and distracted by the abundance that exists on the periphery of attention and in the background of experience. They are receptive to such surplus (through their learning) and willing to make it free (through their teachings). In short, only those who are maximally distracted can assemble a constellational curriculum as rich and varied as Benjamin's intuitive eclecticism. He finds ways to make the knowability of tradition free in the most unlikely of places and through the most unlikely of things. His distracted alertness to the potentiality for knowability to articulate itself is therefore both a symptom of a modern form of poverty (that cannot hold onto attentiveness without it swelling beyond itself) and its homeopathic cure. Simply put, the absentminded examiner is a master of his or her poverty.

The absent-minded examiner is also imaginative. Imagination, for Benjamin, is not a faculty responsible for creating something new. Somewhat shockingly, when viewed from the contemporary perspective that unites imagination with creative economies, the imagination is described by Benjamin as playing a game that involves the "dissolution with its forms."[52] In this sense, imagination "de-forms"[53] but does not negate or destroy. Likewise, it does not produce strong utopian blueprints. In this way, Benjamin separates imagination from strong destructive and creative powers. Instead, what we find is a *poor* power that renders something inoperative just enough for a neglected potentiality or –ability to become free. Importantly, Benjamin highlights the author Jean Paul who "had the greatest imagination" and who "came closest to the minds of children."[54] Imagination, as a kind of pure receptivity, links the adult author to the child. And in turn, this is precisely what made Jean Paul "the outstanding pedagogue that he was."⁵⁵ He was an outstanding teacher because he had approximated a kind of learning that did not separate him from children or his childhood (as in developmental models) but rather reconnected him with childlike capacities in new, alchemical ways. Through his imagination, he was able to (de)form the novel by combining fantasy and realism so as to defy categorization. In this gesture, he did not create something new beyond traditions nor did he abolish traditions so much as disperse and entangle them through various (de)formations. The results of such imaginative and absentminded displacements *teach* an important lesson: that the world's traditions contain a potentiality only the next generation can inherit.

At the same time, Benjamin's positive appraisal of Jean Paul as a pedagogue is tempered by an important distinction between grotesque imagination and romantic irony. At his best, Jean Paul came "close" to children's imagination. That slight distance is important to highlight as it points to a possible critique of Jean Paul's works. On the one hand, the (de)forming powers of Jean Paul's imagination are certainly recognized by Benjamin as having educational power. These powers are identified with the grotesque, which for Benjamin does not "de-form in a destructive fashion but destructively over-forms."⁵⁶ The grotesque "stands at the extreme margins"⁵⁷ of the imagination—a swelling point where imagination seeks once again to become form without passing into a definitive, closed or finite form (hence the emphasis on overforming). The grotesque is the swell within the sphere of the imagination—a contact zone where the imagination touches the potentiality for new formations within its (de)formative process. This is a point of awakening identified by Benjamin as an educational threshold. Yet, Jean Paul's work also diverges from the grotesque, toppling over into the ironic. Ironic detachment remains at a distance from the form it externally relates itself to, and thus, does not truly enter the form in order to deform it from the inside out. Because of this detachment, irony arises through an external compulsion rather than an internal swelling, and in this sense *cannot be* a teaching (as teachings always emerge out of the swell of learning). The grotesque, as Benjamin writes, "comes from within."⁵⁸ For this reason, the grotesque is the proper aesthetic of the educational dynamic where what is visible makes itself free through an internal process of outward-facing destruction-in-exaggeration. The grotesque is not a break from so much as an inheritance of tradition as it deforms itself at its outermost rim into an overformed plenitude. While the criticism of irony's detachment and destructive capacities apply to most of Jean Paul's works, Benjamin also sees in them a latent potentiality for the grotesque that points toward Jean Paul's unique pedagogical persona.

The gesture toward the ironic brings up the question of the comedic role of the teacher. As Matthew Charles has argued,[59] Jean's Paul's notions of humor and comedy were important influences on Benjamin's desire to create an anti-tragic philosophy capable of overcoming the heroism of most educational responses to social fate. Sean Franzel also points out how Jean Paul used humor to criticize certain trends in literary criticism.[60] Humor (1) reclaims the everyday, ordinary, and small (as opposed to an emphasis on the monumentality of history and the deeds of heroic figures); (2) focuses on the impermanence and transience of life (instead of the immortality of great works); (3) "relativizes the great"[61] as a cultural construct (rather than a universal canon); and (4) satirizes the lives of academics (instead of idealizing them). While Benjamin's efforts to undo monumentalist, national history and the tragic heroism of the great writer can take a melancholic turn, other attempts to undermine these conventions can be clearly humorous in nature. As the learner swells up, these points of maximal exaggeration express themselves as comedic gestures that cannot be contained (kept private), but rather must be given away (in the form of a laugh).

In addition, the teacher is passive in a special sense. According to Benjamin, learning is a swelling of a wave from inside tradition. The learner is indistinct from this swelling up of the knowability of tradition. In this sense, the only thing that matters to the learner is "to surrender"[62] to the dynamic motion of learning as it happens. To surrender means that one struggles with learning, but this struggle culminates in a giving that amounts to tradition becoming visible and free in the form of teaching. The learner has to give him or herself over to tradition for teaching to happen. Remember that, for Benjamin, mastery is the abnegation of the will and a giving over to the body and its intuitive, preconscious alertness to a situation. The learner, in other words, has to yield (even if this means betraying his or her professional status or the emulation of accepted models). Drawing on Kafka as well as Benjamin, Paul North theorizes the politics of yielding. For North, yielding signifies the "pull between withdrawing and producing—yielding a yield—such that anything or anyone could belong to anyone or anything."[63] Yielding does not merely produce; rather it yields to a potentiality present in tradition (made visible), and in that yielding, yields teaching, which is given away (made free).

Yielding also implies a giving up of the security of the self and its roles and its locations, and in this sense, is a kind of dispossession rather than possession. Teaching, in giving away the potentiality that it has learned, is a radical state of poverty. It is, as North argues, a "depotentized labor, not equivalent to effort or toil."[64] This is a labor that suspends its operativity within institutions or economies, lacks potency, and thus releases itself from toil. Interestingly, Benjamin argues that learning actually prevents one from taking on a profession, and in the sense suggested by North, is a kind of depotentized labor. North writes, "[S]cholarship, far from leading inexorably to a profession, may in fact preclude it. For it does not permit you to abandon it. In a way, it places the student under an obligation to become a teacher, but never to embrace the official professions of doctor, lawyer. Or university professor."[65] To engage in learning, as Benjamin sees it, is to surrender one's self up to its wave-like movement without a clear destination beyond its own rising and falling. For this reason, learning does not easily permit one to stop learning, as the wave will continue to swell with potentiality. Teaching is not the end toward which learning is perpetually moving. It is only part of the swelling up of tradition's transmissibility, and for this reason, it is a continuation of learning as it spreads outward (is given away). Because of this, there is something perpetually unprofessional about teaching, which returns continually to its origins only to give them away. To teach is ultimately to abandon one's professional status and any assumed authority (potency) it might bestow on one. In this context, we can better understand Benjamin's frustrations with his own university professors. Early in his university career, he complained that in the lecture courses he was forced to attend he witnessed "the shrill brutality with which scholars display themselves before hundreds of people; how they do not shy away from each other, but envy each other; and how ultimately, they ingeniously and pedantically corrupt the self-respect of those who are in the process of becoming, by turning their self-respect into fear of those who have already become something, of those who have matured early, and of those who are already spoiled."[66] Precisely because academic professors have professionalized teaching—and therefore are defined in terms of their possession of knowledge (which induces envy) rather than by the precariousness of their surrender to learning—they denigrate those in the "process of becoming." They are too potent (in control, in power, in potency), and for this reason, have lost the vulnerability of the surrender to learning. Stated bluntly, they are not poor enough to teach!

Importantly, yielding also is connected to comedy. The tragic, since Aristotle, has always been linked to actions, yet the absentminded examiner is defined in terms of depotentized actions or actions *as not* actions. The humorous figure of the teacher as a nonprofessional lacks knowledge and deeds and is therefore outside of the trap of responsibility and tragic guilt. And in this manner, learning and teaching can become joyful even if they are pressed into extreme poverty. It also enables us to see how alertness to just the right moment is a form of perfect *comedic timing*. Between the prolonged, untimely hesitation of the tragic figure (such as Hamlet, for instance, who is overly concerned and paralyzed with questions of right timing or when he should do what), and the appropriate timing of the bourgeois professional (who has exact knowledge of what to do and when to do it according to appropriate rules and regulations) there is comedic timing that intuits *precisely the appropriate moment to act inappropriately*. Instead of success being a willful, intentional action, Benjamin sees it as a "caprice in the workings of the universe" that corresponds to the "idiosyncrasy in the individual."[67] The master might have spent years of training and building up certain habits, but the moment of success is a suspension. The resulting sense of justice is, for Benjamin, comedic in that it does not come about through any good will or utilitarian calculation but through "countless mistakes that end up producing an exact result, thanks to one last little error."[68] The "one last little error" is the moment of masterful comedic timing, which falls off script, stumbles, or bumbles something in just the right way so as to make knowability suddenly light up and become free. The result is an unprofessional, depotentized action that is comically disturbing but in such a way as to activate a peculiar kind of awakening.

The ethics of this kind of teaching directly correspond to its comedic dimension. Reflecting on ethics, Benjamin argues that thus far, philosophy has undervalued the role of politeness in the struggle between morality and existence. Politeness is, for him, both "nothing and everything"[69] simultaneously. Politeness is nothing in the sense that it enables individuals to overlook conflict by producing a beautiful illusion of harmony where it does not actually exist. Because of this, politeness cannot help resolve ongoing conflict—it is a nothing. At the same time, politeness can free itself and a situation from certain conventions by "tear[ing] down these barriers"[70] that separate parties into polarized factions. Imagine how ingrained and obdurate opinions might come to dominate a situation, erecting boundaries that enable individuals to remain entrenched in their positions despite on-the-ground convergences. The only option in this case is to entrench one's self and try to gain the upper hand by remaining "impolite."[71] Opposed to this tactic, politeness can intervene at the most (im)proper moment through a special kind of *distracted* attunement that Benjamin describes as "an alert openness [*wacher Sinn*] to the extreme, the comic, the private, and the surprising aspects in a situation."[72] Politeness can comically disrupt boundaries and barriers by tripping over them, injecting a contingency into a situation in such a way as to loosen positions without directly offending competing parties. In short, politeness can catch enemies off guard in an inoffensive way, and by doing so, opens a space for an awakening. Tripping, on this account, is not haphazard. Indeed, Benjamin argues that "patience" is the "heart of politeness."[73] The comically polite teacher waits for just the right moment to make just one more little error, which in turn, produces educational opportunities by disrupting and disorganizing set, embattled relationships or perspectives. This disruption is polite precisely because its gesture concerns *little* errors that are attuned to the educational potentiality within a situation. In this sense, they are not random, chaotic outbursts that merely disrupt for disruption's sake. Rather, they emerge from a surrendering of the teacher to what remains transmissible in a situation *despite* fixed, rigid, conflicting standpoints and boundaries. Unlike wisdom or virtue, politeness has no tradition of philosophy to draw on to ground it. Instead, it emerges from the poverty of experience in the modern world as a small, impotent, weak resource for defining the ethics of teaching.

Overall, the poverty of the teacher is a historical reality that is tied to the new barbarism of both capitalist fetishism and fascist politics. It is a position of great vulnerability, yet also a clearing for reassessing the origins of teaching. The question therefore should be "What can teaching do if it is radically poor?" By pushing teaching to its point of dissolve (wherein there are no resources for guaranteeing the transmission of knowledge), poverty reveals the fundamentally weak power of the teacher as absentminded, (de)forming, comedic, passive, and polite. The task of the teacher is to make these little things go a long way, as Benjamin might say. And by doing so, give up on the transmission of knowledge by yielding to the only thing that remains in the wake of barbarism: a potentiality to transmit knowability from within the ruins. This would amount to the inheritance of inheritability as such (rather than this or that particular kind of knowledge to be possessed).

The Violence of Teaching

As several scholars have argued, Benjamin's notion of education is decisively violent.[74] Awakenings are rarely willful, intentional acts. Instead, they are often prompted by some kind of force that jolts, shocks, or disrupts one's relationship with a dream. As such, it would appear that there is the potentiality for harm in any educational moment. This violent potential of education is perhaps best illustrated in the unpublished foreword to Benjamin's postdoctoral thesis, *The Origin of German Tragic Drama*. Instead of traditional, academic prose, Benjamin offers up a rewriting of the Grimm brother's version of the fairy tale "Sleeping Beauty."

> I would like to retell the fairy tale of Sleeping Beauty.
> She lies sleeping in her thorn hedge. And then, after so and so many years, she awakens.
> But not because of the kiss of a lucky prince.
> The cook woke her up when he boxed the ears of the busboy. The blow, resounding from the conserved energy of so many years, echoed throughout the castle.
> A beautiful child sleeps behind the thorn hedge of the following pages.
> If only no fortune-hunting prince in the blinding armor of scholarship approach it. For it will bite back during the bridal kiss.
> Instead, a head cook, the author has reserved the right to awaken it himself. The blow that is meant to echo shrilly throughout the halls of academia is long overdue.
> Then this poor truth that pricked itself on the old-fashioned distaff when it illicitly thought to weave a professorial gown for itself in the attic will also awaken.
> Frankfurt, July 1925[75]

As Irving Wohlfarth points out, this second retelling of "Sleeping Beauty" is a complex, imaginative (de)formation of the academic forward that expresses Benjamin's disappointing experience of university life but with a humorous rather than melancholic twist.[76] In fact, Benjamin himself regarded this retelling of "Sleeping Beauty" as "one of [his] most successful pieces"[77] up to that date. As such, we ought to pause to consider its broader, educational implications. The absent, wicked godmother, on Wohlfarth's reading, represents the old, illiberal university that rejected Benjamin's candidacy for the habilitation, and the fortune-seeking prince, with his "modern" approach to scholarship, would be the newly reformed, liberal university intent on rehabilitating the sins of the former institution. But let's focus on the first figure: the illiberal university.[78] For Wohlfarth, the university must maintain the spell of sleep over truth (the princess) through esoteric rituals, elitist standards, and self-aggrandizing assumptions about what counts as knowledge. The reactionary and out-of-touch university appears as a dusty, cluttered attic chamber where the princess eventually pricks her finger. In attempting to make herself a dress, and thus appear appropriate according to the university's standards, she falls into a trap set by the university itself. The very wheel she used to spin the gown was laced with the poison of resentment. Thus, "playing" the game of the university can never be merely superficial. It leaves a lasting sting from which the truth cannot awaken . . . not without violent provocation.

Benjamin is willing to awaken the princess by playing the role of a cook who boxes a kitchen assistant's ears. The cook is not a professional academic. He might not even be considered a "teacher." And yet, he is precisely the poor, weak actor who sets in motion an awakening of profound importance. While certainly an active protagonist in the story, he is also radically passive, surrendering himself to a swell of tensions that had the "conserved energy of so many years" behind it. At a certain inopportune time, this swell breaks through the sleep, crashing down in the form of boxing the ears of a busboy. As such, the cook yields to a latent potentiality for awakening that had been mounting within the dream. His actions are also and equally *reactions* to this swell as it made itself expressively unavoidable and undeniable. Importantly, the princess (truth) could not be awakened in any direct manner. Instead, awakening had to occur through a detour, from the margin, from the lowest point (rather than the highest). The cook thus reveals a necessary feature of teaching in these barbarous times: traditions cannot guarantee that the next generation will awake, and as such, a certain amount of wide-open attunement to alternative, unexpected avenues is called for.

Perhaps the most controversial aspect of "Sleeping Beauty" is the cook's treatment of the busboy, but also, by extension, all those who are affected by the echo of his clap (including the princess). The rapping of the ears is no accident, and speaks to the violence of education—a violence that is implicit in the essence of awakening and, in particular, instruction, which is the crashing of the waves of learning into a teaching. And yet, I will not go so far as to suggest that this fairy tale endorses violence as corporal punishment—an argument that has been proposed by critics of Benjamin such as Axel Honneth.[79] Such criticism fails to place Benjamin's reflections on violence and education in a larger context. To impose the adult world onto the child through coercive force would amount to nothing more than what Benjamin in passing refers to as "colonial pedagogy."[80] Such a pedagogy attempts to master children instead of the relationship between the generations. Benjamin summarizes this crucial distinction as follows: "But who would trust a cane wielder who proclaimed the mastery of children by adults to be the purpose of education? Is not education, above all, the indispensable ordering of the relationship between generations and therefore mastery (if we are to use this term) of that relationship and not of children?"[81] The cook is not the punishing cane wielder who enacts violence over the child. Despite this resistance to coercive force over children, it is indisputable that violence remains an operative category in Benjamin's comments on education, as illustrated by "Sleeping Beauty." I would like to suggest that the distracted and imaginative teacher's violence is qualitatively different from a simple form of cruelty or violence over a child. Here we can once again return to the distinction between cruel irony and grotesque parody outlined above. Because irony erects a distance through a boundary between itself and the forms it comments on, it can cause pain, suffering, and can even destroy the forms it inherits. Its violence is, in short, a destructive violence over another life external to it. This would be the violence of the cane wielder who is interested in the mastery over children. The grotesque, on the other hand, is a power of deformation that is "permeated by a rich flow of events" connected through an exaggerated swelling that "never leads to death."[82] In this sense, the violence of the grotesque is associated with the *creation* of events (as they overform or overflow) rather than with simple destruction. Given this distinction, Benjamin's retelling of "Sleeping Beauty" becomes a refashioning of the ironic violence of boxing ears (culminating in a painful punishment of a child for an unknown offence) into a grotesque violence of awakening (before the pain of the disciplining lesson takes effect within the framework of a passing dream). The alchemical power of the fairy tale interrupts what might be read as corporal punishment of children, giving it a new sense oriented toward emancipation from institutional conventions. In the fantastical logic of the fairy tale, the cook's gesture thus becomes transformed from impolite violence over a child to a comedically polite form of violence for the purpose of awakening the truth (the princess) from slumber.

To further specify the type of violence at stake in a process of awakening, it is instructive to turn to Benjamin's distinctions between mythic and divine violence. He writes, "Mythic violence is bloody power over mere life for its own sake; divine violence is pure power over all life for the sake of the living."[83] Mythic violence creates a transcendental law that is held over life in order to judge which life is to be sacrificed. It creates laws through executive decisions and then proceeds to execute these laws through administrative forms of violence that police and discipline life. The academy (in Benjamin's fairy tale) and its colonialist pedagogy are forms of mythic violence. Such violence is also ironic in that irony rests on a certain distance—a distance that might even be characterized as inducing levels of hardness and coldness through interminable sleep. Such detachment is a precondition for sacrifice through destruction and/or death. Perhaps we can even say that the sleep of the academy is a way of separating a teaching from its origins, enslaving truth (rather than making it free).

On the other hand, divine violence is law suspending. Instead of standing over and against life from a place of superior detachment, it remains immanent to life itself, extending and intensifying it through the swelling of its knowability. Here tradition is neither preserved nor destroyed but suspended just enough so that it can be made visible and free via an awakening. Such violence is not panoptic so much as diasporic, wayfaring, and thus disruptive to any given order of things. Such violence does not rest on laws (developmental, historical, natural, or otherwise) so much as it rests on the plasticity of tradition opening itself up to transmissibility. Outside of the violence imagined by legal theory, divine violence is a "pure means."[84] By this Benjamin means that it is a violence that is not justified in relation to an end (in preserving or founding a law . . . the law of the academy for instance). Controversially, the divine power that underlies this particular form of violence is described as "educative power."[85] To think educative power as a form of divine violence is to divorce educational means from purported educational ends, leaving these ends indeterminate. Such thinking is challenging as educational violence is almost always justified in relation to ends. "This is good for you," "One day you will thank me," "You will see in the future how this is important." Education is for the promotion of the good life or for the harmony of the polis or for economic prosperity. Such ends—acting as Aristotelian formal causes—give education its direction, duration, and authority over the lives of children. Yet, to think of educative power as a kind of divine violence calls such means-end logic into question.[86] Divorced from ends, would not education become a comedy of errors or a grotesque joke? The teacher, an absentminded and unprofessional waste of resources?

Importantly, in Benjamin's essay on violence, he highlights the workers' strikes as embodiments of divine violence. These general strikes unleash the potentiality of an indeterminate future not through action but through inaction (a nonaction or a subtractive action), *preferring not* to work. From the strikes we can see the potentiality for a new society swelling up without this potentiality being wedded to either existing or future patterns of labor. Likewise, in his review of the book *Basic Questions of Proletarian Education* (1929) by Edwin Hoernle, Benjamin points out the importance of Hoernle's examples of "spontaneous school strikes" and "children's strikes during the potato harvest"[87] as moments of education in which children prefer not to participate in the status quo, unleashing secret signals full of the potentiality for a coming school or a coming education. If the figurative strike to the face (by boxing ears) echoes in the world of the fairy tale, then the nonactions of children during the strike take on a collective, historical dimension. The busboys and -girls now box the ears of the cook. The education provided by the strike is not the result of an adult plan or a prescribed developmental model. Instead it is impromptu, interruptive, dispersive, and immanent to the lifeworld of children as it swells up beyond itself to join in the struggle for human freedom. The children's strike is an educational form that is not law preserving or law creating but rather law suspending, unleashing gestures that take up the world while refusing to abide by the rules of that world. The children strike back when their learnings exaggerate to the point where they have to become *precocious* teachers, educating the educators. In this sense, we can read the strike in relation to the (im)proper education theorized by Karl Kraus, which Benjamin recounts as follows: Kraus "never envisaged the child as the object of education; rather, in an image from his own youth, he saw the child as the antagonist of education who is educated by this antagonism, not by the educator."[88]

Poor Teaching versus Agitational Teaching: A Question of Inheritance

If we want to turn to the political dimension of Benjamin's theory of instruction (as a combination of learning and teaching, teaching and learning swelling and dispersing into one another), then we have to be mindful of Jane O. Newman's cautionary tale concerning the National Socialist's appropriation of Benjamin's *The Origin of German Tragic Drama*.[89] According to Newman's scrupulous archival research, scholars affiliated with National Socialism were quick to co-opt Benjamin's writings because of his interest in the German origins of the tragic drama. We could add that Benjamin's interest in the folk (as illustrated in his love of fairy tales and rural, preindustrial toys, for instance), youth movements, and divine violence could, through misreading and misappropriation, also be appropriated for pro-Nazi ends.[90] As I write this in 2018, it is tempting to equate Donald Trump with the persona of the teacher outlined above: Trump's absentminded ramblings and violent rhetoric aimed against the establishment, the media, and elites who refuse to address the plight of the disenfranchised white working-class; his nonprofessional, informal speaking style that appeals to the "everyman" in his use of vulgar, seemingly off-the-cuff humor reinforcing the hegemonic white and masculine vision of "America"; and his insistence on holding popular rallies, even after the election, in more rural locations and venues often neglected by other politicians all form some of the key elements of what William E. Connolly refers to as the "affective communicative" strategy underlying Trump's brand of aspirational fascism.[91] While Connolly neglects to emphasize the pedagogical dimension of these tactics, I feel it is important to highlight that Trump is, either consciously or unconsciously, teaching his audiences valuable lessons concerning how to channel their pent-up, repressed anger into a strong-willed, concentrated form of political power aimed at "making America great again" and "draining the swamp." On this reading, turning to Benjamin in dangerous, poor times might only add further poison to the well. Isn't Trump the embodiment of the cook, violently slapping Americans awake to the hidden truth with his unorthodox, bold, antiestablishment, anti-institutional rhetoric?

Yet, there are also resources from within Benjamin's reflections on education that offer up certain antifascist potentialities against Trump's form of aspirational or neofascism. To make this distinction clear, I want to stay firmly on the terrain of affective communication that threatens to collapse into some kind of fascist political and/or pedagogical form of speech, while at the same time redeeming a fully embodied alter-shock beyond fascism found in the writings we have inherited from Benjamin. Despite superficial similarities, I will argue that Trump bears more resemblance to Leo Lowenthal and Norbert Gutterman's description of the American agitator than to Benjamin's poor teacher. While Lowenthal and Gutterman, writing in the late forties, argued that "American agitation is in a fluid stage" with only a few agitators occasionally coming close to the "national political scene," with Trump we see their full ascension to the highest level of political power and influence.[92] In opposition to the poor teacher, the *agitational* teacher manipulates an audience through certain devices such as doubletalk and false promises, the exploitation of discontent for personal power, villainization of out-groups, unrestrained rants against shadowy enemies, and the dissemination of spurious conspiracy theories that vaguely tap into political, economic, cultural, and moral grievances. As such, Trump-style agitational teaching cannot cause awakenings so much as perpetuate fascist slumber.

To begin, inflammation (swelling) might very well rest at the heart of Trump's agitational rhetoric, yet such inflammation, as Connolly argues, is only half the story. Connolly writes, "Trumpian rhetoric, crowd organization, and shock tactics help to consolidate specific thought-imbued memes into the habitus of followers as they simultaneously create blocks against attending to discordant facts and perspectives. The blockages are as important as the inflammations."[93] Trump inflames sentiment, but in a way that prevents the exaggeration of such inflammation from ever reaching a point of swelling where its internal knowability becomes visible and free. Although manic in his approach, Trump has also mastered a sophisticated kind of control that always manages to put up blockages and filters at the precarious moment of exaggerated inflammation so as to prevent any kind of awakening (in himself or in his audiences) from his phantasmagoria. For instance, very real concerns over deindustrialization in the heartland are intensified, yet subsequently tamped down and routed into fantastical solutions (bringing back coal and steel industries) and fascist suspicions of invaders from Mexico taking jobs rather than swelling outward beyond rhetorical flourishes toward real economic and political contradictions.

Trump's distractedness is a unique mix of mere diversion and laser-focused attentiveness on core issues that support his personal lust for power and fame. In both cases, Trump constrains the wayfaring, dispersive, open and receptive qualities of distraction. Remember, diversion is a *steering away from* something toward something else. Likewise, attention is a grasping and holding onto something in particular that prevents one from openly receiving or yielding to the diverse plenitude of differences in the world. Trumpism, as a new form of agitation emerging from within aesthetic and media trends, is all too good at steering the masses through a complex cocktail of forced diversionary tactics and attention grabbing. Twitter, radio, and Fox News programs act to produce the bewildering sensation of constantly being diverted (away from *real* issues such as collusion with Russia, the evisceration of democratic norms, deregulation policies, inflated national debt, environmental crises, etc.) while simultaneously being told to remain vigilantly attentive (to spurious allegations concerning undocumented immigrants, voter fraud, etc.). We might even be able to diagnose those caught in Trump's stranglehold as suffering from what Susan Sontag calls "Attention Surplus Disorder."[94] Both those who love him and love to hate him stand transfixed, hanging on his every word, generating escalating forms of fanaticism. Such fanaticism prevents the kinds of distraction Benjamin finds essential for individual and collective freedom against fascist unification, totalization, and homogenization. This is not mere speculation. A recent study found that 25 percent of the adults surveyed suffered from obsessive-compulsive disorder related to the 2016 United States presidential election.[95] In the meantime, the potentiality for awakenings beyond the hypnotizing effects of the Trump diversion/attention nexus is bracketed out of existence. What is important to note is how Benjamin finds educational value in distraction. The Benjaminian teacher is distracted by the other perspectives, places, and events that Trump and Trumpers block. As Marina Van Zuylen argues in her review of philosophical and educational reveries, daydreams, and idle ruminations, being *without* distraction is dangerous, often resulting in either vacuous media surfing or narrow-minded fanaticism (both of which are fused in Trump-style reality TV politics).[96]

The violence of Trump's Big Lies is law destroying—not only in terms of actual legal regulations but also in terms of social norms and values. He undermines the public sphere, erodes long-standing civil codes of conduct, and produces a chaotic maelstrom where the only thing that keeps one alive is an unflappable sense of loyalty to the charismatic leader. The lesson in hardness and coldness could not be clearer: to survive, one must stop being a liberal "snowflake" and wage an endless war against all enemies, all the time, on all fronts in the name of loyalty to Trump himself. In a key respect, Trump stands in contrast to Benjamin's notion of educative violence, which does not destroy or preserve so much as suspend in order to make visible and free an untapped potentiality that only surfaces when use and exchange relationships are at a standstill. If "fake news" is a deformation of history, its violence lacks imagination. For Benjamin, imagination (de)forms inheritance in order to open its knowability and transmissibility, yet Trump's declarations simply dismiss, ridicule, and silence in order to shut down further opportunities for learning.

Here we reach what might be the most important divergence between agitational teaching and poor teaching: the relation between education, inheritance, and potentiality. Alexander Garcia Düttmann argues that fascism is never truly revolutionary precisely because it "only re-establishes links with tradition."[97] Take for instance the classical attempts by Nazi educators to inculcate youth to the lie of Nordic racial purity that must be preserved against any kind of contamination. In National Socialist textbooks, Greeks and Romans were held up as examples of Nordic races that betrayed their racial inheritance, causing a weakening of their cultural and political systems. The myth of blood purity had to be sustained, even if, as Gilmer W. Blackburn points out, it contradicted a multitude of historical and archeological facts.[98] The poverty of experience that Benjamin highlights is squarely repressed by a mythical notion of history, where inheritance can be secured by reclaiming a pure bloodline. In his list of key traits defining "ur-fascism," Umberto Eco likewise highlights the "cult of tradition" that informed both the Nazi interest in occultism and a rejection of enlightenment reason, as well as the Italian fascist obsession with the holy Roman and Germanic Empires.[99] In both cases, there was an embrace of twentieth-century technology and industrialization, but without any respect for modernity and its standards of rational, critical, or democratic discourses. For Roger Griffin, fascism is defined by an irrational mythic core that is predicated on a belief in "panlingenesis" or rebirth/regeneration.[100] This rebirth founds a radically new future on a nostalgic longing for the revitalization of precapitalist ritual, cultish pageantry, and spiritual values capable of unifying the masses into a racially pure, strong, and healthy people. In an American context, Lowenthal and Guterman highlight the importance of the fascist agitator's double gesture, which invokes total disaster while offering up a return to "the good old days" as a possible solution.[101] We might also recall Adorno's careful study of the manipulative psychological ploys used by the American radio personality and fascist-style demagogue, Martin Luther Thomas, which attempted to compensate for the shock of the new with an overemphasis on the "old-fashioned" and the "homely" as being "genuine and traditional and as having a sort of patina which the novelties lack."[102] But, as Adorno warns, this nostalgic appeal to the "regeneration" of American values in the face of perceived threats is a disturbing dream in which the "drunkenness of an annihilation . . . pretends to be salvation."[103] In other words, there is no awakening from the fascist agitator's perverse nightmare, which unifies redemption and horror in equal measure in order to redirect revolutionary tendencies toward conservative and reactionary ends.

Trump's phrase "Make America great again" is emblematic of this fascistic cult of tradition and mythic panlingenesis. The phrase works to ignite fascist tendencies because it assumes there is a "we" that needs to take back its lost patrimony. To take it back is to return to it as it empirically was during a romantic, nostalgic time when things were simpler, more pure, more "American." In the past, the "we" finds an actualization (no matter how imaginary) of the greatness that America was that can be known, understood, and possessed once again as a rightful inheritance. In this model, the past as it was lived (by a privileged few whose memory has been refracted through fascist longings) is idealized as a paradise from which society has fallen. By retrofitting the present, some of the past glory can be regained and preserved for the future. Yet this kind of teaching enacts mythic violence over those who do not see themselves reflected in the glory of years gone by. Women, minorities, LGBTQ communities, and other out-groups are written out of this history that must preserve itself against difference. The agitational teaching of neofascism reproduces violence against the oppressed precisely because history is no longer seen as a dynamic, plastic process of catastrophes and awakenings. Such violence is always a means to an end predetermined in advance by a particular vision of history of history as a teleology in reverse order that culminates in a future defined as an imitation or pastiche of what was. Mythic past turns into a mythic future, predetermined at the outset by the "victors" of history. Unable to find resources for awakening within the poverty of experience, this poverty is negated in the name of the fullness and plenitude of a promised land. But this retreat back into tradition and mythic history is, ironically, also and equally a retreat from the inheritance of origins, which always contain something that *was not* in what was. Tradition, for a neofascist agitator like Trump, is separated from origins to become an utterly reified, utterly one-dimensional prop to manipulate the masses into accepting charismatic authority. It is fetishized not unlike a commodity, packaged, advertised, and stamped on a red hat as a slogan. And indeed, this is precisely the kind of branding found in Trumpism as well as any number of neofascist, populist movements around the world.

Trump's teaching misses the dynamism of origins and how these origins offer up potentialities for awakenings beyond the blockages, repressions, and retreats enforced by fascists. Teaching, for Benjamin, is always concerned with inheriting an origin by making it *free*. In this model, what is inherited is the latent potential in the past for further awakenings in the now time of the present. Such potentiality is found on the periphery of the past, in its marginalia, in its discarded and fragmented swelling points. This is neither a return to what was nor a projection onto what ought to be ex nihilo. Rather, it is a return to what never was in the past as an unfulfilled origin of a possible future made free in the present: transmissibility of what yet can be known (knowability). The poor teacher is distracted by the peripheral potentiality missed by fascists, as they are only attentive to history's myth, thus undermining the plastic temporality of Benjamin's redemptive, messianic notion of inheritance. Instead of neofascist imitation of a lost past through the spell of nationalism, we find a suspension that unleashes indeterminate potentialities found in what remains of the everyday, the small, and the transitory traces of a tradition that has been compromised if not lost. While agitational teaching presumes knowledge of the past (in the form of absolute laws and irrational conspiracies), this presumed knowledge prevents alertness to that which is still in potential.

Instead of agitating in order to gain and solidify political power, the absentminded, imaginative, humorous teacher yields, suspends, and potentializes. Yielding to the process of learning and teaching means giving up on one's preconceived knowledge of what was or what is to come, abandoning the self to the knowability and transmissibility of a lingering potentiality found in the buried histories of general strikes or children's strikes (not to mention the dilapidated Paris arcades, trash, old toys, and any number of other odd bits and pieces that seem to distract Benjamin). These are the swelling points of history, where history suddenly awakens to its "poor truth" as Benjamin's "Sleeping Beauty" puts it. It is not the strikes as such that are the point here, rather the virtual swell that remains untapped within them. Such potentiality would be lost to the neofascist teacher who is interested in guarding the mythic past against such swelling. Only the absentminded and imaginative teacher is alert to what remains in the margins and capable of making this excess visible and free for new uses. The authority of the neofascist and his or her certainty (perhaps best exemplified by Trump's phrase "Believe me . . .") in a teleological view of mythic history is rejected for an absentminded (and thus open) approach to the inheritance of a tradition that cannot easily be transmitted as an inheritance and yet leaves the trace of transmissibility in that which remains.

The work of deforming the past in order to keep it open for the future is not only imaginative but also grotesquely humorous! In an attempt to combat Trump's affective communication, Connolly suggests that oppositional groups not fall back on the typical liberal strategy of taking the high ground and turning to reasonable, objective speech situations as the solution to disinformation, Big Lies, and inflamed passions. He warns that factual corrections and reasoned arguments are not enough. Critical self-reflection is important, but so is impassioned speech that can dislodge affectively habituated patterns of listening, seeing, and thinking. Interestingly, Connolly suggests that "at the right moments . . . laughter and satire . . . can do noble work."[104] In particular, "exaggerations, freeze-framings, and satirical repetitions bring out both how Trump works his crude magic on the visceral register of chosen constituents and how his clownish character could eventually become something to resist."[105] Through exaggerated mimicry and parody, the affective logic of Trump's communication is thrown into relief. Mimicry in this sense does not reproduce, but rather produces an affective, intensive resistance through grotesque (de)formations. Such comedy stands in contrast to Trump's own form of aggressive comedic destructiveness. He and his ilk—including Rush Limbaugh, Fox News pundits, and alt-right bloggers—employ cynical irony to induce fear, hate, and further consolidate his base. This humor is *impolite* in a Benjaminian sense as it merely reinforces battle lines between warring factions. For instance, Trump's chosen comedic form was and is middle-school name calling infused with a keen sense of political cynicism, including "Little Marco," "Crooked Hillary," "Sleepy Joe," and "Little Rocket Man." Perhaps this is the final condemnation of the neofascists: they are either too tragic or too ironic to see how redemption is to be found precisely where the labor of violence in relation to law and power is left idle. It is not that they lack a sense of humor (in fact, Lowenthal and Guterman highlight the central role of jokes in the repertoire of the agitator), but rather that this humor is predicated on an impolite, cynical irony that enables law-preserving and law-destroying violence to enact a sacrifice in the name of a Big Lie. For Lowenthal and Guterman, the American agitator is the "least restrained of all figures in public political life,"[106] often employing impolite, bawdy, outlandish behavior and ironic jokes to invoke a "tough guy" aura of "authenticity" while sacrificing those around him or her. The agitational teacher lacks comedic timing, and constantly enacts explosive and impulsive tantrums or blurts out the epic gaff geared toward humiliating those who are least privileged and most vulnerable (for instance, Trump's many spontaneous and unscripted rants against immigrants, people with disabilities, and war veterans). The poor teacher prefers not to engage in such humorous acts of destruction and humiliation, opting instead for humor that can only appear in the margins where parody finds its weak power to suspend for new use the obscenities of the agitator. He or she is absentmindedly attuned to "one last little error" that is the threshold of justice buried in the remnants and fragments of what has been inherited (despite the best efforts of the fascist agitator to destroy). Such a teacher cannot write great myths of what was but only minor fairy tales of what truth remains in potential.

RADIO BROADCASTS

For this chapter, we shift from a general overview of instruction to Benjamin's only sustained attempts at public pedagogy through radio broadcasts. I am referring to his Berlin radio scripts written between 1927 and 1933 and performed on Radio Berlin and the Radio Frankfurt Youth Hour. Reading the remaining scripts for his radio broadcasts carefully, one can determine a set of pedagogical principles at play within them that indicate how Benjamin approached the use of mass communication in a novel way to swell the historical consciousness of children through auditory alertness. While taking an important cue from Sabine Schiller-Lerg's description of Benjamin's radio scripts as a kind of materialist pedagogy inspired by Brecht's epic theater, authors have not taken into account the intimate relationship between the form and content of the radio plays, Benjamin's philosophy of childhood, and the potentiality for the knowability of historical difference.[1] For instance, Klaus Doderer has discussed the educational importance of the radio broadcasts, but his analysis too closely aligns these performances with Benjamin's reflections on children's literature, thus failing to recognize the distinct properties of radio as an auditory experience (rather than a visual one) linked to temporality and history in important ways.[2] Jaeho Kang addresses some of these oversights, pinpointing the particular educational themes of the radio plays—including the participatory audience, the formal structure of narration, and dialogue with invisible listeners—yet, once again, how these various themes connect to the swelling up of historical thinking from within the sonic field is still missing from the analysis.[3] On the flipside, Tadashi Dozono appropriately highlights the centrality of historical thinking for a Benjaminian philosophy of education, yet fails to mention the connections between such historical thinking and Benjamin's own radio practices.[4]

Addressing these oversights, I argue that the radio broadcasts are a specific expression of an instructional practice that rests on the production of *thought sounds* to produce historical awakenings in young audiences. While it is common to equate Benjamin's thought images (*Denkbilder*) with the visual, here I would like to suggest the importance of the auditory and its connection to temporality as defining features of Benjamin's dialectics. A thought sound, in this context, is a thought that cannot be isolated from its auditory form. *Hearing* the content is thus as important as the content itself. Through auditory narration and sonic experimentation, the temporality of experience becomes uniquely accessible/knowable, swelling up with historical potentiality. Furthermore, I will demonstrate how thought sounds enable us to draw together Benjamin's analysis of childhood, his reflections on education, and his actual radio broadcasts.[5] The following is an attempt to begin this project with a particular sensitivity toward (1) the distinct properties of radio as an auditory medium, (2) how a set of pedagogical principles can swell these properties into a thought sound, (3) culminating in historical awakening. Although Theodor Adorno once quipped that the radio listening amounted to nothing more than acoustic flanerie—the catchphrase of the flaneur was, after all, "look but don't touch!"[6]—the following principles will demonstrate that sound does indeed touch the listener in surprising ways, enabling a new potentiality for historical thinking to become audible (rather than visible), and thus free.

In this sense, I will take Benjamin's observation that "teaching and research should again part company" so that each can establish "rigorous new forms."[7] Indeed, Benjamin argues that "we should not look to research to lead a revival in teaching; instead, it is more important to strive with a certain intransigence for an—albeit very indirect—improvement in research to emerge from the teaching."[8] If this is the case, then we should perhaps shift gears from the *theory* of instruction outlined in a previous chapter to Benjamin's own practice where we find a "rearrangement of the subject matter" that "give[s] rise to entirely new forms of knowledge."[9] One teaches because learning has swollen to the point of becoming free (citable), and in turn, this citability (manifest in the rearrangement of the subject matter in the form of lectures or notes) produces another round of unanticipated, unpredictable learning. In the spirit of Benjamin's injunction, I will turn to his radio broadcasts in order to understand how his practical engagement with the medium of sound through radio pedagogy not only embodies his philosophy of instruction but also produces a new kind of knowledge: a truth innervated through sonic potentialities.

Radio, Time, and Historical Consciousness

Before outlining the key principles of his radio pedagogy, one problem should be addressed, and it concerns the sensual life of the child so often highlighted in the secondary literature. For Benjamin, childhood is uniquely connected to seeing (and thus to a phenomenology of the gaze/vision). In his brief essay "A Child's View of Color," Benjamin argues that "the child's view of color represents the highest artistic development of the sense of sight; it is sight at its purest, because it is isolated."[10] He also states, "[C]hildren do not reflect but only see."[11] Such speculations are further reinforced by Benjamin's own childhood experiences. Recalling a stained glass windows in an abandoned summerhouse, Benjamin writes, "Whenever I wandered about inside it, passing from one colored pane to the next, I was transformed; I took on the colors of the landscape that—how flaming and now dusty, now smoldering and now sumptuous—lay before me in the window."[12] Importantly, the young Benjamin *took on* the color in such a way that his very being was transformed. In this sense, childhood is uniquely linked with the visual field and the ability to have pure visual experiences that enables the child's very being to be described as "sight at its purist." In a short dialogue titled "The Rainbow: Dialogue on Fantasy," Benjamin pursues this phenomenological point further, arguing that children are capable of having an innocent, sensual experience of color through the pure receptivity of fantasy: "The one who sees is wholly within the color; to look at it means to sink the gaze into a foreign eye, where it is swallowed up—the eye of imagination. Colors see themselves; in them is the pure seeing, and they are its object and organ at the same time. Our eye is colored."[13] In imagination, there is no longer any separation between subject and object, for the eye itself becomes colorful. On this view, imagination is pure in so far as it is uncontaminated by forms, objects, or dichotomies of any kind. Within the purity of childhood imagination, Benjamin argues that "color is something spiritual."[14] Color is spiritual in the sense that it does not exist within the boundaries of space or time. Instead, it consists of "an infinite range of nuances"[15] that are nondenumerable and nonlocatable. As such, a child's phenomenological experience of color is distinctly different from that of the adult's. According to Benjamin, adult vision is "abstract from color" reducing color to a "deceptive cloak for individual objects existing in time and space."[16] Here we can think of the adult philosopher whose reflections on color revolve around the question of whether or not colors are actual properties of objects or merely mental perceptions. Color, on this view, becomes trapped within a mind-body dualism, either revealing or concealing features of reality. For the child, the experience of color bypasses these more or less abstract questions concerning substances and properties, and instead speaks directly to submersion and absorption into the phenomenon. An expression of this immediacy is found in children's drawings, which, for Benjamin, are not figurative (and thus concerned with space, time, laws of form, and objects) but purely colorful. Coloring-in has a "purer pedagogical function"[17] than painting precisely because it throws into relief this most basic—and colorful—form of attunement. While this heightened receptivity might emerge through other aesthetic experiences, it is somehow watered down or distorted. For instance, in relation to music, the child's receptivity is "sterile."[18] The claim here is not simply that Benjamin was interested in the particular properties of the visual experience of children but rather that he conceptualized childhood as a spiritual visual experience. Hence his abiding interest in the colored illustrations in children's books. Because of this tight connection between childhood and the visual, the secondary sources on Benjamin have a tendency to also concentrate on the literary and imagistic.[19]

And it is certainly true that in Benjamin's writings on childhood, picture books loom large. He writes, children "learn from the bright coloring"[20] of illustrated books. They learn less about the outside world (as depicted) and more about their internal capacities for imagination (to receive color). Benjamin speculates as follows:

> After all, the role of children's books is not to induct their readers directly into the world of objects, animals, and people—in other words, into so-called life. Very gradually their meaning is discovered in the outside world, but only in proportion as they are found to correspond to what children already possess within themselves. The inward nature of this way of seeing is located in the color, and this is where the dreamy life that objects lead in the minds of children is acted out. They learn from the bright coloring. For nowhere is sensuous, nostalgia-free contemplation as much at home as in color.[21]

The particular education found in colored illustrations leads inward rather than outward. It consists of an education in and for imaginative expansion as experienced by children. Black-and-white illustrations, on the other hand, appear incomplete and lead children to fill them in with scribbles of their own. Such scribbling is the first pass at learning about writing. Benjamin thus summarizes, "For no other pictures can introduce children to both language and writing as these [meaning black-and-white illustrations] can."[22] Indeed, it is in the world of monochrome pictures that "children awaken"[23] from the dreamy imagination of color to face the external world. We might even argue that the mark of writing is the precise trace of space and time overtaking the pure fantasy of color.

Given this background, Benjamin's radio broadcasts pose a distinct problem: If children are phenomenologically defined in terms of pure vision and imagination, then what happens when one shifts to the auditory dimension? What are the stakes in this sensorial alteration? Is there another "awakening" that happens when listening is privileged over seeing? There are two obstacles to answering these questions. First of all, Benjamin seems particularly suspicious of sound. In a letter to Theodor Adorno, he pessimistically points out that the advent of sound in films is an operation "designed to break the revolutionary primacy of the silent film, which generated reactions that were hard to control and hence politically dangerous."[24] Second, one could easily make the argument that the turn to radio was based in practical, financial considerations and thus was a less than ideal outlet for Benjamin's educational practice. Given more amenable historical circumstances, perhaps Benjamin would have been a children's book illustrator. Despite his critique of the sound film and evidence warranting a purely pragmatic interpretation of his radio plays, I would like to explore the educational and philosophical implications of the move to radio. As stated above, the pure receptivity of childhood is best expressed through the visual grasp of color (the child's eye *is* colorful for Benjamin), and that when this receptivity is related to music (sound) it is somehow sterilized (less vivid and less immediate).[25] If we take Benjamin at his word here, several conclusions can be drawn. First, the experience of *hearing* is uniquely different for children from *seeing*, and thus the radio might have a particularly unique educational function to play in the life of a child. Instead of celebrating and encouraging the aesthetic experience of the dreamscape of color, radio offers an acoustic experience of the world, which is an aesthetic shift *away* from childhood sensibilities. Stated differently, sound *interrupts* the child's submersion into the color field of the pure imagination. The radical nature of this shift cannot be underestimated. For Benjamin, the human body can be divided into two kinds of senses. On the one hand, the body is the "organ of active relations" of "perception of form and movement, hearing and voice," while, on the other hand, there are also "passive relations" such as "the perception of color."[26] When the body draws a contour line, it creatively produces an image of something that it appropriates. Yet, the body cannot create color, it can only yield to it. Color is pure, spiritual reception (rather than creation), and therefore a "primal phenomenon."[27] The sensation of color is subjectively passive whereas the sensation of sound is active. A passage from one to the other thus signals a modification in the relationship between primary and secondary senses.

The nature of this shift from passive to active relations is essentially an introduction to that which is missing in the fantasy of color: the knowability of temporality. An example of an awakening to temporality can be found in the thought image titled "News of a Death" from the 1934 version of Benjamin's *Berlin Childhood around 1900*. Here, Benjamin argues that déjà vu should not be understood in terms of images but in terms of sound. He observes, "Shouldn't we rather speak of events which affect us like an echo—one awakened by a sound that seems to have issued from somewhere in the darkness of past life? By the same token, the shock with which a moment enters our consciousness as if already lived through tends to strike us in the form of a sound."[28] Sound has the ability to produce a shock related to the happening of events, revivifying them by returning them to consciousness. Sound can call children into the past (as in an echo) and can thrust them into the "invisible stranger"[29] of the future. In short, sound is linked to a growing sense of temporality that is missing in Benjamin's descriptions of color. In this sense, I agree with Eli Friedlander's analysis that there is a clear distinction between seeing color and hearing sound. The former is associated with the dream, and the latter with awakening, and in particular, awakening to temporality.[30] Recall the boxing of the busboy's ears in Benjamin's retelling of "Sleeping Beauty." While we might intuitively focus on the act of boxing, it is the sound of the cook's gesture that echoes through the academy, and it is this *sound* that causes the academy to begin to awaken to the knowability of truth.

At the same time, I want to suggest that the distinction between color and sound is not so radical as it might first appear and that sound exists *in potential* within the fantasy of color. And in this sense, I agree in part with Uta Kornmeier who, as opposed to Friedlander, argues for an interplay of different senses, thus deemphasizing dichotomies between color fields and soundscapes.[31] To mediate these positions, I argue that sound *swells* from inside the movement of color, and this swelling makes a latent temporality audible (and thus knowable *as* temporal). In this sense, the movement of color (before and after) can inflate itself to the point of temporalizability. This is the process of awakening that underlies both the connection and disconnection between passive and active, fantastical and historical dimensions of Benjamin's reflections on childhood.

For instance, Benjamin highlights how children are fascinated by how "colors shimmer in subtle, shifting nuances" or "make definite and explicit changes in intensity."[32] He goes so far as to argue that color is "fluid, the medium of all changes"[33] for children. Because colors have this shifting quality, there has to be some notion of movement *within* the color field, even if this field is ultimately a spiritual, pure realm existing before the advent of spatial and temporal intuitions (as in Kant's critical philosophy). Even if there is not a subject or an object present in the color field, there is at least a before and an after that can be sensed as colors change. This phenomenologically basic sense of before and after that occurs with the movement of washes of color in the imagination is latent with a temporal dimension that is not yet knowable to the child. Sound is the sudden audibility of this spatial inscription of before and after, ripping it out of the spiritual and into the historical. On this reading, the historical would be the transformation of before and after into *earlier and later*, sensorially swelling to consciousness that which otherwise would remain implicit within the receptivity of fantasy. As such, thought sounds are small messianic educational displacements within, yet beyond, the color field.

Evidence for this view is provided by Benjamin's unusual description of memory within the horizon of color. "Picture books," Benjamin writes, are for children "paradise" in which they "learn in the memory of their first intuition" of color, which is a "memory without yearning."[34] Remembrance without yearning (for a nostalgic return or a hopeful change) is akin to movement *without* a sense of temporality. Pure movement in the color field would be experienced without loss, as there is no past, and without expectation, as there is no future. Such a temporality would be purely plastic with neither a beginning nor an end.[35] And yet, it is important to note that for Benjamin, this state without yearning is still a form of *memory*—memory of a movement outside of temporal consciousness.

Sound can only be heard (and recalled in the form of an echo) precisely because this pretemporal memory is always already working within color. As the example "News of a Death" illustrates, sound is an event that shocks the child out of the color field by introducing the *moment* into experience—the moment of death. Death is an event that punctures the endless movement of color with an earlier and a later. Further, this argument helps clarify the relation between sound, temporality, and déjà vu. The originary moment of temporality could only ever be an experience of déjà vu precisely because temporality is experienced twice: first as a swelling up within the movement in color and then as a making audible this movement through the echo. The shock of sound is, as Benjamin puts it, "as if already lived through" precisely because it is first and foremost a movement submerged within the waves of shimmering color. What is important in my argument, is that this new temporality—with its yearnings—is not the negation of color so much as color awakening to the knowability of the temporal dimension of its movement. The shimmering and fluttering waves of color swell into sound waves that emit audible frequencies, and with this expansion, activity appears within receptivity, history within the spiritual.

In fact, several of the radio plays are overtly concerned with the shift from seeing to hearing, and how this sensorial shift marks an opening to the knowability and transmissibility of temporality or, in its worldly formulation, historical thinking. In the radio script titled *A Visit to the Brass Works*, Benjamin begins with the following challenge:

> I can imagine that upon hearing something like 'A Visit to the Brass Works' on the radio, a listener might think: 'Oh dear, another of those harebrained topics. You have to see something like that, you can't describe it.' If that listener did not turn off his [sic] radio a few seconds ago, then I beg him [sic] to be good enough to give me just a few moments more, because it is precisely to him [sic] that I wish to speak.[36]

It would be a mistake to assume that the following detailed description of the brass works is a mere substitution for seeing. While apparently highlighting the limitations of the auditory over the visual, Benjamin abruptly reverses this line of reasoning, suggesting that when one sees the brass works in the first person, one is overwhelmed with the sensory experience and thus unable to contemplate the totality of the works.

Benjamin then suggests, ". . . one can say that the closer one wants to get to what is going on in such an immense plant—should one witness such an operation some day—and the more one longs to understand a little bit of it, the further one has to distance oneself from it."[37] Radio listening provides the critical distance needed to pull one out of submersion in the visual field (of color) so that one can reflect on the *history* of the brass works. Here Benjamin highlights the unique properties of the auditory dimension introduced through radio as an educational form.

Based on this line of reasoning, we can offer an educational and philosophical justification for radio as an educational form (rather than a simple pragmatic/biographical footnote). Through auditory experience, a child awakens to the temporality of the world (history) from within the movement of the color field. The choice of radio for inaugurating a shift is not a coincidence. The waves of color as they change are the preconditions for the waves of sound, which are temporalizing. With every word that Benjamin speaks, the radio broadcast anticipates its own *end* (its death). Indeed, Benjamin frequently makes asides to his audience concerning the length of time that remains or that there is not enough time. For instance, in the play on the brass works, Benjamin states, "If you now know how infinitely much there would be to say [about this topic], to ask about all of this, and if you remember that we only have twenty minutes for our conversation, then you will see that there is no point running ahead in our seven-league boots, and that we should rather take our time at a few, individual stations."[38] Benjamin calls attention to the finitude of time, and what can be done within a set span. Although possibilities are infinite within a color field, historical time offers certain constraints that necessitate choices of where to start and what to do before time ends. The auditory realm of radio awakens children to this set of limitation that are always bound by an earlier and a later. In this sense, radio swells children into the *historical capacities of youth* through a full-bodied alter-shock to the visual system. Indeed, the major defining feature of youth for Benjamin is precisely an awakening to history. Unlike children, youth feel themselves "related by blood to history—not to that which is past but to that which is coming."[39] Youth find themselves engaged in a struggle against schools and the family, which attempt to stifle their awakening—thus keeping them in a position of eternal childhood (a fantastical, imaginative realm) or pole-vaulting them directly into adulthood (which lacks spirited resolve over the fate of values). Drawing attention to the awakening of temporality draws attention to the need to make decisions and actions (concerning what to do with the time that remains before its end), which do not concern children. These are the preoccupations of youth. In short, the radio format points the young audience toward the problem (and possibilities) of existing within the history of the world. Through the instruction about brass works, it becomes clear that Benjamin's educational concern is twofold: to teach about the brass works, but also, and perhaps more importantly, to alert the child to the knowability and transmissibility of temporality (history) within the color field as it swells up through sound waves. It is the very medium of the radio broadcast that might have the most violent yet educative effect on children who are otherwise drawn into the spiritually transcendent experience of color. Thinking historically therefore is dependent on a more fundamental sensorial shift within *and* away from the visualization of color. Imagination might (de)form via color, but this is also a moment of creative formation of something yet-to-come: the historical being of youth.

Principles of Radio Pedagogy

As stated above, the goal of radio broadcasting for Benjamin is to provoke a moment wherein children become estranged from submersion in the spiritual, pretemporality of the color field. Radio is a youthful educational form that enables children to enter into history through the production of dialectical thought sounds. Through sound, experience is suddenly temporalized, and because of this, the potentiality for thinking historical difference (earlier and later) emerges. Benjamin often begins his radio broadcasts with some kind of riddle or challenge to think historically. For instance, when starting the broadcast of "Berlin Guttersnipe," Benjamin playfully and provokingly asks his audience, "I bet that if you try, you can remember seeing wardrobes or armories with colorful scenes, landscapes, portraits, flowers, fruits, or other similar designs inlaid in the wood of their doors."[40] In this challenge, Benjamin attempts to prompt historical memory of things passing away. Such a challenge cannot be easy for children who, if Benjamin is correct, experience the world through a quasi-spiritual gaze with no earlier and later present, no yearning, no loss, no sense of death. The fundamental shift from visual submersion in the color field to an auditory experience of temporal unfolding means that the broadcaster must take care so that the violence of this sensorial reconfiguration does not completely paralyze the child. Indeed, the stakes of learning to listen only become clear against the backdrop of the primacy of color, vision, and passive relations in childhood. The following provides a set of pedagogical principles extracted from the radio broadcasts that could be read as educational rules-of-thumb but also as ethical measures against sensorial paralysis or sonic manipulations of various kinds. In other words, these rules of thumb make sure radio remains a *polite* educational form. To be clear, my point is that radio is potentially educational in its form (as a medium of sound). The following principles merely amplify this potential capacity to produce historical awakenings (letting it swell up to the point where it becomes transmissible in the form of a teaching). In this sense, we once again find Benjamin wrestling with the connections between teaching, learning, and the inheritance of tradition. Only this time, he offers up an educational form (radio), which can produce the unique capacity for historical thinking via thought sounds.

The Principle of Storytelling

Scholars such as Richard Wolin[41] have found it difficult to square Benjamin's simultaneous interest in redeeming the potentiality of the past through the precapitalist practice of storytelling and his eager embrace of the most advanced forms of modernist culture and technological innovation. While this remains somewhat of a theoretical aporia—with Benjamin often flipping back and forth from these two perspectives as if they were mutually exclusive Gestalts—what I want to argue here is that he actually finds a way to mediate them in his practice of radio pedagogy.[42] As argued at the outset of this chapter, if we turn directly to real instructional practices, then new research and new knowledge can be generated. In this sense, we can look to Benjamin's radio pedagogy to potentially "solve" certain aporias that appear in his theory, and in particular, the aporia of the poverty of experience brought about by modern technologies (such as radio).

In his famous essay on storytelling, Benjamin highlights how our "ability to exchange experiences"[43] is disappearing and how intergenerational wisdom is "dying out" because capitalism has "removed narrative from the realm of living speech."[44] In other words, there is a growing gap between a fragmented, decaying, and reified sense of personal experience and a collective sense of history that is intergenerational and enables the individual to mediate experience through the meanings and traditions of the past. To deal with this problem, Benjamin opts for a redemptive strategy that finds hope in the marginal practice of storytelling.

For Benjamin, the story (as opposed to the epic, the novel, or mere information) has a particular structure. Stories (not unlike fairy tales) present life as an intelligible and coherent whole, where experience and meaning are interconnected. This is what makes stories readily communicable to younger generations. They are also a form of premodern craftsmanship that involves hands, bodies, gestures, as well as spoken words. In short, they are collective, embodied performances. And most importantly, the storyteller is a *teacher* who initiates a special kind of *intergenerational communication* through which historical experience can travel. The storyteller also has an "incomparable aura."[45] As we know from Benjamin's work on art in the age of mechanical reproduction, aura is linked to a sense of distance, ritual performance, permanence, authenticity, presence, and irreplaceable singularity. We can easily imagine these same features being attached to the storyteller, granting him or her a certain amount of what Benjamin might refer to as cult value. This value is generated through an emphasis on the presence of body, narrative, and spoken word. Sound and body are connected through the gestures of the storyteller, who not only stands before an audience, but also speaks the story. In light of Benjamin's analysis, technologies of mass reproduction such as the radio are a decisive threat to the auratic embodiment of the storyteller, thus limiting the potential for the transmission of inheritance across generations.

The redemption of a marginal and antiquated practice such as storytelling (and its cult value) in order to solve the pressing problems of modernity's poverty of experience stands in stark contrast to Benjamin's overtly Marxist proposition in "The Author as Producer." Here he argues that only the most advanced literary techniques can determine whether or not an artist is following the correct political tendency (and we might add, educational tendency). What communist art needs is not "spiritual renewal," but rather "technical innovations."[46] A work of literary art will be progressive politically if it follows the most advanced artistic techniques and adopts the most cutting-edge technologies and regressive if it follows traditional, outmoded artistic practices. Revolutionizing the processes and techniques of the artistic modes of production, and thus struggling with the internal problems of form that are proposed by the introduction of new materials, styles, modes of mechanical (re)production, and so forth exposes a utopian fragment of a possible future within the present, seemingly impoverished and barbaric, moment. Instead of returning to the auratic power of ritual, tradition, and storytelling, as opposed to the latest technologies (e.g., radio), we have a vision of art that explodes aura in the name of collective experimentation and political appropriation of the modes of artistic production.

While Benjamin might not have been able to *theoretically* mediate these two positions, his radio plays mediate them through pedagogical *practice*. The radio plays redeem storytelling but through the most advanced, mass communicative tool available. This strange hybrid transforms both Benjamin's understanding of storytelling and technical, artistic innovations. For instance, storytelling is no longer bound to the embodiment of gestures. Instead, the voice is distinctly disembodied—the body is replaced by voice mediated through technology. Closeness and presence are replaced by distance (from the auditory source) and displacement (one can now listen anywhere with anyone while doing anything). Benjamin explicitly points this out when he comments that children will never know if they meet him in the streets. In addressing his audience directly, Benjamin speculates, "Maybe someday I'll meet one of you there [in the markets of old Berlin]. But we won't recognize each other. That is the downside of radio."[47] While Benjamin seems to lament the loss of visual identification, I would argue that this dimension of listening to the radio (minus *seeing*) only heightens the temporal aspect of the experience. Further, the aura of the unique, irreplaceable storyteller also withers. The mechanical filtering of the disembodied voice does not enable auratic enchantment/attachment to the storyteller, allowing for the sound of the story to take on a life of its own beyond the teller. In this sense, the oral storytelling of the radio rests somewhere between the authority of the storyteller (granted by physical presence, or the correspondence between voice, gesture, and body) and the democratization of the book in absence of such a presence. Thus, the cult value of the story is decreased, while its educational value is increased, dispersed, and made free through the mechanically mediated voice of the broadcaster now detached from its source and put into public circulation. Storytelling is brought back from oblivion by the very same technology that put it under threat in the first place, taking on a ghostly, disembodied afterlife. Aura dissipates, leaving a hollow within sound for a new kind of thinking to emerge that has distinctively political valences (as we will explore below). In short, radio redeems the educational value of storytelling but in a transformed frequency, one that is not beholden to either the specificities of a particular body/set of gestures or auratic cult value.

The Principle of Catastrophe

Many of the radio broadcasts concern catastrophes, including the eruption of Vesuvius that covered Pompeii in lava, the earthquake that destroyed the capital of Portugal in the eighteenth century, a Canton theater fire from 1845, a railway disaster in Scotland in 1879, and a Mississippi flood in 1927. Benjamin's emphasis on catastrophes is interesting for two reasons. First, the category of catastrophe crosses the natural and historical divide and is thus connected with themes found in stories and fairy tales. In Benjamin's reflections on Nikolai Leskov's story "The Alexandrite," Benjamin emphasizes a strange detail of this most peculiar stone, which grants an "ability to see in this chrysoberyl a natural prophesy of petrified, lifeless nature—a prophesy that applies to the historical world in which he himself lives."[48] In other words, the stone embodies a paradoxical sense of *natural history* wherein the atemporality of naturally occurring rock (lifeless and petrified) reveals the temporality of human history (alive and dynamic). Stories often mediate between this dichotomous pair of opposites, demonstrating how nature reveals the historical and how history can often become petrified and lifeless. The catastrophe thus rests on a dialectical cusp that separates and conjoins nature and history, and as such, serves as a powerful pedagogical tool for introducing the historical to the child who him- or herself is largely outside of history yet has the ability to awaken to history. Volcanos in particular seem to rest at a key juncture between nature and culture for Benjamin. In *The Arcades Project*, Benjamin argues that the beauty of Paris is akin to the beauty of great landscapes, and in particular "volcanic landscapes."[49] He elaborates, "Paris is a counterpart in the social order to what Vesuvius is in the geographic order: a menacing, hazardous massif, an ever-active hotbed of revolution. But just as the slopes of Vesuvius, tans to the layers of lava that cover them, have been transformed into paradisal orchards, so the lava of revolutions provides uniquely fertile ground for the blossoming of art, festivity, fashion."[50] Here the allegorical nature of revolution (which is largely impossible to envisage) is equated with lava and the generative flowering of experimentation, which the volcanic destruction opens up. Neither fully human/historical time, nor merely geological/natural time, the time of catastrophic eruption is the time of potential revolution.

In this manner, the catastrophe concerns a rupture with both geologic and chronological temporalities. The catastrophes that concern Benjamin are abrupt and violent events that shake civilization and open up new, unforeseen possibilities. There is no progress or development, only repeated emergencies that remind us of the finitude and precariousness of existence. In this sense, they teach that the impossible happens. Concerning the railway disaster at the Firth of Tay, Benjamin writes, "Today I'll be telling you about a railroad catastrophe, but not only because it's a horrible and frightening story. I also want to place it within the history of technology, specifically of railroad construction."[51] Rather than dwell on the sensationalism of a particular episode, he frames the catastrophe as *revealing* something about the history of technology as such. He continues, ". . . I want to present this accident as only one minor incident in a great struggle, a struggle in which humans have been victorious and will remain victorious if they do not once more destroy the fruits of their own labor."[52] The hopeful note of optimism in human capacities for progress is undercut by the final turn of the sentence that warns of the propensity of human labor to destroy itself. Thus, catastrophe is internal rather than external to the historical becoming of technology. Triumphalist history as a unified process is undercut by the ongoing insistence of catastrophic breaks.

But perhaps even worse, the modern era has seen the absolutization of the catastrophe. Famously Benjamin writes, "That things are 'status quo' *is* the catastrophe."[53] The state of exception has become the rule. Yet rather than see this as a complete disaster, Benjamin finds a small opening within the global catastrophe. "Redemption," he speculates, "depends on the tiny fissure in the continuous catastrophe."[54] In this sense, there is a potentiality for redemption, a swelling up of alternative histories within yet against catastrophe, which gives hope to the hopeless. Benjamin's radio broadcasts point the audience toward these tiny remnants, these seemingly irrelevant details within the rubble of catastrophe where truth still sleeps, ready to be awakened.

Such truth cannot take the form of progressive overcoming nor nostalgic return to an age free from the destructive powers of catastrophes. Historical consciousness without nostalgic longing is a fundamental lesson of Benjamin's radio pedagogy. Regarding this point, Benjamin speaks of the disappearing dialects found in Berlin markets, "When you hear a speech like this, there's no need to mourn old Berlin, because it can still be found here in the new Berlin, where it's as indestructible as our speaker's collar stiffener."[55] If catastrophes are the rule and not the exception, then so too there remains an indestructible kernel lying in wait within a tiny fissure that persists despite the surrounding destruction—an unfulfilled remnant that is not found in the past but rather emerges in present ruins as a promise of a different future. One of the goals of Benjamin's radio pedagogy is to make the young listener sensitive to the dialectic between catastrophic destruction and the persistence of this unfulfilled potentiality in the rubble, which is indestructible. This fragment of the lost, forgotten, and decaying (yet indestructible) has what Paul North might refer to as a *negative aura*, or an aura that is neither negated nor restored.[56] This would be an aura *as not* an aura, or an aura whose cult value has been eroded by continual cataclysmic disruption. Negative aura decays, yet its atomic half-life stretches out its existence into a seemingly indestructible span of time, thus preserving the hope for a different future. In this sense, radio pedagogy sensitizes the listener to its trace amount, transforming the ear into a messianic Geiger counter.

What is important in focusing on catastrophes as paradigms of temporality is that they present time as neither geological stasis nor chronological progress. The first lesson in history is that time *is* a rupture (there is a before and an after), a contingency, and thus a radical opening capable of redeeming an indestructible potentiality for difference. While the form of radio pedagogy generates its own seismic shift from seeing to hearing, the content of this pedagogy likewise provides thought sounds of equally volcanic ruptures on the broader scale of human worlds. In this way, form and content mimic one another, reinforcing the unique importance of the plastic temporality in Benjamin's radio experiments.

The Principle of Irrelevance

In his radio broadcasts, Benjamin praises the work of the German writer E. T. A. Hoffmann because he can make visible and free the extraordinary out of the ordinary. Benjamin observers that what made Hoffmann so unique was his "gift of beholding in every phenomenon, whether a person, a deed, or an occurrence, the most unusual things, to which we have no relation in our everyday lives."[57] He could uncover the demonic and the supernatural within the most taken-for-granted and seemingly banal gestures and habits of his surroundings. He was, for Benjamin a "physiognomist of Berlin"[58] who decoded the whole from details, the general from the particular. And in so doing, he transformed the irrelevant and superficial details into allegories. Here the average and the mundane are redeemed from the meaningless ritual performances of city life in Berlin. The key to unlocking an alternative reality rests in cultivating an acute sensitivity toward the purportedly irrelevant. The fantastic possibilities unconcealed by the physiognomist would be missed by anyone who was too preoccupied with the business of getting by or getting along with the pragmatics of city life. Hoffmann had the uncanny ability to focus in on the trivial, and through this investigation, profess their destinies.

Like Hoffmann, Benjamin also praises the forgotten book illustrator and painter Theodor Hosemann for his physiognomic appreciation for the beauty of the typical details of Berlin. While elite critics dismissed Hosemann's art as kitsch, Benjamin highlights his ordinariness, inelegance, and lack of refinement as somehow containing a radical social and political potentiality. Such potentiality is missed by the cultured but can be appreciated by "the common people and children."[59]

Hoffmann and Hosemann's shared principle of irrelevance emphasizes that which is ignored by museums and schoolhouses. Commenting on a commonly used textbook from the time, Benjamin remembers the following:

> Back then what especially struck me about the book was that most of its pages were divided into large and small print. The parts in large print covered princes, wars, peace treaties, alliances, dates, etc., which we had to learn, though I did not enjoy doing so. The parts in small print dealt with so-called cultural history, including the habits and customs of people in earlier times, their convictions, their art, their knowledge, their buildings, and so on. Learning these things wasn't required. We only had to read them over, and this I enjoyed greatly. As far as I was concerned, there could have been even more of it, no matter how small the print.[60]

There are several important points to be taken away from this passage. First, historical thinking concerns marginalia, which is always eclipsed by great events, epic heroes, and grand political gestures. Like Hoffmann, Benjamin finds a negative aura within that which has been placed on the sidelines of official historical narratives. Such ephemera provide moments of rupture with school book chronologies, thus maintaining a revolutionary kernel within the everyday. Second, this investigation of minor history is pleasurable precisely because it is *not* required, and thus is a kind of educational experience that is *free* from the need to produce learning outcomes. It serves no practical purposes, and thus flies below the radar of educational measurement and calculation. As such, minor history is illicit. If minor history is tolerated, it is only in small print, as an aside that no one pays attention to (except Benjamin, of course).

Minor history is history told from below in order to pick up on the traces of that which would otherwise be regarded as meaningless or insignificant. While equating history with physiognomy might sound suspicious (given physiognomy has been linked with various forms of racism), Benjamin's point here is that his notion of a minor history is not reducible to a set of mere sociological facts about a place and a time. Partly empirical observation and partly imaginative storytelling, minor history cannot be simply additive. The irrelevancy principle that underlies minor history calls for a paradigm shift in who is seen as a historian, how history is written, and the fundamental lessons it tells. To start from the margins is to reshape the scope and form of history as the textbook depicts it. It is an effort to (de)form and (re)form how history expresses itself on the surface of lived experience (hence the reference to physiognomy). Such marginalia includes forgotten heroes, artists, and common folk. Benjamin seems to revel in history from an oblique angle, focusing on forgotten and obscure figures such as the children's book illustrator Hosemann, the unusual case of Kaspar Hauser, bootleggers, gypsies, witches, and bandits. In all cases, he avoids easy moralistic interpretations of those individuals and groups that history has deemed "evil" or "mad" or "criminal." Instead, most of these figures and groups come to represent the intolerance of powerful religious or state institutions. This does not mean that they are romanticized, but rather that the physiognomy of radio pedagogy sensitizes children to the unspoken that remains in the shadows of the stories that Western Enlightenment tells about itself.

Benjamin urges his young listeners to become *minor* (pun intended) historians and to *speak* their own stories from below and from outside of official institutions. To do so, the city of Berlin becomes a schoolhouse presenting an unofficial and unsanctioned narrative of civilization. "Just open your eyes and ears," Benjamin beseeches his youthful audience, "when you're walking through Berlin and you'll collect many more such stories than you've heard on the radio today."[61] Children should become physiognomists of their own worlds.[62] From radio listeners, they too can become producers of minor histories. The activity of listening leads to discovery and production. And when they tell their own stories, the ordinary will become extraordinary, the irrelevant will become charged with the utopian. The market place can become a "veritable academy for Berlin dialect,"[63] a diasporic counterinstitution to the schoolhouse. There, in the streets, no one is around to certify what has been learned, how to learn, when to learn, or where to learn. This is education in suspension of its institutional logics—thus transforming into an unsanctioned form of poor education. In this sense, there is a complete decentralization of learning as well as resistance to any official control over knowledge. There is only the pleasure of suddenly tripping over the miraculous or demonic fragments of an alternative universe that splinters the present with an unanticipated potentiality for something else/somewhere else that can appear right alongside the venders and street urchins of the market. As Benjamin summarizes, "For even the most ordinary weekly market has some of the magic of oriental markets, such as the Samarkand bazaar."[64] In sum, physiognomy of the irrelevant detail can be transformative.

Indeed, Benjamin saw evidence of this in his trip to Moscow where he witnessed emancipated children who interacted very differently with art museums than their bourgeois cousins. He observed: instead of contemplating masterpieces chosen by the curators and experts, a child of the revolution "acknowledges very different works as masterpieces," based on what "relate[s] to him, his work, and his class."[65] In this sense, children were emancipated from the expertise of the curator, and were actively producing their own criteria for what counted as a "masterpiece." Of course, this might very well appear as irrelevant to the adult who is in the know. But what Benjamin seems to have found so inspiring is the possibility for interjecting an alternative understanding of art into a space that would otherwise be strictly policed. The child as an emancipated curator of his or her own life world interrupts certain kinds of hierarchical control over who gets to decide what counts as relevant or irrelevant in the first place.

The Principle of Inlay

History for Benjamin is not a linear, teleological story of incremental and cumulative progress. It is a series of catastrophes. But these catastrophes do not merely happen in succession, one after another. Nor do they take place in vacuums. Histories overlap, contaminating the present with splinters, fragments, and remnants. To attempt to pedagogically convey the overdetermined nature of the historical present, Benjamin equates historical thinking with the handicraft of inlay. He writes,

I bet that if you try, you can remember seeing wardrobes or armoires with colorful scenes, landscapes, portraits, flowers, fruits, or other similar designs inlaid in the wood of their doors. Intarsia is what it's called. Today I'd like to present you with some scenes inlaid not in wood, but in speech.[66]

The shift here from image to speech is important to note, as Benjamin attempts to create a sonic soundscape that includes multiple, overlapping histories that collide in the present, swelling with a new sense of historical difference and potentiality. He then proceeds to extract a description of the Tiergarten in Berlin from the autobiography of Ludwig Rellstab from 120 years in the past and then to inlay into this description another description of the Tiergarten from the present. This inlay technique allows for comparisons across time in order to illustrate differences and continuities, but also to illustrate how spatial relations become temporalized and vice versa. Historical moments are neither identical nor absolutely different from themselves. Each moment is composed of the *nonsynchronous* overlapping of different historical moments that can be tapped into through the work of inlay.

Historical inlay is replicated on the level of sound itself. In the radio play titled *Much Ado about Kaper*, Benjamin begins with "*The sound of whistles and horns from a ship*,"[67] which are emitted in a dense fog. The fog makes it impossible to see anything (except the fog itself), thus undercutting the reliance on vision to navigate the world. Instead, the audience is prompted to rely on hearing. The play then proceeds through a series of auditory inlays that fold together the whistling of the main character, Kasper Hauser, with the whistling of a locomotive, the sounds of animal voices and human voice, the inner monologue of Kasper and the external sounds of the city. Benjamin encouraged children to be *alert* to this diasporic soundscape with its multiple, overlapping valences. Indeed, he even made a game of it. Children were asked to guess what all the sounds meant and to send their opinions to the radio station for a small prize. In this way, listening itself could become audible and thus free.

In short, radio pedagogy is a careful placement of overlapping temporal and sonic layers for the purpose of interrupting one-dimensional forms of seeing and thinking about history. While the textbooks speak of a single, monumental narrative progressing forward toward the absolute, for Benjamin, nothing ever dies or fully disappears. Rather, echoes remain to interrupt the linearity of experience. The inlay is therefore both a remnant of a catastrophe (the ashes of class struggle) but also the utopian hope for something different (a classless society). It functions as a reminder of what was and what could be—both of which are experienced *now*, in the potentiality of the present to be heard (in all is distracting diversity).

The Principle of Remembrance

One of the key enemies of Benjamin's work as a whole is commodification of social reality, or, stated differently, the universalization of the commodity form. Because of this phenomenon, it is particularly striking that Benjamin would spend so much time collecting, writing about, and discussing toys, which have become the supreme example of the commodification of childhood. Indeed, he even speculates that there should be a special radio show dedicated to this topic for children. While this idea might seem naive to us today—as children are typically inundated with nothing but advertisements for toys—it is interesting to see the novelty of the idea from Benjamin's perspective. Perhaps something more than naive fancy is at work here—something that is distinctly related to a historical materialist interest in time.

For Benjamin, toys are not simply commodities. Rather, they contain within them a certain messianic potentiality to disrupt their own commodity status. In "Old Toys," Benjamin argues that "once mislaid, broken, and repaired, even the most princely doll becomes a capable proletarian comrade in the children's play commune."[68] Old toys do not imitate adult reality (in a reproductive manner), but rather contain within them a promise of a postcapitalist society in miniature form. What is decisive in this analysis is the interplay between play and the object for unlocking this potentiality. Thus Benjamin writes, "[W]e must not forget that the most enduring modifications in toys are never the work of adults, whether they be educators, manufacturers, or writers, but are the result of children at play."[69] Play transforms the typical princely doll into a harbinger of a communist utopia. This does not mean that the toy has no agency in this process, quite the opposite. Benjamin writes about *old toys*. The transformation of the prince into a proletariat can happen only when the toy has been "mislaid, broken, and repaired"—a point that has been missed by astute Benjaminian scholars such as Carlo Salzani,[70] who have written on the importance of toys in

Benjamin's work. The toy must be untimely, or out of time in order to be played with. It must be broken, or somehow fragmented in order for play to transform it into a remnant of another future within the present. Hence Benjamin's fascination with nineteenth-century Russian toys that he saw at the Kustarny Museum in Moscow. For Benjamin, these toys were a kind of trace of a quickly disappearing folk culture, materially expressed in their "fragile condition."[71] What is important about this observation is that the toy has to have a certain *temporal distance* from its point of purchase. For play to unlock the secret potentiality of the toy, the toy must be separated from the process of production and circulation. The only real toy is the toy that has been abandoned, stowed away, lost and then rediscovered years later. The precise reason for this is that the toy-as-commodity is too much a part of the *adult* economy to truly be a toy, and thus an object of the *child's* world. To say a toy is old is therefore a redundancy, for only old toys can be toys. Only when a toy from the past is rediscovered does it open itself up to play. As such, toys are distinctly temporal objects, distinctly historical. Perhaps we can even say that to play with toys is to *inlay* a different, explosive temporality into the present—one which is not reified under the commodity form.

Benjamin's radio scripts dealing with toys address this precise tension between the toy as a commodity and the toy as a toy. He pinpoints this issue at the end of his first installment of his "Berlin Toy Tour."

> I'm worried sick I'll soon be swamped with mail, letters along the lines of: 'What? Are you completely mad? You think that kids don't already whine from morning to night? And now you're putting ideas in their heads and telling them about thousands of toys that, up until now, thank God, they knew nothing about, and now they want all of them, and probably things that don't even exist anymore?' How should I answer them? I could take the easy way out and beg you [the children in the audience] not to repeat a word of our story, don't let them in on a thing, and then we can continue next week just like today. But that would be mean. So it's left to me to calmly say what I really think: the more someone understands something and the more he [sic] knows of a particular kind of beauty—whether it's flowers, books, clothing, or toys—the

more he [sic] can rejoice in everything that he knows and sees, and the less he's [sic] fixated on possessing it, buying it himself [sic], or receiving it as a gift.[72]

Here Benjamin warns against the quick-and-easy equation between toys and commodities. But his radio analysis concerning the problem of commodification is distinct from his essays on old toys and toy collecting. Instead of discovering old toys to physically play with them or to collect them, he opts for *re-collecting them*. The memory of old toys brings joy. Whereas any physical toy contains the residue of commodification within it, and thus is always already primed to enter back into an exchange relationship with other commodities, memory has a "particular kind of beauty" that preserves the autonomy of the toy from the logic of the market, staving off the desire to possess, buy, and own the toy. To fixate on possession means that one is fixated on the commodity side of the toy rather than on the playful side. Yet, remembering is a way of possessing something without possessing it, a way of possessing that which is absent. As such, it is a noncommodified use of toys. Perhaps we could even go so far as to argue that *only in memory can we ever really play with toys*. We can only play with echoes.

We can push this line of inquiry even further. To remember old toys means that the untimely quality of the toy is brought to the foreground and that this unique temporality ultimately eclipses the physical presence of the toy object, making it redundant. The toy dissolves into time. When we remember old toys we play with them, but what we are really playing with is time itself now made visible and free (rather than locked within the physicality of the toy object).

Such a notion of play is perhaps too internal and privative for some. How does one play with others when the toys are not physically present to mediate between children? One can play through sharing memories. In other words, one can only play when internal memories are unfolded in the form of spoken stories. The playful exchange of memories through storytelling is not equivalent to exchange within a capitalist system as memories cannot be assigned an abstract value, nor can the exchange of stories ever be quantitatively evaluated. The memory of toys *redeems* them from their fate as mere commodities, and their sharing through stories that are told and listened to opens up an intersubjective space that is not reducible to commodity exchange relationships. Here is a different kind of play—a play that is not predicated on the presence of objects or their production and circulation within exchange relations, but rather on their temporal traces left embedded in memory and then spoken about. Perhaps this is one manifestation of what Benjamin meant when he called for "emancipating the toy"[73] from industrialization. The radio broadcasts about toys are therefore Benjamin's way of playing with toys through the sharing of and listening to memories in the absence of visual cues or tangible objects. This sharing is the most direct way to jumpstart a sense of history—especially in children who, as Benjamin wagers, find particular pleasure in merely listening to his descriptions of toys from long ago.

Authoritarianism on Air: Benjamin versus Adorno on Radio Pedagogy

This view of radio is redemptive, saving something of storytelling from within the very technologies that put it at risk. Through a set of pedagogical principles, Benjamin was able to harness the educational potential of the radio for producing sonic awakenings in children. Theodor Adorno, not surprisingly, would have been more skeptical of this move. For Adorno, the technological mediation of the radio demanded attentive listening while at the same time *negating* the potential for listening in any serious way. In short, radio cannot produce thought sounds infused with power to produce historical awakenings. For instance, the radio and its electrification of sound are part and parcel of both the commodification of experience and the rise authoritarianism. Adorno summarizes, "The standardization which we mean is the more or less authoritarian offer of identical material to a great number of people." This standardization of sound for broadcasting is not arbitrary but rather "the essence of radio itself."[74] For Adorno, standardization through new technologies is a symptom of the dialectical connection between fascism and the liberal democratic mass culture of the United States. A rather unique example of this analysis can be found in Adorno's criticism of the radio symphony, which, for him, is a total contradiction. The intensities of sound that characterize the live performance of a symphony are flattened out when broadcasted, causing the symphony to disappear at the very moment it is brought to the ears of the masses. "As soon as it [the performance] is reduced to the medium range between piano and forte, the Beethoven symphony is deprived of the secret of origin as well as the might of unveiling."[75] In short, the technical features of sound mediation via the radio *make listening impossible*, preventing sound from producing true musical thought (or, for Benjamin, awakenings). The radio therefore manipulates sound to the point where sound is homogenized and standardized, transforming qualitative difference into quantitative frequency. Fascist hardness and coldness as well as technological fetishization are soon to follow. The ear is numbed to the rebellious qualities of musical interruption, and interest in musical experience is exchanged for the "agency" to control volume levels to accommodate sound to the interior space of the home. "Regressive listening,"[76] as Adorno was apt to say, is indicative of the consumer model of subjectivity found in mass culture but also in the authoritarian personality of the fascist. In his work on the culture industry with Max Horkheimer, Adorno makes a similar claim. "In fascism radio becomes the universal mouthpiece of the *Führer*."[77] The voice of the leader becomes omnipresent, but this banality makes the voice only more powerful. There is no longer an outside or a place immune from the spread of political propaganda. The authoritarian voice becomes naturalized as part of the everyday background noise of life and then internalized as part of one's own psychological disposition. Advertising is similar; its pervasiveness makes it invisible, but this invisibility is its greatest asset. Within the "immanent tendency of radio . . . recommendation becomes command."[78] This subtle shift from freedom to choose to a command unites the voice of the Führer and the voice of the salesperson. There is no option not to obey the call of duty (to follow or to make a purchase). Radio levels the differences so that commands infest the sphere of the everyday. In this sense, radio, or so it would appear, is the problem instead of the solution to the question of awakening (musical or historical).

Given Adorno's pessimism concerning the radio, it is interesting to note that he, like Benjamin, was deeply interested in redeeming the educational value of the medium, wrestling it away from its own, internal fascist tendencies. Thus, it is instructive to read Adorno's analysis of NBC's *Music Appreciation Hour*, a radio program dedicated to the instruction of children. Adorno's criticism of this program is too expansive for me to cover in full. But what I want to do is highlight some of the failures of the program in Adorno's eyes with particular emphasis on the interplay between form and content in Adorno's argument, and how the two reinforce certain authoritarian potentialities in radio.

According to Adorno, the fundamental problem with NBC's *Music Appreciation Hour* is that it does not provide authentic experiences for children to listen to music. Adorno writes, the program "leads to a fictitious musical world ruled by names of personalities, stylistic labels, and pre-digested values which cannot possibly be 'experienced' by the audience of the Music Appreciation Hour, since the program presents the material in a way designed, wittingly or unwittingly, to foster conventional, stereotyped attitudes, instead of leading to concrete understanding of musical sense."[79] The standardized form of listening stands in sharp contrast to Adorno's description of the power of sound to jolt a child into a musical awakening. Akin to Benjamin, Adorno writes, "[T]he deciding childhood experiences of music are much more like a shock. More prototypical as stimulus is the experience of a child who lies awake in his bed while a string quartet plays in an adjoining room, and who is suddenly so overwhelmed by the excitement of the music that he forgets to sleep and listens breathlessly."[80] In other words, musical sound can *innervate the body* of the child to the point where he or she cannot sleep. This is precisely the intense kind of full-bodied alter-shock that radio standardization prevents.

How does radio pedagogy like the *Music Appreciation Hour* denude sound of its educational value for musical awakenings? First, the pedagogical approach adopted by the program's conductor, Walter Damrosch, dissects sounds into parts divorced from a dialectical relation to the whole, leading to the fetishization of instruments and their purported personalities. Children are told to be attentive to the "personalities" of individual instruments, and in so doing, they lose a more global alertness and openness to the movement of music as it swells up. In attempting to hear particular instruments, the child never hears the symphony as such. As Adorno worries, "A child who waits, when listening to a Haydn symphony, for the entrance of the flute, the violins, or the kettle drums, misses the music itself and becomes what may be called 'technique-minded'; that is to say, the child concentrates on recognizing each instrument."[81] The child does not cultivate the art of hearing. Instead, he or she becomes *hard* of hearing. Hardness of the ear means that the radio has promoted the closing off of the auditory faculty from the power of the symphony. The resulting "fetishistic attitude toward music"[82] means that child is more excited to point to a recognizable sound than he or she is to experience the radical presence of music that might be difficult, strange, unfamiliar, and shocking. For Adorno, this minor point has political implications as the model of listening being advocated results in "men [sic] becoming emotionally more closely bound to the tools themselves (the means) than to their human function (the end). . . . There is a grave danger to the psychological development of young people involved here. . . ."[83] The grave danger is the implicit cultivation of the kinds of hardness and fetishism that are the psychological foundations for fascism. These radio programs also cultivate coldness toward the range of emotional and psychological responses that music can produce. Adorno highlights how the programs overemphasize the fun and enjoyment of music. All affect becomes one-dimensional. The result is that music is cast as nothing more than a consumer good whose end is to supply satisfaction. Hence, the hidden reproduction of a broader logic of capitalist consumerism: "Something must be pleasing and worth its money to be admitted to the market."[84]

It is important to note that the *Music Appreciation Hour*'s pedagogical principles are not simply different from Benjamin's principles but actually *invert* them. For instance, while Benjamin focuses on history as a catastrophe, the radio program presents musical history as a linear story leading from one great figure to the next. Instead of helping students face the disruptive fact of historical transformation, history is heavily censored to protect children from any content that might be disturbing to them or possibly confusing. Furthermore, this sanitized history of great geniuses (each building off the work of their predecessors) only has room for the famous, and therefore excludes the irrelevant, marginal, or the problematic. According to Adorno, the criteria for being included in the curriculum of the *Music Appreciation Hour* is nothing more than "success," as it is borrowed from the world of "business competition."[85] Adorno worries that this means those composers who are less productive might be excluded from the lineup, and that difficult, modernist composers might be censored. The result would be a degraded and impoverished notion of musical quality. The program "presumes an artificial, unilateral, evolutionary development of music serially in time"[86] that fails to capture the intricate inlay of temporalities Benjamin attempted to weave into his broadcasts. And finally, Adorno worries that the approach to memorizing facts and figures (not to mention the memorization of melody lines) reduces the act of hearing music to nothing more than "commodity listening" through which music becomes "property"[87] to be recited on a test for a passing grade. The "hording of information about music"[88] replaces the fleeting, spontaneous, and immediate experience of hearing—an experience linked to the full-bodied shock effect that sound can produce. The remembrance of the *event* of hearing becomes reduced down to the grasping of bits and pieces of information that are stored up to be recited at a later date to demonstrate what one has "learned."

At the head of this pedagogical failure is the *Music Appreciation Hour*'s conductor, Walter Damrosch. While Benjamin emphatically downplays his own aura as a radio storyteller, Damrosch uses the medium to produce a new kind of *authoritarian aura* through his voice and his magical control over the orchestra. Indeed, the study guides that accompanied the *Music Appreciation Hour* repeatedly emphasized Damrosch's ability to wave his magic wand (his conducting baton) and cast a spell. A "false halo"[89] was produced around Damrosch as a "spiritual leader"[90] of music. The lesson learned from the resulting cult of personality was a "reactionary attitude"[91] with decisively "authoritarian tendencies."[92] Significantly, the mass inculcation of children to the sound of authoritarianism invaded the home in the guise of "harmless" if not overtly benevolent educational programs. Whereas Benjamin *gives his voice away*, encouraging children to turn away from him, outward toward the city, Damrosch's voice is authoritarian in that it demands attentiveness to his expertise.

But, as Adorno is quick to point out, this is not Damrosch's fault. Rather it is part of the "one-way structure"[93] of radio as such—a structure leading unilaterally from the disembodied voice of the charismatic, spiritual leader to the ears of the students. Listening, on this reading, loses its shocking, educational value. And in turn, coldness, hardness, and fetishization find their way into the most banal of radio programs. In fact, it is important to highlight how Adorno's critique of the authoritarian tendencies of the radio come out of an analysis of a purportedly democratic program meant to be for the public good. Instead of an extreme example of fascist radio propaganda, Adorno's keen ear throws into relief how form and content of everyday radio programs reinforce a standardized approach to listening that, in the end, hardens the ear, frosts over the heart, and encourages fetishistic attitudes toward serious music. But this makes Benjamin's struggle within *and* against radio all the more impressive. Compared to Adorno's rather paltry suggestions for "improving" the *Music Appreciation Hour*, Benjamin's experimentation is nothing less than exceptional. Benjamin actively *(de)forms* the medium of radio, encouraging the kinds of sonic experimentations and forms of alert listening that might still be able to shock the perceptual system into historical awakening. Interestingly, while the *Music Appreciation Hour* reduces music to the linear, homogenous temporality of capitalist production and consumption, Benjamin finds room to recover alternative temporalities that can swell forth, spill over, and ultimately fan out, leading ears away from the radio and into the city. His dialogical approach and his interactive games seriously challenge the one-way direction of radio, working on and over the material conditions for radio production to make it more participatory and active. His pedagogical principles thus are an intervention not only into the content of the radio but also the implicit form that the radio prepackages sound into.

Conclusion: Sonic Inheritances for the Present Age of Images

What does Benjamin's reflections on sound, radio, and auditory education have to say to us, *today*? In the essay "The Author as Producer," Benjamin argues that the political tendencies of art are only guaranteed through correct literary tendencies. Artists working with the most advanced technologies and techniques are more politically progressive than those who might espouse political slogans but are working in reactionary aesthetic forms. Given that we live within the "pictorial turn"[94] or, stated differently, within a "photographic universe,"[95] it might seem as if the political tendencies of education can only be secured if we embrace technological tendencies of the image. Indeed, both Benjamin and Adorno accurately saw the importance of the rise of the mass image, and quickly shifted gears away from radio toward film. In our more contemporary era, cell phones, tablets, laptops, and other digital devices ensure the ubiquity of screen images far beyond what Benjamin and Adorno could have imagined. On this front, Fredric Jameson's call for an "an aesthetic of cognitive mapping,"[96] which draws its inspiration from cartography (as a visual medium), seems to be the most apt inheritance of Benjamin's notion of a dialectical image capable of embodying the necessary (though contradictory) interconnectedness between visual space and historical disruption.

As the same time, I want to highlight a potential worry when emphasis on the visual image marginalizes the need for an analysis of the educational relevance of sound-based pedagogies. It is worth pointing out that ultra-right-wing pundits such as Rush Limbaugh, Sean Hannity, and Glenn Beck consistently rank in the top five most influential and widely listened to radio personalities in the United States. There is no question: to this day, fascists rule the radio airwaves, and these airwaves have a wide audience. It would appear that fascists—then and now—understand the importance of controlling sound through an authoritarian voice.

Because of radio's connections to the far right, those on the left should not foreclose on radio as a contested educational terrain worth fighting for. While ideological critique of Limbaugh, Hannity, and Beck is important, perhaps more pressing is an examination of their pedagogical principles. Like Damrosch before them, Limbaugh, Hannity, and Beck use radio to further promote coldness, hardness, and fetishism through the authoritarian voice. The result is that the potentiality of sound to produce historical awakenings is not made audible or free. Instead, radio becomes a tool for imposing a linear, one-dimensional, highly selective notion of mythic history over and against the plastic diffusion of minor histories. Here we might also cite Katja Rothe's useful argument that radio for Benjamin is a kind of experimentation where sensations in excess of the imagination are introduced without predetermined ends attached.[97] Radio's experimentation with sensation stands in contrast to uses of radio for either repression or ideological conformity. Neofascism, I would argue, does exactly this: it denudes radio of its latent, experimental dimension by privileging its function within an ideologically narrow economy. Attentiveness to the authoritarian voice of the charismatic leader replaces open alertness to the diasporic welling-up of sound as it emanates from and entangles us with the echoes of history found distributed throughout the world. If this is so, then the potentiality for sound-based media to awaken children to historical difference is at risk in today's neofascist radio hegemony. Perhaps we can appropriate a well-known slogan of the left and rewrite it as a kind of sonic challenge for current radio pedagogues: "This is what democracy *sounds* like!"

CHILDREN'S THEATER

In the last chapter, we explored how radio—in both form and content—encourages a certain kind of awakening: an awakening to history. Radio acts as a technological conduit for the swelling up of thought sounds from within the color field of early childhood. This movement into youth is also an opening up of the self to history. In this chapter, I will outline how theatrical performance offers two further swelling points that (1) extend the mimetic dimensions of play outward into collective, performative manifestations and (2) intensify the futural vector of childhood fulfillment. Both (1) and (2) stand in stark contrast to bourgeois individualism and fascist, retrospective nostalgia for a lost, "fulfilled" past. While there is much written about Benjamin's reflections on children's theater,[1] in this chapter, I want to explore the specifically antibourgeois and antifascist implications of this educational form, and in doing so, shed new light on the importance of children's theater today.

But before I begin, it is important to highlight how Benjamin's essay "Program for a Proletarian Children's Theater" (heavily influenced by the Latvian actress, director, and communist Asja Lacis) should not be isolated from Benjamin's other, more famous, engagements with theater. For instance, it is peculiar how there is little commentary in the secondary literature on Benjamin's interest in the connections between theater and children in *The Origin of German Tragic Drama*. A lack of attention to the connections between the *Trauerspiel* and children's theater might very well be because the mourning plays are characterized by decay, brutality, hauntings from the past, and sadness whereas Benjamin's reflections on children's theater are full of lively gestures, playfulness, the shock of the future, and revolutionary exuberance. As such, there seems to be a distinct difference in mood, content, temporality, and aesthetic orientation between the two manifestations of theatrical performance. And yet, there are implicit and explicit connections binding the two forms. Of course, the very word *Spiel* rests within the gap that unites and separates theatrical performance and children's games, thus speaking to an element that crosses the rift. Citing Novalis, Benjamin makes the curious observation that the equivalent of the *Trauerspiel's* interest in the fragmentary, the untidy, and the disorderly is none other than "children's nurseries."[2] For Novalis, this is grounds for suspicion, but we might better see it as offering an insight. Further, Benjamin makes explicit connections between the *Trauerspiel* and children's puppet theater, highlighting the work of puppeteer Joseph Anton Stranitzky who popularized the role of Hanswurst (a comical character later replaced by Punch) in the 1700s.[3] But perhaps most important, plays by the major Silesian playwrights that Benjamin cites in his thesis on the mourning plays were designed to be performed by adolescent schoolboy actors who were students at the Protestant schools of the major Silesian city of Breslau. They were written as part of the early modern, central European performance tradition of the school drama (*Schuldrama*). As Jane O. Newman points out, key baroque plays—with their seductions, murders, and executions—were educational forms designed to shape the youthful male actors into "subjects destined for positions in the early modern administrative bureaucracies of the holy Roman Empire, the cities, and the smaller principalities of eastern central Europe."[4] In this sense, Benjamin's concern for the relation between children, education, and theater is longstanding. Indeed, I would like to suggest that the later interest in proletarian children's theater is, in some sense, a critique of the German tragic drama as an educational form, shifting emphasis away from socialization (as Newman highlights) to revolutionary, collective performance. In one, children are coerced to conform to an adult world whereas in the other, children actively play with the adult world in such a way that a future dimension swells forth from within and beyond it.

Mimesis beyond Bourgeois Discipline

Benjamin repeatedly insists on the centrality of mimetic play as a defining feature of the lifeworld of children. Indeed, in childhood play we witness the last vestiges of humankind's gift for seeing and producing similarities. For instance, Benjamin observes, "play is to a great extent its school. Children's play is everywhere permeated by mimetic modes of behavior, and its realm is by no means limited to what one person can imitate in another. The child plays at being not only a shopkeeper or teacher, but also a windmill and a train."[5] Importantly, this means that children are ontologically open to otherness—organic and inorganic. Their worlds lack the solidity of boundaries defining self and other, inside and outside. Benjamin writes, "Couldn't it be the case that childhood makes a start with the most remote things?"[6] In other words, the child's sense of self does not start from an internal, unified sense of "I" so much as with an entanglement with otherness beyond itself. Benjamin even goes so far as to state that while mimesis enables a child to become similar to dwelling places, objects, animals, and so forth, it never allows one to become similar to one's self. Mimesis refutes self-sameness or self-similitude. Instead, it emphasizes the continual swelling of the child outward to touch upon the most remote things in their experience. Adults simultaneously rely on this mimetic fact—as it is the origin of the potential for socialization—and discipline it in order to ensure conformity to certain, preestablished norms, rules, and behaviors.

Nowhere is this disciplining more apparent than in Benjamin's reflections on his childhood experience in the commercial photography studio. What is interesting for us is how this studio acts as a kind of bourgeois children's theater, complete with a stage, dramatic lighting effects, props, and even a "script," all of which produce a dramatic scene captured in a still image. While the juxtaposition of photographs of children and children's theater might at first appear rather odd, Benjamin himself makes a similar comparison. In the section titled "A Childhood Photograph" from his essay commemorating the tenth anniversary of Kafka's death, Benjamin begins with a description of a photograph of Kafka as a child, which I shall discuss in more detail below. Opposed to the "torture" of the image, Benjamin proposes the "fulfillment" of the Nature Theater of Oklahoma from Kafka's novel *Amerika*.[7] Whereas the former represents the disciplining of mimetic powers, the latter represents the full swell of mimesis through collective, improvisational gestures that innervate and extend the body outward to the most remote relationships. In Kafka's writings, gestures are "too powerful for our accustomed surroundings and break out into wider areas."[8] These gestures, unleashed by the Nature Theater of Oklahoma, are infused with certain signals from the future that connect them to the mimetic gestures in Benjamin's analysis of children's theater. In both cases, what is at stake is the suppression or intensification of an awakening process through gestural comportment: awakening to the potentiality for collectivizability through mimetic performance.

To begin, Benjamin remembers the contrived, artificial, and highly constrained atmosphere of the photographer's studio. The photographer, as educator/director, demanded a deployment of the mimetic capacity of his actors to conform to the preselected objects on the set. "Wherever I looked," writes Benjamin, "I saw myself surrounded by folding screens, cushions, and pedestals which craved my image much as the shades of Hades craved the blood of the sacrificial animal."[9] The mimetic potentials of play are turned against the child who is sacrificed for the purposes of getting the right shot. On my reading, sacrifice here is not the loss of an essential or integral sense of self but rather of the spontaneous playfulness of mimesis that defines the lifeworld of childhood. Benjamin makes this point clear when he writes, "Thus, we [as actors on the photographer's stage] made ourselves more like the embroidered cushion that someone had pushed toward us, or the ball we had been given to hold, than like a moment from our real lives."[10] Emphasis here is on how the props are "pushed" onto the children from *outside* their real lives. Mimesis is commanded or dictated by a transcendent power (of the adult) rather than immanently emerging from the "real" life of Benjamin's younger self. The result is a stilted performance as seen in the "tortured smile" on Benjamin's tiny face and an overall "distorted" sense of being that comes from manipulation.[11] Displacement of self through mimetic play might very well be a natural propensity for children, but when this capacity is co-opted by adults and coerced into a contrived performance, it withers. The child subsequently feels violated by the command to stand, act, look a certain way. Instead of mimesis enabling the child to touch the most remote things, it coils in on itself, creating a sense of isolation and fixity that would otherwise dissipate in the diasporic movement of mimetic entanglement. Paradoxically, Benjamin recalls how mimetic powers made "me similar to dwelling places, furniture, and clothes" but "never to my own image, though" and this "explains why I was at such a loss when someone demanded of me similarity to myself."[12] Through mimesis, the self finds itself in disseminating itself into otherness, yet in the photographer's studio, this tendency to extend outward becomes highly constrained by disciplinary command to remain *who* you are. The child is forced to stabilize him/herself. Instead of a self that is only defined in excess of itself, the young Benjamin is obligated to reify the self into a property of itself. He is forced to resemble himself, which is precisely an impossible command given that mimetic compulsion is always an exodus or an innervating and extending activity beyond limits and boundaries of "self" and "other." In the moment when the self becomes a property, it can be controlled through apparatuses of shame. But perhaps even more importantly, as property, the self must be *defended* against invasion and contamination. Thus, the self hardens over, protecting itself from certain externalities that are now viewed as a threat. In the process, the capacity of mimesis to leap toward that which is most remote becomes increasingly domesticated and denuded of its powers.

The photograph of Walter and George Benjamin taken in 1920 is strikingly frozen, stiff, and without life. The children are absorbed into an image that speaks simultaneously to their cultural heritage (through their Tyrolean garb) as well as the wealth, prestige, and values of their bourgeois upbringing. Another famous image of the young Benjamin taken in 1897 standing alone, in quasi-military uniform, holding a flag and sword also conveys this sense of isolation and mortification. The artificial feel of these images should not be dismissed as mere reflections of certain technological limitations of photography (as family photographs of children taken today contain many of the same elements). Instead, they reveal an essential truth about bourgeois subjectivity: that it simultaneously *affirms* mimetic capacities for producing similarities while also *negating* these vary same capacities. The result is a form of theatrical performance that promotes artifice, fake posturing, and rigid conformity to stereotypes of cultural identity and civic pride that are outside of the child's world.

It is interesting in this context how a portrait of the young Kafka exhibits a small and "pathetic" form of resistance to the abuse waged against childhood mimesis in these photographic images. Surrounded by oppressive props and holding an equally ridiculous broad-brimmed hat worn by Spaniards, Kafka would "surely be lost in this setting were it not for his immensely sad eyes, which dominate this landscape predestined for him."[13] The "infinite sadness"[14] of Kafka's eyes puncture the artifice of the staging, revealing the destructive dimension of bourgeois discipline over the mimetic powers of the child. Importantly, Kafka's eyes leap out of the dead and frozen performance to connect with the viewer—inviting a moment of mimetic displacement through an exchange of glances (even if this similarity is faint, or a mere trace). As the Kafka image suggests, Benjamin's analysis of childhood photographs is not disparaging of the medium itself (a medium that is sensitive enough to pick up on the subtle qualities of Kafka's eyes) so much as the theatrical staging deployed by the commercial photographer.

Benjamin's analysis of the negative effects of the disciplinary apparatus of commercial photography in bourgeois society on the mimetic potentialities of childhood stands in stark contrast to his observations of children's theater in revolutionary Russia. One of the most important aspects of Benjamin's trip to post-revolutionary Moscow in 1927 was witnessing the unleashing of the energy of children from the disciplinary constraints imposed upon them by adults. If, as Marx once hypothesized, revolution will unfetter the restrictions of bourgeois ownership over the mode of capitalist production, then so too will revolution loosen the moralizing constraints placed over children. Benjamin observed that "Moscow swarms with children."[15] This is not to deny the suffering of such children or to be indifferent to the trauma and poverty of war experienced by orphans lingering in the streets. Instead, it is to emphasize that while poor and suffering, the children were nevertheless busy with various projects, clubs, and gangs that could be organized through children's theater. Such organization emerges from *within* the real lives of the children and thus stands in contradistinction to the forced organization imposed on the child by the photographer in the example above. Furthermore, children's theater capitalizes on mimetic play but does so in a way that does not negate it but rather creates a stage for enhanced innervation and extension into collective, material forms of play that resist bourgeois isolation and atomization. In short, while the educational logic of bourgeois photographic theater is to prevent the swelling of the lifeworld of the child into collective, innervated forms of action, this is precisely what is encouraged in proletarian children's theater.

For the bourgeoisie, mimetic play must be disciplined. This discipline takes two forms: psychological and virtuous character development. Summarizing, Benjamin warns, "Psychology and ethics are the poles around which bourgeois education theory revolves."[16] The two poles work together in order to produce the "useful, socially dependable, class-conscious citizen."[17] This citizen is class conscious in the sense of recognizing class distinctions so that they can be maintained through a division of labor. Psychological development orients education toward a specific goal, dictated in advance by the existing social order: a predetermined notion of citizenship and character development that sustains the bourgeois sense of self. Emphasis on developmental models is conveyed to children through catchphrases, such as "This is good for you!" or "Silence is golden!" Yet there is a fundamental educational problem here. Benjamin offers the stark warning that "mere catchphrases have no power over children."[18] Interestingly, mimesis does not seem to work in relation to such catchphrases. When discussing his mimetic "compulsion," Benjamin notes that it "acted through words" but "not those that made me similar to models of good breeding."[19] Mimesis builds similarities between bodies and materials through the use of words as connective tissue, but words do not work in this fashion when it comes to imposed catchphrases that enforce certain developmental and ethical norms of "good breeding." Notice how the phrase "good breeding" simultaneously implies both genetic and ethical dimensions. Life itself becomes part of an ethical equation binding the child to a particular set of expectations, norms, and values that are inscribed in and through genetic breeding. Yet, it would seem that mimesis always distracts the child from abiding by these predetermined pathways leading to certain socially reliable and dependable roles (that correspond to and give proof of good breeding). Because of the inability of catchphrases to spark mimetic similarities on their own, they must be *enforced* through discipline. The punishment is shaming the child. Interestingly, Benjamin argues (perhaps naively) that revolutionary society only disciplines young adults, never children. He writes, "The proletariat *disciplines* only the proletarians who have grown up; its ideological class education starts with puberty."[20] This means that ethical shaming does not happen with proletarian children. Instead of shaming children when they do not conform to the discipline of the adults, Benjamin flips the script and argues that "The discipline that bourgeoisie demands from *children* is its mark of shame."[21] It is shameful precisely because the imposition of ethical catchphrases curbs children into domesticated conformity with bourgeois virtues that are unable to challenge class divisions (merely reinforce them).

Proletarian children's theater truly capitalizes on the mimetic faculty's unique ability to touch the most remote things through two complementary forms of swelling: innervation and extension. In the moment of performance, "New forces, new innervations appear—ones that the [adult] director had no inkling of while working on the project."[205] Innervation here includes "creative" and "receptive" variants.[23] In this sense, proletarian children's theater is decisively "noncontemplative."[24] It works through mobilizing the physical and psychical energies of children as they encounter the world. Mimetic performance is receptive in the sense that it is open to touching remote things *without shame* and without moral censure. The self only finds itself in dispersing itself through innervated forms of receptivity to the world around it. Receptivity is a kind of perceptual sensitivity to the agency of otherness. Instead of reducing otherness to sameness or to a simple resource to be manipulated, mimetic receptivity is akin to looking at an object in order to "invest it with the ability to look back at us."[25] The exchange of glances with the material world described here resists transforming objects into brute matter (resources or property). While reification might be violent, the open receptivity to the exchange of glances described in mimetic receptivity is a nonviolent form of communication. One can think here of the exchange of glances described above in relation to the image's ability to capture the sadness of Kafka's eyes, and thus open up a space for mimetic play between self and other. The image allows the viewer to receive the sadness, not through empathy, but rather through a mimetic power to perceive a look. But if mimesis were merely receptive, it would amount to nothing more than reproduction, or, even worse, recapitulation of the status quo. To counter this assumption, Benjamin emphasizes that mimesis is equally creative. In this sense, Benjamin's refunctioning of mimesis in children's theater is not dissimilar from Brecht's theory of gestus, which likewise criticizes the notion of mimesis as mere imitating.

There are three mechanisms through which mimesis is creative or generative. First, mimesis is creative in the sense that it produces new assemblages of bodies, actions, and gestures that are displaced from their conventional places, functions, and meanings in a social order. For instance, an example of nonsensuous similarity produced through displacement is the word "mummerehlen."[26] Because the word for aunt (*Muhme*) meant nothing to the young Benjamin, he transformed it into the name of a spirit creature mummerehlen (as an innovative juxtaposition of the words for aunt and person). Displacement is also accompanied by variations that suspend and render inoperative purposes. Thus "playing war" does not merely reproduce the violent ends of actual war. Through displacement, the gestures of war are opened up to possible variations beyond violence. Stated differently, mimetic variance deactivates violence while maintaining (preserving) the gestures of war in a suspended state. The gap between means and ends is a potentially creative space of mimetic performance with gestures. Again, in relation to Brecht's epic theater, we should remember that for Benjamin, gestures "interrupt someone engaged in action" by suspending ends. Once ends are deactivated, gestures become "quotable" within a variety of new situations.[27] They are, in other words, open to variations. And third, mimesis is creative through comical inversion. As Benjamin writes, performance in children's theater takes on the form of a "carnival" where everything from the adult world is turned "upside down."[28] In the short piece titled "Conversations Above the Corso: Recollections of Carnival-Time in Nice," Benjamin engages in a fanciful conversation with two characters, one, a friend named Fritjof, and the other, a mysterious Danish sculptor inspired by massive rock formations. Discussing the nature of carnival-time, the Dane states the following: "The carnival is an exceptional state [*Ausnahmezustand*]. A descendent of the ancient saturnalia, when everything was turned upside down and the lords waited on the slaves."[29] Instead of a state of exception from above (commanded by a transcendent power), here we have a state of exception from below, from the people themselves. Applying this logic to the children's performance, we can read it as a kind of carnival inversion of the adult world, turning it upside down.

Through displacement, variation, and inversion, mimesis becomes creative. This creativity unlocks a "secret signal"[30] of an alternative life possible within the present. As Benjamin writes, creative mimesis taps into "powerful energies of the future"[31] whose uses are yet to be determined. Through these innervating energies, the body's capacities to receive new sensations extend outward. The body becomes sensitive to communication with the most remote things—things that now glance back in a communicative moment. By inviting communicative exchange, the individual body becomes amplified, swelling through collective infusions of forces, actions, and gestures. These work on and through tissues and perceptual attunements that are now sensitive to and permeated with entanglements that infuse the present with energies from the future. Thus, innervation implies extension, and extension into collective modes of being further intensifies innervated tissues, organs, and perceptions to produce creative moments out of displacements, variations, and inversions. The energies released are a challenge to bourgeois discipline and attending class-consciousness precisely because they gesture into an as-of-yet unforeseen future.

"Improvisation," as Benjamin writes, "is central" to this project of innervating and extending.[32] "Performance is," continues Benjamin, "always aimed not at the 'eternity' of the products but at the 'moment' of gesture."[33] Proletarian children's theater is thus concerned with the time of production and of creation decoupled from a fetishization of a product or end. In this sense, it stands in stark contrast to bourgeois notions of property (which absorb means into an end, mystifying the production process) but also developmental theories of childhood which always point away from the present toward a specific end point (such as the development of specific skills to prepare a child for life as a citizen or worker). Instead, what we find in children's theater is an embrace of performance as a kind of pure means, or as a spontaneous expression of the lifeworld of the child as it encounters otherness, inflates itself and expands its sensorium in unpredictable ways.

At this point, we can summarize some rather stark distinctions between the bourgeois photographic theater and the proletarian children's theater. First, emphasis in the photographic process is on following orders dictated from above and outside the lived world of the child. Instead of engaging the entire life of the child, the child is cut off from this flow of life and inserted into a prefabricated setting that reflects adult interests and concerns. The result is a *decrease* in creative innervation. Innervated bodies are forced to be still, take an artificial pose, and play out a predetermined script that determines ends in advance. In short, receptive innervation is disciplined to take on certain national and social symbols without variation and/or inversion. Even the displacement of adult poses and dress loses any creative thrust precisely because there is no opportunity to play with the elements (through various combinations and juxtapositions) or their intended function (through innovative use). By forcing children to wear certain dress, there is a crisis in mimetic receptive perception. The communicative potentiality between child and object is prematurely foreclosed. Both the child and the surrounding objects are left lifeless, dead, inanimate, gazing past one another (rather than catching each other's glances). Perhaps we can argue that when receptive mimesis is decoupled from creative mimesis through the structure of the command, the result is precisely the kind of "torture" experienced by the young Benjamin. Mimetic play becomes a bourgeois display of itself (its identity, its nationality, its wealth and security) to itself. Hence the importance of the photograph over and above the performance. The photograph is aimed at mythic eternity. The photographic image can be owned, grasped, held close as evidence of a certain continuity of self and/or nation-state. It is kept safe in family albums or displayed with care on mantelpieces in glass frames so as not to be damaged. Commercial photographs of this kind therefore provide reassurances to mask the essential fragility and precariousness of the bourgeois identity and class positionality. When the end product—the image—is replaced by improvisational performance, such security is abandoned for a more open-ended set of risky entanglements that always threaten to undo the constraints of the self (rather than solidify them). In proletarian children's theater, the adult director has no control over the outcome; no authority to discipline youthful bodies in accordance with set standards, norms, and values; and no list of prepared catchphrases to elicit shame. Simultaneously, the outcome ceases to be a principle concern. Rather the point is what happens on the stage as bodies innervate and extend through mimetic displacement, variation, and inversion.

But this does not mean that the adult abandons children to their own devices. The role of the adult in this process is, first and foremost, negative: not to impose developmental or ethical norms and values. Instead, the adult should observe children and their lifeworld so that the "*entire life*" of the child be "engaged" in the performance.[34] In this sense, observation replaces instruction as the main educational gesture of the teacher-as-director. Benjamin writes, the "neutralization of the 'moral personality' in the leader [adult director] unleashes vast energies for the true genius of education— namely, the power of observation."[35] No longer playing the role of the enforcer of aesthetic principles, ethical character, or developmental pathways, the adult is released to *observe*—perhaps for the first time—the sheer life of children. Bracketing presuppositions about how the theater *ought* to function, what children *ought* to learn from performance, or how they *ought* to behave, Benjamin turns instead to children with fresh eyes to see what they are learning and how they are behaving within their lifeworlds. Instead of being attentive to certain aspects of this lifeworld, the observant adult is characterized by a diffuse alertness and openness that enables *true* observation to occur. Indeed, we might go so far as to argue that observation of a lifeworld in all its multifaceted dimensions is only possible through a certain heightened, absentminded, and imaginative state that is no longer restricted to any one focal point of directed attention (as might concern the photographer in the studio). In this sense, distributed observation interrupts predetermined theories of development or civic virtue, sustaining the possibility that there remains within children something indeterminate that can swell up and is unexpected.

Only then can the adult help to organize the powerful forces of children's play into theatrical performance, or, as Benjamin writes, release children's experiment from the "hazardous magical world of sheer fantasy and apply them to materials."[36] This is the second role of the adult in children's theater. Directing is equated with observation and the subsequent organization of things and relations into performance, which shifts the ground of childhood experience from imagination and fantasy (color) to encountering materials (colors and sounds—colors innervated through sounds, sounds made colorful), from pure reception to reception and creation through innervated performance. This important shift is an educational movement that constitutes an "indirect influence" on the children always "mediated through matter, tasks, and performances."[37] In other words, the adult director—not unlike Benjamin as a radio broadcaster—acts to organize collective innervation and extension. Awakening is akin to expressing the potentiality of *collectivizability* of the child's body. In collective, I include human and nonhuman actors that partake in the performance through which the body swells up beyond its sensorial limitations via innervation and extension. The adult must be put into contact with children in order to organize performances that bear the educational value of awakening to the potential for collectivizability.

The role of the adult director is not to act as a model to be emulated or as a judge to evaluate so much as an observer and organizer. At the same time, Karen Burk, drawing on the work of Giulio Schiavoni, argues that the role of the adult in children's theater cannot be easily equated with Benjamin's reflections on instruction introduced in the first chapter of this book. For Burk, there is something anti-pedagogical about the children's theater model because the role of the director is not instructive so much as mediatorial.[38] I would not go this far, but rather argue that the theater director embodies a specific form of pedagogical intervention, a specific manifestation of the wave of learning. Here the director's learning of the lifeworld of the child (through observation) swells up to the point where it is made visible and free in the form of organization. Also, it is important to note that the organizing of the theater does not come about as a response to the needs of the children or their interests. Rather it comes about from the observations the adult makes concerning the dynamics of collectivizability that emerge from within a social situation as a whole. If anything, this act of mediation through observation and organization gives an even more immediate sense of the magic of the threshold (*Schwellenzauber*), as Benjamin describes it, than direct instruction. Stated differently, the adult director in children's theater truly embodies the radical *poverty* of the instructor, and this poverty is positive rather than negative.

Indeed, in a text dedicated to Brecht, Benjamin draws on Herr Keuner who thinks poverty is "a form of mimicry that allows you to come closer to reality than any rich man can."[39] This is perhaps nowhere more true than in the poverty of the teacher-as-director of children's theater who does not have the knowledge, skills, or dispositions of the bourgeois educator but for this very reason is able to listen and observe children with great attunement. The poverty of preconceived disciplinary knowledge opens the director to mimetic similitude with the children observed, producing the preconditions for immanently playful and imaginative organization (rather than organization from above).

The existence of a proletarian audience is also important for defining performance as a swelling and spreading out of play (its transmissibility). The performance "need[s] the [proletarian] class as audience."[40] Benjamin continues: "And it is the prerogative of the working class to have a completely fresh eye for the children's collective, whereas the bourgeoisie is unable to perceive it."[41] The working class audience—based on its position within the division of labor—is capable of seeing the importance of collective performance in ways that the atomized bourgeois spectator could not. Even if we doubt the class essentialism of this argument, what is important to note is how Benjamin emphasizes the complex educative set of relationships that emerge through children's theater. On the one hand, children actively learn to experience their mimetic powers, awakening to collectivizability as a form of life that is internal to the movement of mimesis outward toward the most remote things. At the maximal point of this learning process, a performance swells up, turning outward into a teaching. The performance transmits collectivizability, making it visible and free for an audience. Benjamin suggests a working-class audience is most appropriate because it is already primed to receive this teaching, re-energizing its own collective possibilities for revolution (see below).

But the performance does not present a model or ideal that (1) the director has in mind ahead of time and (2) toward which the audience can aspire. Rather, it sets the stage for an awakening of the audience to its own immanent powers of collectivizability. This collectivizability is then aimed at an open question. In other words, a specific form of collectivity is not presented as an answer to the problems of the division of labor. Rather, the process of awakening to the potential for collective formation is stirred through the improvisational performance and then made visible and free for the audience.

Beyond Fascist Wish Fulfillment

In proletarian children's theater, children awaken their powers of collectivizability through mimetic play that innervates and extends their individual bodies through communicative networks with a diverse array of others (animate and inanimate). Sensuous similarities do not simply repeat what already exists, rather, through displacement, inversion, and variation, sparks of something new are introduced into the present. This secret signal from the future circulates amongst performing bodies and then turns outward, toward the audience, making itself visible and free. The performance found in children's theater is thus a swollen, expanded, inflated form of the mimesis in individual play. Or, stated differently, it expresses the fullness of childhood play. In fact, Benjamin asserts that children's theater guarantees children "the fulfillment of their childhood"[42] through an engagement with the whole of life. This lifeworld is not an abstract entity, but rather a perceptual plentitude overflowing with communicative potentialities between people, things, and environments. We should not read fulfillment here in the sense of a return to a fixed essence or an uncontaminated and pure manifestation of childhood in isolation from external contaminants. Instead, fulfillment is precisely the capacity for childhood to reach beyond itself through mimetic entanglements that touch what is most distant from it. In this sense, a fulfilled childhood is a childhood that is maximally grotesque and monstrous (meaning it cannot be defined in and for itself without taking into account its continual perceptual and communicative contamination)! A full expression of this capacity for grotesque (de)formation would be a childhood that is not prematurely disciplined to accord to specific, predefined definitions of a reliable and dependable life (within a certain division of labor), but rather a childhood that is allowed to swell up with the intensities of innervation and expansion that naturally coalesce through performance. Collectivizability is the ability to live a collectively full life beyond bourgeois isolation, individualism, and shame, making itself knowable and available for new use.

But we must be cautious here, as some might argue that this vision of surging, collective energies, undisciplined by bourgeois norms and values might smack of fascism. Yet fascist forms of collective energies are always disciplined. Indeed, they overcome the isolation and individualism of bourgeois society by *maximally* disciplining mimetic innervation so as to conform to a singular, romantic model of the ideal Aryan citizen without time or space for displacement, variation, or inversion. In this sense, fascism is not the negation of bourgeois society so much as an intensification of certain disciplinary, normalizing principles already at work within it. For instance, fascist parades and other forms of performance are not experiments in innervating collectivizability but rather are instruments for legitimizing clearly defined collective formations. The fascist collective is defined by clear boundaries that limit the powers of mimetic semblance to the *closest* things rather than the most remote. Further, the indirect effects of the poverty of the teacher-as-director found in proletarian children's theater are decisively rejected in fascist education for the authority of the teacher-as-agitator. The agitator does not listen and organize so much as silence and impose. In fact, enforced mimesis must be agitated in order to be jumpstarted. It does not spring from within the lifeworld of the child, and therefore must be prodded to conform to catchphrases that threaten shame or torture as possible punishments. The teacher-as-agitator values conformity to a determined, nostalgic wish fulfillment (best encapsulated in catchphrases of racial purity or traditional values), and in doing so negates the fulfillment of childhood as it swells up and extends into difference and otherness. For one, fulfillment is closed and overdetermined by adult wish fulfillment, while for the other, fulfillment is open and permeated. The coldness and hardness of the fascist perceptual system prevents receptivity toward the glance of otherness from penetrating the body. The result is a form of mimetic imitation that is torturously conformist rather than creative. Finally, the tragedy of fascism is foreign to the comedy of proletarian inversion and carnival eruptions. In short, as Miriam Bratu Hansen argues, Benjamin's interest in *Spiel* (and its collectivized manifestations) begins with *both* a desire to critique liberal-capitalism *and* a concerted effort to prevent a fascist, military catastrophe.[43]

If there is indeed this undercurrent in society through which liberalism and fascism flow together, then we can return to the photographic images of Benjamin introduced at the outset of this chapter as embodying a certain kind of protofascist nostalgia for the countryside, for folk life, and for military performance and pomp. The torture that Benjamin describes when he is subjected to conforming to these tropes opens up an ominous portal into a dark future where bourgeois liberalism and fascism suddenly emerge as dominant social and economic formations of the new twentieth century. The frozen, petrified, staged bodies of Walter and George Benjamin come to embody the coldness and hardness of fascism in a nascent stage of development. As opposed to the receptivity and creativity of innervated and extended bodies, here we have bodies that are forced to conform to types imposed from the outside by those who have failed to observe the lifeworld of children. Stiffness, artificial rigidity, and an indifferent detachment in these youthful bodies speak to the kinds of coldness and hardness that will only grow into maturity as the century progresses. Teetering between bourgeois discipline and fascist manipulation, these tiny bodies expose a defining fault line that will cause catastrophic ruptures in the near future.

Liberalism and fascism are both counter-revolutionary disciplinary movements that first prevent collectivizability from becoming knowable and then project fulfillment into an impossible, exclusive past where there is no room for the secret signals of the future. Opposed to this, Benjamin writes, "Revolutions are innervations of the collective."[44] Revolution is first and foremost a recomposition of bodies through extension and intensification. Bodies of the oppressed take on forms and gestures that are not their own, while gestures of refusal intensify, multiply, and invert hierarchies and divisions separating society from itself. These forms of innervation produce a disorderly mass that can no longer be manipulated by fascist rule or restrained by protofascist coldness and hardness. For Benjamin, the recomposition of innervations must happen on two levels: the natural, organic, bodily level and the collective, social, and technological level. As suggested above, Benjamin argues that fascism blocks both forms of innervation. Criticizing the fascist phrase "blood and soil," Benjamin argues, " 'Blood' runs counter to the utopia of the first nature [bodily innervation], which strives to make its medicine a playground for all microbes. 'Soil' goes against the utopia of the second nature [collective, social, and technological], which for fascism is realized only by the type of man who ascends into the stratosphere in order to drop bombs."[45] On my reading, the purity of blood in fascism undermines the extension and intensification of bodies, which always swell up toward otherness, entangling themselves with materials, roles, and tasks over which they have no claim (only a passing similitude) and yet nevertheless make a claim. Fascist soil is only constituted through its destruction. The immunization of fascist soil against invaders results in an autoimmune disease that turns against life in the very name of its preservation. At base, there is a sadistic death drive at work here that undermines the revolutionary potentiality for the new as it arises out of the indeterminate comingling and intensive distractions of bodies. Akin to revolution, the mimetic performance of children's theater is a nondestructive encounter with difference through inflamed tissues and perceptual systems that open up gestures, actions, and relations to new use. Animation extends and intensifies, thus resisting the determination of its coordinates by either (1) bourgeois property or (2) fascist blood and soil.

In today's society, what is the role of this "proletarian" formulation of children's theater? For instance, Brechtian epic theater is, for Benjamin, politically relevant precisely because it successfully translates certain methods of montage and technical processes of film and radio into theatrical forms.[46] How could a similar translation happen in relation to children's theater? This is a particularly interesting considering that Benjamin explicitly situates children's theater within the context of the proletarian revolution in Russia. Zipes poses this question directly, arguing that any notion of children's theater has to face the reality of globalization, the rise of media spectacles, and advanced consumerist culture—all of which enforce catchphrases and discipline over (and against) the natural mimetic play of children at an alarming rate.[47] Calling for an "unspectacular" form of children's theater, Zipes hopes that Benjamin's formulation can take new shape within the capitalist West. I agree with Zipes, and his examples of innovative children's theater, including his own experiments with the Neighborhood Bridges theater company, are helpful in imagining how to fuse play and reality in such a way as to interrupt the predetermined identities, thoughts, and feelings manufactured by adults and imposed on children so as to transform the division of labor into a kind of secondary nature. Yet at the same time, I argue that Zipes overlooks the most important obstacle facing children's theater today: the rebirth of global fascism, which always threatens to appropriate collective formations in the name of a nostalgic return that is exclusive rather than inclusive, that is tragically violent rather that comically performative, that is disciplined from above rather than playful from below.

The educational use of children's theater resides in its capacity for amplifying both first and second order innervations so that collectivizability can be known—not so much cognitively as known viscerally through the body itself. In this sense, the theater can become a miniature expression of that which is truly revolutionary: gestures released from determinate ends, able to become something else through improvisational displacement, variations, and inversions. Instead of destroying the world (as in the fascist fantasy), performance produces flashes of an alternative world right now, in the bodies of children as they collectivize through material assemblages, improvisational gestures, and comical disruptions of the norms and values that bind individuals to reliable and dependable social roles. In this sense, perhaps the greatest weapon against neofascist tragic irony is the comedy of children's theater.

PART II

COLLECTIONS

In this chapter, I am interested in exploring in some detail the tight connections between education, collecting, and childhood found in Benjamin's work. A critical jumping-off point is Benjamin's observation concerning the "Untidy Child" from *One-Way Street*: "Each stone he finds, each flower he picks, and each butterfly he catches is already the start of a collection, and every single thing he owns makes up one great collection. In him, this passion [for collecting] shows its true face."[1] Howard Eiland points out that in such passages, the child becomes a prototype for many adult characters, including the collector, who appear throughout Benjamin's *The Arcades Project*.[2] Likewise, Graeme Gilloch writes, "Benjamin's critical historiography is formed through the interplay of the adult-as-recollector (producer of a new history of humankind) and the child-as-collector (creator of new relationships between social, natural and material domains)."[3] As Gilloch observes, for Benjamin, there is indeed an interface between the activities of the adult (recollecting) and the activities of the child (collecting). But I argue that these formulations are only partly correct, as they miss how collecting is an educational form.

We find important connections between education and collecting in *The Arcades Project* passed over by both Eiland and Gilloch without comment. In his sprawling, unfinished, text that charts the rise and fall of the arcades in nineteenth-century Paris, Benjamin makes the following, rather brief and elusive observation, "Collecting is a primal phenomenon of study: the student collects knowledge."[4] There are several aspects of this citation that are crucial to point out. First, collecting is a *primal* phenomenon of study. This means that collecting is *essential* and *foundational* to any theory and practice of study. All studying is a

113

form collecting (of course, this does not always mean that all collecting is studying; consider, e.g., collecting souvenirs).[5] Second, it is important that Benjamin focuses on *study*, which is a particular form of learning. Perhaps the quintessential studiers for Benjamin are the strange students found in Kafka's stories and novels who are "pupils who have lost the Holy Writ [*Schrift*]" and thus "have nothing to support them."[6] Kafka's eclectic studiers do not have an instructor and therefore no one to provide a teaching. They have either no access to an instructor or have swelled to a point where the instructor is no longer needed to provoke learning. In a brief review of his friend Franz Hessel's book *Walking in Berlin: A Flâneur in the Capital*, Benjamin makes a crucial distinction between learning and studying that has not yet been adequately appreciated by those interested in the educational dimensions of his work. Between learning and studying, writes Benjamin, rests "an entire world."[7] The key differences, according to Benjamin, are that (1) "learning [*lernen*]" aims at "duration" (that which lasts or endures) and study does not, and (2) "anyone can study [*studieren*],"[8] whereas learning seems reserved for only particular kinds of people.

To understand this distinction, one must remember the description that Benjamin offered concerning the essence of education described in the first chapter on instruction. Learning—as a swelling up of a wave—has a prolonged duration, and this extended temporality enables learning to aim at what endures. As it extends and intensifies, it presses knowledge to its absolute limit or threshold where truth (as that which makes knowledge possible yet persists beyond any individual act of knowing as a virtual potentiality to be given way) can be encountered. The educational forms thus far encountered (instruction, children's theater, and radio plays) prolong and stretch out learning, giving it duration (through pedagogical tactics, organizing, and script writing, respectively) so that it might aim at that which endures (and as such, might even turn into a teaching of its own). A teacher, director, or broadcaster is there to maintain learning, allowing it to swell to a certain fevered pitch where it expresses the truth of its own conditions of possibility (knowability). This prolongation of learning enables learning to aim at truth as that which is inside yet beyond situated knowledge claims. Yet study is nondurational, meaning that it is an intense, punctuated, and rather ephemeral eruption of a learning opportunity that may or may not last. It lacks a teaching or a teacher to sustain it for any prolonged period or to anchor it in a particular place and time. Because it is sudden, unexpected, and unintentional, anyone at all, as Benjamin writes, can study—there are no prerequisites (such as time and resources to engage in extended learning). Without duration, study cannot aim at what endures, and as such, study rarely crashes into a teaching (making itself free). What it makes knowable may remain implicit in the experience as such without encountering its own knowability (or ability to be known as its virtual component).

In the second half of this book, I explore *moments* of study that might otherwise be passed by as lacking educational relevance because of their contingent, ephemeral nature. At stake is the messianic redemption of those forms of educational life of anonymous "anyones" who do not have teachers and do not have teachings to guide them. It is my argument that Benjamin attempted to archive fleeting moments of study through various *weak* and *poor* educational forms such as collections, memoirs of straying through cities, children's word games, and so forth. Each form attempts to recall, remember, or express a studious moment in order to push it toward a threshold of truth, lending it a minimal duration necessary for knowability to be sensed (even if it is never thematically articulated as such or turned outward into a teaching).

In this chapter, I turn to Benjamin's re-collections about collecting in order to unpack the relationship between study and collecting knowledge. To do so, I first have to outline Benjamin's theory of touch. Touch is a small gesture that (1) lacks duration that (2) anyone can perform. It is ephemeral, yet contains within it a certain study value (it makes things, in their particularity, known or familiar). The collection is an educational form precisely because it enables study value to potentiality turn into a wave of learning. The collection is a body of embodied memories that, even if for a moment, enables the collector to discover a hidden truth that endures within and yet beyond every individual touch: the traceability of fate.

Touch

Touch is a way of studying one's environment that does not rely on mental oversight or conscious intentionality. As Benjamin writes, "Tactile reception comes about not so much by way of attention as by way of habit."[9] Tactile reception—touch—happens without mediation by mental faculties. While the mind is distracted, the body *feels* its way around, intuitively, building up sensorial familiarity with what it encounters. The body seems to automatically study its environment by absorbing it into adaptive gestures that, over a period of time, can become habits. This kind of incidental educational experience is not bound by any restrictions in terms of who can study, when, or where. If Benjamin is correct, tactile receptivity *as* embodied study is always already happening whenever and wherever bodies and environments meet.

Paul North highlights the centrality of touch in Benjamin's work and its connections to distraction. Touch is a sensually distracted "letting go and passing by"[10] of experience without the need to consciously recognize the experience as one's own. As such, touch lets go of the need to anchor the self, thereby opening the self up to an indeterminate stream of experience below the radar of mental intentionality. And as the hands move across objects, various tactile sensations outrun the ability of apperception to grasp and synthesize such sensations into a coherent experience identifiable as "mine." In this sense, touch exposes the self to difference at the most basic level of experiential engagement with the world. Instead of possession (in terms of apperceptional unity and synthesis), touch concerns dispossession (in terms of a dispersal of self). For North, there is a particularly educational meaning to this fleeting gesture. He writes, "The laws of touch are 'rich in teaching,' for Benjamin, because they teach in a future tense in which reception runs ahead of itself out of fear that if it stops for an instant it will lose itself and its object, becoming transfixed in a stupefied present."[11] Touch does not have a duration (as it is too fleeting to be measured), and because of this, its teaching is not concerned with learning, which extends an "I" through a certain temporal duration. Here the unified "I" must learn to learn differently, or study its own dispersion. Because the law of touch is not unidirectional, there can be no strict division between active subject and passive object. Instead, in touching something, that thing also touches the subject in such a way that the reception of sensation outruns the capacity of the subject to claim ownership.

There is a reciprocal interpenetration of subject and object here that is never encountered in gazing. Gazing always sets the subject at a distance. And this distance offers protection against contamination. The power of the gaze is its remove from its object, which can henceforth be *objectified*. Likewise grasping something attempts to continually force the object to retain its objective status as an object of possession under the will of a subject that grasps. The grasping in such cases fends off contamination precisely by willful domination and control. To grasp is to stand over and above the object by exerting force and intentional will. Gazing and grasping thus are similar gestures: both set apart, concern duration, and enforce a certain unilateral line of force leading from subject to object. Yet, to touch is to glance off of something just long enough to sense its presence and to be sensed by it in a nontotalizing way. Touch is, on this account, radically exposed to the possibility of momentary reversibility of subject and object through the haptic palpitation of surfaces.

Evidence of touch is hard to find, as it only leaves faint traces on surfaces of objects. Groves, folds, marks, dings, scrapes, stains, scratches, patina—all are indicators of traces of touch. Unlike aura, trace, for Benjamin, is "appearance of a nearness, however far removed the thing that left it behind may be."[12] A trace is the mark of an intimacy or closeness. Something was once close at hand. It was produced but also consumed, or used in specific ways. A trace is a remnant of the entwinement of subject and object in a glancing moment when hands palpitated surfaces, fingers turned pages, thumbs pressed in, elbows rested, and bodies imprinted. If touch absorbs its environment, then traces are the remnants of how the environment equally absorbs bodies in movement. Traces are the marks of ephemeral, nondurational, preconscious ways of letting go and passing by that nevertheless leave fragmentary hints of momentary, studious relationships.

Collecting

Now we can turn to collecting as a particular way in which the study value of touch becomes thematized. Collecting is perhaps most commonly connected up with Benjamin's interest in the flaneur. Yet there is an important distinction that is lost when we collapse the two. In his essay on Eduard Fuchs, Benjamin observes, "Romantic figures include the traveler, the flaneur, the gambler, and the virtuoso; the collector is not among them."[13] But why the distinction? In *The Arcades Project* Benjamin argues that "Collectors are beings with tactile instincts. Moreover, with the recent turn away from naturalism, the primacy of the optical that was determinate for the previous century has come to an end. . . . The flaneur optical, the collector tactile."[14] Indeed, for Benjamin, the motto of the flaneur is "Look, but don't touch!"[15] Whereas the flaneur emphasizes the eye (the gaze), the collector emphasizes the hand—one moves out to get a broader view while the other moves in close to touch.[16]

There is a strange mimetic relationship between the collection and the collector. At the end of his famous essay titled "Unpacking My Library: A Talk about Collecting," Benjamin states that it is not so much the books that come alive in him but rather that "it is he who lives in them" as if they were a dwelling into which he "is going to disappear inside."[17] Collectors give themselves over to collections to such a point that without them, collectors might even become "invalids."[18] A series of similarities thus accrue between collection and collector that, over time, make them indistinguishable from one another.

This entanglement complicates any notion of possession as mere ownership over an object. It is true that Benjamin states, "Collectors are people with tactical instincts" and that "property and possession belong to the tactical sphere."[19] It would seem then that touching is akin to possession and thus ownership. For instance, Benjamin writes that the disposition of the collector toward his "possessions stems from an owner's feeling of responsibility toward his property."[20] Yet, I would argue that there is a more subtle dimension of tactility that butts up against such notions of property and possession. For Benjamin, the collector is "motivated by dangerous though domesticated passions."[21] On the domesticated side of the equation we might situate the bourgeois habit of ownership and property. Ownership reinforces an active sense of self that dominates the world of passive things/resources. As any Marxist would point out, this results in a reification not only of the material world but of the self as well (now monetized). On the dangerous side of the equation, perhaps there is something about collecting that upsets this kind of property relationship and the concomitant reification of self. Indeed, could we not argue that in collecting, the subject engages in self-forgetting to the point of dispersing the self into the collection? Duration, on this reading, would amount to an attempt to prolong a haptic encounter—a fleeting touch—to the point where touch, rather than ownership, can be thematized. The collection would therefore be an organization of material encounters in such a way as to *make haptic knowledge knowable (visible rather than invisible) as the truth of our embodied engagement with the world.*

To make touch touchable, to make traces traceable, the collector must also be touched through his or her touching of the collection. This point is made explicit in "Unpacking My Library" when Benjamin writes,

"As he [the collector] holds them [his books] in his hands, he seems to be seeing through them into their distant past as though inspired."[22] Here the collector thinks through hands, through the faculty of touch in order to read the history of touch as it is inscribed within and on the surface of things. This is a marginal history of the intimacy of subjects and objects producing and using each other (without consuming each other), leaving only minimal traces. Benjamin makes a clear connection between the trace and collecting. In a review of Gabriele Eckehard's *The German Book in the Baroque Epoch*, Benjamin writes, "It would be better to characterize the community of genuine collectors as those who believe in chance, are worshippers of chance. Not only because they each know that they owe the best of their possessions to chance, but also because they themselves pursue the traces of chance in their riches."[23] Aura is timeless, transcendent, and distant (it has duration), but the trace is contingent, immanent, transitory, and for these reasons, nondurational. Just like touch, trace also fades and becomes illegible. Indeed, a trace appears only in so far as it is constantly disappearing.

But this does not mean that objects simply disappear into dust. Collecting preserves the traces so that the *fate* of objects can be knowable. Fate, for Benjamin, is composed of traces. Study concerns isolated, unintentional, chance meetings that flit by, leaving only traces behind—internal traces in the form of habits and external traces in the form of marks and imprints. Collecting is a gathering of these traces on and through objects in such a way that the collector can learn about the fate of objects in an extended and intentional sense. "The period, the region, the craftsmanship, the former ownership—for a true collector, the whole background of an item adds up to a magic encyclopedia whose quintessence is the fate of the object."[24] The fate is not a mere catalogue raisonné that can be verified through empirical research. Rather it has a certain "magical" quality that is greater than the sum of the facts accrued about it. Fate, in this case, is the image of an object that emerges when the feelings induced by touching traces become traceable, outlining a "whole background." The intangible qualities of traces that seem to run ahead of our slow-moving, subjective recognition, suddenly swell up in their significance, outlining a historical context beyond any one, particular trace.

Only when objects have been saved from *both* use and exchange value can this fate appear. Benjamin writes that the existence of the collector is tied to ". . . a relationship to objects which does not emphasize their functional, utilitarian value—that is, their usefulness—but studies and loves them as the scene, the stage, of their fate."²⁵ The resulting fate of objects preserved in tenuous traces is not a linear, chronological story so much as the accumulation of the wear and tear, production and use/exchange that are as consequential as they are inscrutable. In sum, a collection traces traces, or makes chance traces traceable in the form of fate. While the truth of aura only comes through a separation from touch/trace, fate is a truth that is within touch/trace as its most swollen edge.

Collecting and Allegory

Because collecting is the collecting of traces or fragments of a moment of touch, collecting is also connected to allegory. The tactile truth that is made explicit in collecting is, at its base, deeply allegorical. In the following passage, Benjamin makes clear the connection between brooding, allegory, and collecting:

> The brooder's memory ranges over the indiscriminate mass of dead lore. Human knowledge, within this memory, is something piecework—in an especially pregnant sense: it is like the jumble of arbitrarily cut pieces from which a puzzle is assembled. . . . It is the gesture, in particular, of the allegorist. Through the disorderly fund which his [sic] knowledge places at his disposal, the allegorist rummages here and there for a particular piece, holds it next to some other piece, and tests to see if they fit together—that meaning with this image or this image with that meaning. The result can never be known beforehand, for there is no natural mediation between the two.²⁶

The collector engages in a kind of puzzle over fragments inherited from the past (an "indiscriminate mass" of traces). Fate becomes a patchwork of traces, or memory shards, that tenuously hang together in the form of a collection. The resulting image of the collector recalls the *tikkun* or Jewish mystic who collects broken pottery shards in order to reassemble the vessel and thus finish the collection—knowing full well that such a project is both necessary and yet indeterminate.²⁷ This characterization of the work of the collector offers the first point of contact between collecting and allegory. But, as we shall see, this contact introduces certain problems into our positive assessment of the educational value of collecting. In this section, I will pursue some of these problems, and through the analysis, reaffirm certain points made above, but with a new twist.

Benjamin's interest in allegory beings with his early research into German Baroque mourning plays and ends with his work on nineteenth-century Parisian arcades. In *The Origin of German Tragic Drama*, Benjamin highlights the specific logic of allegory. For instance, Baroque fascination with allegory is connected with a catastrophic vision of history. "This is the heart of the allegorical way of seeing, of the baroque, secular explanation of history as the Passion of the world; its importance resides solely in the stations of its decline."[28] Allegorical knowledge lives between historical actualization and catastrophe. It therefore concerns what is fundamentally *unfulfilled* in the past. Whereas the symbol suggests completeness, allegory proposes the exact opposite. This also means that allegory does not appear to contain truth (as the eternal and durational) in itself.

The symbol offers fullness and unity of meaning, yet allegory suggests a total dispersal of meaning into fragments. "Any person, any object, any relationship can mean absolutely anything else."[29] Nothing is more important than anything else, and as such, experience—in an allegorical sense—becomes flattened out. There is no centralized, guaranteed tradition or symbolic system that can suture back together sign and signifier, life and significance. Finally, Benjamin emphasizes the excesses of possessive subjectivity in German Baroque tragic drama. "If the object becomes allegorical under the gaze of melancholy, if melancholy causes life to flow out of it and it remains behind dead, but eternally secure, then it is exposed to the allegorist, it is unconditionally in his power. That is to say it is now quite incapable of emanating any meaning or significance of its own; such significance as it has, it acquires from the allegorist."[30] The object disappears under the allegorist's gaze. The external world, if it is to have any meaning at all, must reflect back to the allegorist his or her willful powers to possess. There is no truth here, only inward-turning relativism and subjectivism.

In his later work on the Paris arcades, Benjamin once again returns to allegory as an adequate description of the fragmentation of life and the loss of meaning under capitalism and commodity exchange. Capitalism further hollows out any organic sense of unity, stability, and auratic authenticity that could provide the necessary background for sustaining a firm relationship between signifier and signified. Just as stable meaning is hollowed out in allegory, so too is use value hollowed out under capitalism, leaving only empty exchange value. Benjamin writes, "How the price of goods is arrived at can never quite be foreseen, neither in the course of their production nor later when they enter the market. It is exactly the same with the object in its allegorical existence."[31] In this sense, allegory expresses the essential feature of the commodity form and is thus a symptom of capitalism's deteriorating effects on experience and life. Nowhere is this connection more ominously spelled out than when Benjamin writes, "The allegories stand for that which the commodity makes of the experiences people have in this century."[32]

Given this disparaging description of allegory, it poses certain problems for our positive understanding of the study value of collecting. Indeed, Benjamin goes so far as to make the following claim concerning allegory: "Mortification of the works: not then—as the romantics have it—awakening of consciousness in living works, but the settlement of knowledge in dead ones."[33] If collecting and allegory are connected, and allegory *prevents* awakenings (which is the educational expression of swelling), then collecting cannot be educational. It would be a mere symptom of that which prevents any kind of awakening from happening. Even worse, the allegorical emphasis on death, decay, brooding, and "mortification"[34] would suggest that it is also connected to protofascist hardness and coldness. Whereas life swells with innervative tendencies, allegory solidifies and petrifies, putting the collector to sleep. Thus, any connection between collecting and allegory means that an educational interpretation of collecting might be undermined. At this point, one might disparage and simply exclude collecting for Benjamin's constellational curriculum. Yet this approach would deny how collecting is an integral part of childhood, and it would seem to neglect the features of collecting Benjamin appreciates the most. Another alternative might be to simply negate the allegorical dimension of collecting through some kind of Hegelian, dialectical overcoming. Allegory, it could be argued, is an inessential or superficial aspect of the concept of collecting and thus can be excluded from the further development of collecting as an educational form. But, like the previous option, this one seems undesirable as it denies that allegory is, in fact, at the heart of the modern experience of life, and as such, cannot be easily dismissed as merely a castoff. As a third option, I suggest the following: finding minor points of swelling within allegorical mortification that push it to a studious threshold. This would amount to the smallest of messianic shifts that nevertheless change everything.

To begin, Benjamin's interpretation of Baroque allegory's negativity could be read in a *positive* light. Simply put, allegory reveals the *false* totality and artificial unity of the symbol. From an allegorical perspective, any given organic totality is always already full of ambiguity. Allegory disperses meaning, and by doing so, makes it impossible for meaning to be controlled or assigned value within a totality. For this reason, there is something democratically anarchic about the allegorical surplus produced in the modern era. Allegory enables us to turn toward the failed and the incomplete as containing some kind of relevance—granted a *poor* or *weak* relevance. Thus, allegorical thinking is an *initial* pivot toward the marginal and the discarded, those crucial bits and pieces of historical detritus that are essential for Benjamin's understanding of awakening. Even as it mortifies objects, allegory includes a promise to redeem human history from mythic historical symbols.

Likewise, because allegory is *internal* to the commodity, it can press the commodity form to its swelling point, enabling the commodity to become knowable *as* a commodity. Importantly, "More and more relentlessly, the objective environment of human beings is coming to wear the expression of the commodity. At the same time, advertising seeks to disguise the commodity character of things. What resists the mendacious transfiguration of the commodity world is its distortion into allegory."[35] Whereas advertising attempts to gloss over the fractured, empty, and mortified body of the commodity with the phantasmagoric dream of commodities as whole, full, and alive, allegory stays true to the commodity's split nature, and as such, awakens us from its magical spell. Paradoxically, allegory exposes the *truth* of the commodity form as something knowable.

In both cases, allegory's negativity draws out the smallest and most tenuous of swelling points, thus beginning an educational process of awakening from a phantasmagoria of symbols and commodities. But for us, the question of allegory's emphasis on possessive subjectivity still stands as a major problem in relation to collecting's positive educational value. The collector focuses on fragments, stitching them together in a vain attempt to reassemble the past. No single piece has any intrinsic value, therefore all can be manipulated or arranged in multiple configurations without end. The emphasis on unfinishability makes the collector brood over the collection, not unlike the melancholy of the allegorist. And, like the allegorist, the collector is concerned with possessing objects.

If there is meaning, it is the result of the collector's *will* and *power* directed at mortified objects. But here we can return to the previous section, and in particular, Benjamin's observation that collecting is *both* a domesticated *and* dangerous passion. Now we can add to our analysis by making an important distinction. As quoted above, Benjamin warns, "If the object becomes allegorical under the gaze of melancholy, if melancholy causes life to flow out of it and it remains behind dead, but eternally secure, then it is exposed to the allegorist, it is unconditionally in his power." Notice that the unconditional power Benjamin describes has to do with the melancholic *gaze*. It is when objects are submitted to the gaze of the allegorist that they petrify (and thus prevent awakenings from happening). Not unlike Medusa's gaze, the allegorist freezes objects, and, once suspended in perpetual hibernation, they are submitted to his or her unconditional power. Certainly, gazing is part of collecting, yet, as Benjamin emphasizes, the real passion of collecting is *touch*. In fact, we can find an interesting synesthetic glissade in Benjamin's description of the haptic habits of the collector. As cited previously, he writes, "As he [the collector] holds them [his books] in his hands, he seems to be seeing through them into their distant past as though inspired." The collector *sees through his or her hands*. Seeing through hands is, indeed, touching. Touch puts us in touch with objects, disturbing any sense of unilateral power over objects by an excessively possessive subject. Benjamin further disrupts extreme forms of possessive subjectivity when he observes that the "order" of a collection is not imposed from the outside by the collector. Rather, the collection is a "disorder to which habit has accommodated itself to such an extent that it can appear as order."[36] The collector yields to the collection, gives him or herself over to it in order to dwell inside it. Habit rather than the gaze makes possible the order of the collection, giving the collection the feel that is the gateway to fate.

As such, we can speculate that the allegorical gaze of the collector submits objects to his or her power (the power to order, command, control, and so forth), and the collection merely topples over into a domesticated prop for sustaining the dream of bourgeois ownership and commodity fetishism. On the flipside, the allegorical touch (contingent, unintentional) brings the collector close to the collection to the point where they mimetically merge. Here, tactility is redeemed as the origin of the collection, returning property back to the tactile sphere, and thus to the possibility of awakening the subject to the historical fate of objects (their truth) through touch (rather than despite it).

In sum, objects enter history through touch. This touch glances over a long, complex, contingent process of fleeting relations of production and consumption that are inscribed on surfaces of objects in the form of traces. When collected together, these traces can be encountered as fate. But this fate is never complete knowledge, reconstructed perfectly to coincide with "how things were." It cannot be fully verified or objectively measured, even by historical sciences. Instead, its truth is precisely its tactility; its fleeting moment of appearance and disappearance as subject and object touch on that which swells up between and beyond both: fate. In this way, the collection touches on what has been touched, swelling the remnants of nondurational study into a learning.

Intimate Portraits of Two Collectors

Eduard Fuchs presents us with our first example of the educational logic of collecting. Fuchs was not so much a researcher or scholar as he was, first and foremost, a collector, and this emphasis on collecting is, according to Benjamin, absolutely essential for understanding Fuchs's educational innovations. Indeed, Fuchs began collecting in response to a certain educational crisis within the Social Democratic Party in Germany in the late nineteenth century. Historical materialism, at that time, had largely neglected the arts and the humanities, reducing them to mere diversions or stimulations lacking revolutionary relevance to the struggles of the working class. Natural science dominated the theoretical and educational landscape of the left. The only alternative was cultural history—a discipline which abstracted culture from its social and economic context, reifying it. Culture became thinglike and cultural history took on a "fetishistic quality."[37] This fetishism is reflected in the great museums and art houses. These institutions focus on "showpieces" or masterworks, and in the process, focus more on the "master's signature"[38] than the objects themselves.

Opposed to both the dismissal of culture and its reification, Fuchs offered an alternative approach. Instead of culture as a thing, delivered over as if readymade for commodification, Fuchs conceptualized past culture as "uncompleted"[39] traces of a vast network of social and economic relations. This insight liberated Fuchs from certain strands of aesthetic idealism focused on questions of beauty, harmony, and so forth. It also disrupted the unity and continuity of the canon of great art. He "strayed into marginal areas—such as caricature and pornographic imagery—which sooner or later meant the ruin of a whole series of clichés in traditional art history."[40] Mass art(s) disrupted the simple, linear story of high culture and the collecting of master works as representations of mythic history. He also shifted emphasis away from authenticity and aura to focus on each historical era's approach to technological reproduction. Opposed to bourgeois moral taboos, Fuchs was fascinated by the grotesque and exaggerated dimensions of mass art. In fact, Fuchs's famous phrase "Truth lies in the extreme"[41] is later inherited as a methodological principle by Benjamin: truth as the maximal swelling point of knowability must be sought in the grotesque.

Fuchs himself was passionate about collecting. As Benjamin observes in relation to Fuchs, "The collector's passion is a divining rod that turns him into a discoverer of new sources."[42] This passion is not reducible to a personal interest or possessive subjectivity (as discussed previously). Instead, it is a giving over of the self (or an act of self-forgetting). "As a rule," Benjamin writes, "collectors have been guided by the objects themselves."[43] Instead of fame, fortune, or prestige, Fuchs abandoned himself to the act of collecting, responding to the objects he encountered no matter how grotesque. Not unlike Benjamin's example of the collector absorbed into his collection, so too does Fuchs take on traits of his most passionate obsession: Daumier's prints. Benjamin summarizes as follows:

> And as a collector, he [Fuchs] has cleared the way to these things [disgraced and questionable cultural forms] all by himself, for Marxism showed him merely how to start. What was needed was a passion bordering on mania; such passion has left its mark on Fuchs' features. Whoever goes through the whole series of art lovers and dealers, of admirers of paints and experts in sculpture, as represented in Daumier's lithographs, will be able to see how true this is. All of these characters resemble Fuchs, right down to the details of his physique.[44]

Fuchs and his collection become increasingly inseparable, one mimetically resembling the other. When Fuchs touches his collection, the collection touches him, each altering the other. The collection is a trace of this passionate love affair between subject and object.

In the marginal, the grotesque, the disgraced, and the excluded remnants of culture, Fuchs discovered traces of the history of the unwritten anonymous masses. Benjamin summarizes, "Whether devoting such attention to anonymous artists and to the objects that have preserved the traces of their hands would not contribute more to the humanization of mankind than the cult of the leader—a cult which, it seems, is to be inflicted on humanity once again—is something that, like so much else that the past has vainly striven to teach us, must be decided, over and over, by the future."⁴ The political turn here is not to be glossed over. Historical materialism ought to disrupt the cult of the leader by orienting attention away from great works, monuments, and mytically historical narrative, and focus instead on the traces of the hands of the masses found in fragments of their cultural history. These tentative traces—so important for historical materialist education—offer up a brief glimpse into an anonymous history of production and use that can only be known through passionate collecting. The educational value of collecting is in the assemblage of fragments and marginalia so that this "lost" history can swell up in the present, filling the present moment with knowability.

The second collector we can discuss is Benjamin himself, especially the portrait of himself as young collector in his memoir *Berlin Childhood around 1900*. In a thought image from the appendix titled "Desk," Benjamin discusses his habit of collecting old exams as a child and hiding them away in his desk. He writes, "Particularly rewarding was the perusal of old exercise books, which held a quite special value for me, insofar as I had succeeded in preserving them from the clutches of the teacher, who was entitled to keep them. I would rest my gaze on the corrections he had made in red ink along the margins, and the sight would fill me with quiet pleasure. For like the names of the deceased inscribed on tombstones, whence they dispose of no power for good or ill, these marks in my exercise books had spent their force in past appraisals."⁴⁶ There are several important points to make about this passage. First, Benjamin insists on collecting "old" exercise books, or exercise books that no longer have any value to the teacher. Indeed, they are on the verge of being thrown away. While commentary on Benjamin's work on collecting emphasizes the suspension of use and exchange value, what this passage indicates is that collecting also suspends *examination* value: the value of the test to measure, assess, and evaluate educational progress or regress. All their powers have been spent on "past appraisals" and thus remain in a state of suspended animation.

Second, it is in this strange state of inoperativity that Benjamin finds a new form of pleasure. He reads the marks not as correcting marks but as marks that no longer fulfill their destiny. When the mark is operative, it induces a *distance* between the student and the teacher. The teacher has the expertise to judge, and the student is subjected to this judgment. The mark inscribes this judgment into the educational record books so that it becomes a kind of profile of the student. It is the student who is marked just as much as the examination. The mark is also a central feature of the learning-testing ritual in schools. The ritual of learning to be tested and testing in order to learn inscribes the student into a quasi-religious form of educational baptism.[47] If the examination mark always holds a power over the student through ritualized distance, then the mark attains a certain kind of aura. This aura grants the examination mark a power that other marks do not have. Like the work of art, the examination mark embodies a special authority that is sustained through the distance between student and teacher and through the ritual transaction that takes place between them via the apparatus of testing and learning.

Whereas the teacher's authority imbues the mark with a certain aura of power and value (examination value), the interruption and suspension of this authority leaves only the materiality of the red mark as such—a red mark that suddenly can be pondered as a red mark (rather than as a powerful, auratic mark of the teacher's expertise to judge). The mark's functionality fades away until only the ruin of the mark remains on the page. The aura of the mark wanes, and the mark becomes a trace. As a trace, the materiality of the mark draws *near* the student, and this nearness produces an intimacy important to understanding the pleasure that study takes in the fate of the mark as a remnant of touches (including the "clenching" of the teacher's hands). If the mark no longer judges, then what was in the background of the mark can shift into the foreground: the fate of the mark on the page and the gestures of the teacher's mark making.

Third, Benjamin speaks of collecting as resting (*ruhen*) his gaze on the marks. While this might seem to privilege the gaze (and thus lock us into the problem of allegorical appropriation), I would like to emphasize the importance of *resting* the gaze in the above passage. The resting gaze is not simply a gaze that is focused, attentive, and at work. "Resting" can also be read as the neutralization of the work of the gaze. Like the inoperative marks on the page, I want to interpret the resting gaze as a suspension of its powers to possess. On this interpretation, the gaze mimetically folds into its object, both of which are deactivated. The resting gaze does not exhibit its possessive powers so much as it yields to the logic of the out-of-work object, opening itself up to the ability to be touched.

Here the connection with the tombstone becomes important. The names on tombstones no longer do any harm or good to the deceased buried beneath or future generations who have forgotten the past. In a sense, there is an allegorical connection between such names and the marks in Benjamin's notebooks: both are inoperative traces. Once the power of these traces has faded, their fate becomes visible and thus traceable, producing new pleasures not depended on their original, personal or private values.

One more example of collecting from Benjamin's childhood is important to highlight. In "Butterfly Hunt," Benjamin describes chasing down and collecting butterflies during occasional trips in the summer months. In the moment of the hunt, Benjamin would find himself locked within a mimetic relationship with his prey. He recalls "Between us, now, the old law of the hunt took hold: the more I strove to conform, in all the fibers of my being, to the animal—the more butterfly-like I became in my heart and soul—the more this butterfly itself, in everything it did, took on the color of human volition; and in the end, it was as if its capture was the price I had to pay to regain my human existence."[48] Notice how this study of the butterfly happens in and through the "fibers" of his being, in his "heart" and "soul." Even the "spirit of the doomed creature entered into the hunter"[49] upon his triumphal return, thus problematizing the lust for possessive ownership that originally fueled the enterprise. Study is located in the nondurational, haptic moments when subject and object touch each other. This is largely fueled by preconscious, contingent, and embodied forms of navigation. And through this extension and intensification of mimetic study, a whole world of the butterfly is experienced, including the "wind and scents, foliage and sun," as well as the "destruction, clumsiness, and violence"[50] that comprise the phenomenological feel of the situation. But this intuitive sense of this situation is never made explicit in the moments of haptic study as they unfold moment to moment. Instead, the collection itself (or, as the case might be, the adult re-collection of the collection process over a prolonged duration of time) enables the whole world of the hunt, in all its manifold dimensions, to swell up and become traceable.

Antifascist Studious Life

In conclusion, we can now pull together some of the political implications of the collection as an antifascist educational form. On the one hand, it seems ridiculous to suggest that collecting might stand against fascist and neofascist educational forms. After all, the Nazi's horded massive collections of Europe's most esteemed treasures for the never realized Führermuseum, planned for Linz, Austria (Hitler's home town).[51] Yet it is important to end this chapter with some critical distinctions. First, the Nazi's looted their collections. For them, collecting always concerned power and possession, forcibly pilfering treasures from Jews and other occupied peoples in order to consolidate a self-reinforcing image of Aryan superiority. In this sense, the collection becomes a weapon of mythic history. It is predicated on a law creating and law supporting violence, and in turn, exerts a violent force over those who do not accord with its teachings. History is obsessed with the duration of the Aryan nation in its organic unity and stability. Its collections subsequently symbolize this totalization, where every trace of otherness is eradicated or ridiculed, every subaltern history is destroyed. Perhaps we can even say that such collecting practices are anti-allegorical, as meaning must be fixed, stabilized, and massified to the point where there is only one, singular historical narrative without any sense of the traces of multiple, anonymous, oppositional struggles opening up fissures and cracks on the margins. Instead of these historical traces, we are locked into a biological destiny that culminates in Aryan domination.

As I have argued throughout this chapter, for Benjamin, collecting concerns exactly the opposite. The collector touches the marginal and the ephemeral elements left out of history, and in turn, is touched by the collecting process in ways that suspend and render neutral any kind of unilateral possession, looting, and grasping. Second, Nazi collecting was about definitively defining the identity and purity of the German race. Opposed to this ideology of purity, the essence of collecting for Benjamin lies in the contamination of swelling—in undoing the boundaries separating self and other through nonappropriative mimetic entanglements. The tip of the swell is the fragile moment when the self gives way to the potentiality to change into otherness, where loss becomes promise, where historical fragmentation becomes future possibility. A swollen crest cannot sustain the boundaries defining itself and its possessive sense of "mineness," and must yield to whatever is yielded through the process of exaggerating, intensifying, and extending. Hardness and coldness resist the vulnerability of touch, retreating from haptic engagement with otherness into a detached, controlling gaze. As such, the fascist leaves no traces, only symbols of domination. While these distinctions are important to note, the critical distinction is itself educational. Indeed, we might go so far as to suggest that fascist "collecting" erases study—as an indeterminating, nondurational, nondirected activity open to anyone (regardless of racial heritage). Collecting, on Benjamin's reading, is an educational form that undoes the binaries of fascism, creating diasporic, mimetic engorgements that are inclusive rather than exclusive, that are decisively *degenerate*, *grotesque*, and *exaggerated* in ways that would be repelling to Nazi tastes.

Nazi's collected artifacts in order to produce symbols of their racial superiority. Here I am reminded of Benjamin's early essay on Goethe's *Elective Affinities*, where he warns against the false totality of the symbol and its seductive sense of self-sufficiency. A collection of symbols creates a mythology that, according to Benjamin, "petrifies" the human being under the sign of a threatening and tyrannical force of nature.[52] The Nazi celebration of nature over politics (in the form of racial heredity) calls for a collection of symbols epitomizing this totalizing force. In turn, the symbols of racialized mythology reinforce the hardness, coldness, and manipulativeness of the protofascistic personality. Opposed to this, Benjamin calls for an inexpressive power that shatters the mythic symbol into shards or "fragments of the true world."[53] The inexpressive does not come from outside. Rather, it is the swollen rim or tip of any expression or trace as it reaches its maximal limit through allegorical touch. It is the potentiality of the trace's traceablity. This inexpressive poor power does not have the certainty of the symbol on its side. Instead, it can only gesture toward that which is present in its absence: a history whose knowability rests in the eternally fragile nature of traceability.

While the lines between classical fascistic collecting and Benjamin's collecting are clear, perhaps another challenge awaits when confronting neofascism. Here I am thinking of the paradigmatic case of white nationalist and right-wing extremist collecting in the United States: gun hording. Just 3 percent of American gun "super-owners" now own 50 percent of the country's civilian firearms.[54] These are predominately white, male, older, and nonurban owners—a key demographic that supports Trumpism in order to protect their right to collect guns. Here is a subaltern collecting practice by those on the political fringe. It is a collection that speaks to a fear of loss of economic power and political marginalization by those claiming to be a silenced, anonymous mass of anyones. Even so, I would argue that such collecting practices are the purest symbolization of the fascist fetishization of technology over the vulnerability of touch. Indeed, they are the perfect embodiment of the *weaponization* of the collection under fascism. Opposed to this use of the collection, Benjamin offers an alternative—one which is decisively antifascist precisely in its willingness to give itself away, to make humble, to embrace the perforation of boundaries, to render inoperative the mythic power of symbols rather than wield it, to yield to the earth rather than rule over it. The collection of our times ought not be weapons that destroy or create the law, but rather a gathering of old, grotesque, and forgotten objects that suspend the law in order to allow anyone at all to study it without end, without destination, and without fear.

CITYSCAPES

The indeterminacy of study introduced in the last chapter on collecting will now enlarge itself further. The mimetic displacement of the subject into the private collection will become innervated to the point where the subject disseminates itself throughout a cityscape. As Benjamin became more and more interested in cultural criticism through his reflections on modern life, he also undertook a broader, expanded, swollen approach to educational issues. Suddenly environments—such as the city—or events—such as collecting and speaking—could take on educational dimensions autonomous from specific institutional forms (such as schools or museums) and specific actors (such as teachers). If instruction does not necessitate the presence of a student, then the education that I am about to discuss does not necessitate the presence of an intentional teacher (children's theater being the only educational form that seems to demand both simultaneously). The result is a decisively urban style of studying that can only be enacted through the "art of straying."[1]

Stephen Dobson places Walter Benjamin at the heart of debates concerning the informal, noninstitutional education offered up by cityscapes.[2] He highlights the rich resources Benjamin brings to his analysis of cities and how they teach the senses through an education of experience (*erfaringpedagogikk*). Adding to this argument, I want to further highlight the role of distraction in this informal education. While traditional schools might focus on cultivating and sustaining attentiveness, the city offers a different lesson—one that unleashes the positive potentialities of distraction. And while distraction might be commonly seen as the antithesis of an educational virtue, in Benjamin's city writings we find a key distinction between mere distraction as diversion and productive distraction as diffuse openness and alertness that has educational implications. This means (1) reconnecting distraction to the context of the city and (2) making its educational use visible and free. The triangulation of education, city, and distraction has been critically overlooked in most of the secondary literature on Benjamin. Take for instance Jonathan Crary, who criticizes Benjamin for creating a duality between distraction and attention instead of seeing them on a continuum. Crary misses the subtlety of Benjamin's reflections on distraction on two accounts. First, the continuum that Crary posits never allows us to investigate the nature of the continuum in terms of a swelling up of attention to a state of its own dispersal. Missing is the plenitude that resides in distraction as the maximal point at which attention begins to transform into something else. Instead, Crary seems to relegate distraction to nothing more than a watered-down modality of attentiveness (or lack thereof). Second, if Crary rightly locates the problem of attention "at the heart of the functioning of a capitalist consumer economy,"[3] he misses the tight connections between distraction and the city that are crucial to Benjamin's analysis. Indeed, Crary only mentions the impact of the metropolis on modern attention in his epilogue, and does so in largely negative terms. Thus, he marginalizes distraction's most acute social and educational location: the cityscape. The two oversights are linked. Timothy C. Campbell's interpretation of Benjamin is perhaps even more problematic.[4] Whereas Crary at least recognizes distraction as a defining feature of Benjamin's work, Campbell completely erases it, arguing that Benjamin's concepts of childhood and play concern the interrelationship between attention, play, and creativity. Again, this reading is symptomatic of how the relation between attention and distraction is never fully clarified, and how discussions of distraction, children, and creativity are abstracted from historically specific manifestations (in relation to city life, for instance). Paul North's interpretation of Benjaminian distraction suffers from the opposite problem.[5] Unlike Crary and Campbell, North is to be commended for his attempt to think distraction beyond the mere negation of attention, and in the process, he discovers a new form of antifascist subjectivity and massified collectivity. But at the same time, he underplays the ways in which this new, unruly, diasporic mass emerges in and through city dwelling. The following analysis will attempt to accomplish precisely what these critics have failed to do: provide a positive theory of distraction as both a personal and public educational phenomenon directly connected to city experience.

To do so, I will first provide an overview of the various modes of distraction found in Benjamin's philosophy of the city. Here the city will emerge as a phenomenological point of confrontation between states of distraction, each competing with one another. Then, through a careful analysis of several phenomenological descriptions of wandering in the city taken from Benjamin's writings, I will illustrate how city life calls for a different form of attunement to the world than that found in schools. This different kind of attunement, for Benjamin, culminates in the art of straying as an educational potentiality unique to city life.

A Tale of Two Distractions

As already discussed in an earlier chapter, Benjamin's notion of distraction is not the opposite of attentiveness, but rather its maximally swollen edge where it disperses itself into an open, nondiscriminatory state of heightened alertness. It is poor attentiveness, or an attentiveness that gives itself away. For Carolin Duttlinger,[6] Benjamin's interest in the question of distraction became increasingly more and more dominant as he focused on the conditions of modern life, especially in cities. Indeed, the full educational potential of distraction as open alertness is best exemplified in his writings on cities. And, in particular, it is through his phenomenological description of the preconscious ways in which bodies and city environments interact that we can reach a deeper understanding of the connections between distraction, education, and sensorial extension and intensification. But the city is not safe nor a sanitary site for such an educational experience. Discussing Bertolt Brecht's poetry book, *Handbook for City-Dwellers*, Benjamin writes, "Cities are battlefields."[7] The battlefield of the city is composed of many competing interests on various economic, political, and social scales. But here I emphasize the city as a kind of phenomenological battlefield between different forms of distraction: mere diversion versus productive distraction. This battlefield will have to be our starting point for reflecting on how it is that distraction, for Benjamin, can ultimately open up to a new kind of educational life through artful straying.

First, mere diversion is scattered throughout the cityscape in various intoxicating forms, preventing any kind of educational awakening. Through obsessive cataloging of modern life in the city, Benjamin collected evidence of the spreading of divertive intoxicants through social relationships, industrial production, institutions, and urban advertising. For example, citing the poet Charles Baudelaire, Benjamin refers to the first department stores as shrines embodying the "religious intoxication of great cities."[8] Further, Benjamin describes the world's fair as a "phantasmagoria which a person enters in order to be distracted."[9] In both cases, the captivated spectator of department stores and world's fairs is held in throng by "*divertissements*"[10] that do not sell particular items so much as a consumptive, divertive lifestyle. Once a place wherein people could communicate with one another through the bourgeois public sphere,[11] the cityscape increasing replaces communication and intersubjective recognition with the proliferation of talking objects, crass advertisements, and phantastic ghosts. The allegory of the phantasmagoria was particularly apt for describing this modern cityscape, as a phantasmagoria was a popular form of magic-lantern show that appeared in Paris during the Revolutionary and post-Revolutionary years. The lantern operator projected shadows, including heroes and villains of the Revolution, as well as the purported ghosts of loved ones, onto a wall, magnifying their presence through the use of mirrors, smoke, and so on.[12] For Benjamin, this strange apparatus became a paradigm for thinking about the effect of spectacle, image, and commodity fetishism in nineteenth-century Paris.

The origin of this phantasmagoric intoxication rested in the split nature of the commodity structure itself. Just as Marx once derived the whole system of capitalist relations from the irreconcilable cleavage between use and exchange value at the heart of even the most basic commodity,[13] so too did Benjamin derive the phantasmagoria of the city. The commodity as such offers the "glitter of distractions"[14] as its main feature. This means that the commodity contains the kernel of the ghostly spectacle of the nineteenth-century city in miniature form, deflecting workers away from the class struggle, thus supporting the perfect illusion of access, entertainment, and ease offered up by a consumerist dream. For instance, commodities are produced through human labor power, yet when they enter into circulation they seem to become animated by their own, internal, supernatural energies. Commodities are therefore *haunted* by the labor power that created them, but also, they actively mediate between humans in the public sphere, transforming immediate recognition into distorted projections of capitalist design.

Thus far, distraction is nothing less than one of the conditions for and results of capitalist alienation. Yet Benjamin also provides us with a more affirmative and productive notion of distraction—one that is not easily reducible to mere diversion or inattentive, intoxicated entertainment.

Drawing on my earlier comments on distraction as absentminded alertness and openness, I suggest we stay firmly on the terrain of distraction and yield to it in order to see what appears, what alternative potentialities might await us. To be clear, such a turn does not result in simple indulgence in the stream of images that fly by or mere absorption into the flow of the city. Rather it embodies a special kind of examination of experience that can be called an art of straying. This art is absentminded but is also alert and open to the knowability of its own conditions of possibility through an innervation and extension of the mimetic interplay of city and self. Another way of putting this might be that distraction reaches a maximal threshold of swollenness that implicitly reveals its origins in the life of the city.

Duttlinger rightly posits the affirmative features of distraction as a combination of openness and alertness. Yet the question remains: How does the city *teach* one to be distracted? At stake here is understanding how city experience *undoes* the cognitive basis for attentive focus, thus loosening up the mind through innervation of a bodily sensorium that is betwixt and between old and new habits. As such, we must complete Duttlinger's analysis with a supplement that emphasizes the embodied dimensions of encountering cities found in Benjamin's writings.

In the essay titled "The Work of Art in the Age of Mechanical Reproduction," Benjamin tightly connects the concept of distraction with the sensorial experience of walking the city. As Graeme Gilloch points out, there are two ways in which the city educates the senses through distraction.[15] First, there is the mental distraction necessary for habits to take root in our bodies. In this first model, the mind is absent while the body trips its way through the city. Buildings, writes Benjamin, are appropriated through tactile use, not by mental oversight or reflection, resulting in the possible formation of new habits. "Tactile reception," argues Benjamin, "is accomplished not so much by attention as by habit."[16] Key here is that the mind is *not* attentive to what is happening in the particular instance of a haptic encounter. The mind is absorbed in the diffuse cityscape, while the body goes about its preconscious, tactical navigation of whatever comes along and presents itself. The result is an incidental form of educational life that happens below and above the level of the attentive subject.

At the same time, there is another form of distraction: one that shocks, interrupts, and suspends habits. Benjamin cites both the speed and intensity of city life as inducing a "shock effect."[17] When dealing with the fast pace of city life, perception cannot rest on an image or object for long. Habituation is repelled by the sheer velocity and frequency of change. The number of images, people, and experiences encountered in the cityscape open the possibility of continually dislodging the very habits that the same environment induces. Instead of simple discontinuity, which might have paralyzing effects, we can also think of shock as a moment of innervated swelling of the senses that pushes the senses to (de)formation. While these two states of distraction might appear to be separate and even antithetical to one another, I would suggest that they ought to be read together as two sides of the informal education of the city. Education, on this reading, would be a sensorial wave, pulsing between sedimented and emergent habits. Unleashed in such threshold states is what philosopher Marina Van Zuylen might call a "plenitude of distraction" or a surplus of potentialities for sensing and being differently that come about through innervation and extension of the body's capacities for stimulation.[18]

Benjamin refers to this paradoxical state of being in an indeterminate flux as "reception in distraction."[19] Importantly, reception in distraction critically challenges the transcendental conditions for reception in attention, shifting from attentive mindfulness to absentminded entanglement. In the philosophical tradition (from Kant on), apperception is responsible for unifying all experiences and affixing a sense of mine-ness to this unity. Such apperceptual unity is, on my reading, central to achieving attentiveness and focus on a particular thing. There is an implied "I" that is capable of grasping an experience as its experience. Without the synthetic unification provided by apperception, according to a very worried Kant, "it would be possible for appearances to crowd in upon the soul,"[20] creating a disintegration of the self and its ability to hold onto the particularity of this or that object of reflection. The "I" would turn into a crowd, and the self would become an uncontrollable, undomesticated rabble. External multitudes would invade the ordered sanctity of the soul, resulting in a mixing of internal and external, singular and plural, and thus devastating the unity, autonomy, and attentiveness of the Kantian subject. In short, the "I" would be crowded out; the gates would be flooded; all hell might break loose. Perhaps even more troubling, Howard Caygill argues that Benjamin's description of city life challenges Kant's basic categories of understandings.[21] In place of Kant's transcendental deduction of the fixed categories of quantity, quality, relation, and modality from the unity of apperception, Benjamin now derives a new set of categories from city experience itself. In addition to Caygill's list, which includes porosity, threshold, and shock, I would add distraction. These immanent and deeply historical categories speak to an anonymous, transitive, and diasporic sense of self missing in Kant's system—or at least only appearing in the margins as a danger to be avoided at all costs. The threat to educational experience is clear: how can such a dispersed self collect itself in order to be attentive? Yet, for North, the disruption of the work of apperception has decisively *positive* educational implications, and therefore there is no need to retreat back into the safety of attentiveness. He writes, "In order for apperception to renounce its teaching habit and learn to learn, it will have to become susceptible to teaching [through the shock of distraction]."[22] Once suspended, apperception ceases to function as the grounds for attentiveness. The result is not the end of education but rather the beginning of an education in and through open alertness. The crowding out of the "I" in Kant's formula is not simply negative, but rather enabling of a new kind of attunement that is not predicated on divisions between self and other, private and public, inside and outside. Such alertness is the *result* of the distracted moment of habitual (de)formation when the crowd of appearances invades the soul. Once the transcendental ground for self-security and self-certainty, apperception gives itself away—yields to the crowd. Apperception abandons its previous function, and a new education becomes possible—a properly *urban education* in which the self playfully mirrors the multiple branchings and side streets of a decentralized, sprawling, phantasmagoric cityscape as it swells with open alertness.

Perhaps we can summarize the distinctions drawn out from Benjamin's work as follows:

1) Attentiveness 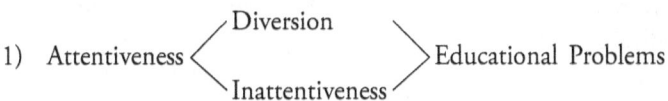 Educational Problems

a. When one starts by prioritizing attention, then distraction can only be seen in a negative deficit and thus educationally problematic.

2) Distraction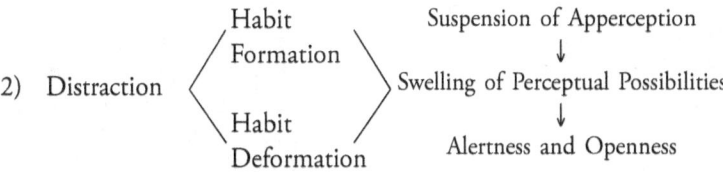

a. When one starts from distraction as such (without seeing it as merely a derivation of attentiveness or as its deficit), then two states of distraction emerge with unique educational possibilities.

Children and Newcomers

We are now in position to turn to several small examples of this movement from sensorial (de)formation to open alertness in Benjamin's work. The first concerns a childhood experience of Berlin as recalled by Benjamin and the others are taken from Benjamin's adult travel writings. In all cases, what we find are educational moments wherein the stimulation of the city leads to embodied, perceptual (de)formations that do not paralyze so much as open the subject up to an exaggerated state of reception in distraction (open alertness). What is received in such instances is the knowability of the city as such (its feel, intensities, and rhythms). It is important to consider both a memoir of a past city from childhood and the more journalistic writing of a city experienced for the first time from an adult perspective as these two images capture the important use of temporal and spatial distance Benjamin evoked in his writings on cities.[23] At stake in both cases is not the city as it is lived in the day-to-day but rather the surprise of the city as it first swells up in one's experience as a zone of perceptual plentitude.

A small yet important example of the connections between distraction, the city, childhood, and education can be found in the scene titled "Sexual Awakening," which appears in the appendix of Benjamin's *Berlin Childhood around 1900*. In this autobiographical description, Benjamin recalls a scene from his youth of getting lost in Berlin during the Jewish New Year. On his way to fetch a distant relative he found himself in unfamiliar surroundings. "Whether because I had forgotten his address, or because I could not get my bearings in the neighborhood—the hour was growing later and later, and my wandering more hopeless."[24] At first, the young Benjamin was filled with anxiety that he might miss the ceremony, that his (imposed) orientation and direction would be interrupted. But then something happened. At the apex of anxiety, he had another, this time unexpected and shocking, emotional reaction, "this one of utter indifference ('So be it—I don't care')."[25] Anxiety and indifference combined, producing a third wave of pleasure. The "sensation of pleasure" was the result of a "profanation" of the holy day by the "pandering"[26] street. Benjamin's younger self did not fully understand the nature of such pleasure, but the newly "awakened instincts"[27] seemed to indicate the emergence of a latent sex drive that would tie Benjamin even more closely to the city and its illicit secrets. Suddenly pleasures and drives cathected to the religious observances of his parents give way to something emergent, something awakening, that came from the city yet folded into the self, crowding out any sense of habitual fixity. Perception became full of an erotic charge that was distracting precisely because its destiny was (at that moment) unknowable.

Walking with his mother through the "urban labyrinth"[28] opened up a space tinged with diffuse, erotic potentialities that had the distinct political potential to critically undermine existing social and familial relationships defining the bourgeois family. The idea of somehow (and perhaps naively) believing he could one day repudiate his mother's authority as well as her class background was derived from these walks. Benjamin writes, "Yet even in those far-off days, when my mother used to scold me for my contrariness and my indolent dawdling, I obscurely sensed the possibility of eventually escaping her control with the help of these streets, in which I seemed to have such difficultly finding my way."[29] Thus, rebellion against hierarchies of control arrived with the "help of these streets" that prompted his "dawdling." Here we see a glimmer of a desire to "never . . . form a united front with anyone."[30] In this sense, the outside or external world of the Berlin streets and the internal psychosexual makeup of the child merge into a mimetic reflection of one another: both undermining any notion of a unified and/or hierarchically ordered set of self and social relations.

As the young Benjamin touches the streets, so too do the streets touch him, producing a dispersal of the self outward into the unknown, erotically infused, and potentially dangerous avenues of Berlin. Thus, the mysterious pleasure that is aroused becomes a politically creative catalyst for imagining another way of relating to self, others, and environment. Unlike Plato's harmony between the justice of the soul and the justice of the city, we find a mimetic syncopation of disruptive and (de)forming forces that prefer not to be organized in terms of an organic, unified, hierarchical whole.

The city suspends plans and directions while producing new kinds of unanticipated and shocking perceptual pleasures. As the self becomes spatialized, it undergoes a kind of diasporic movement outward, discovering emergent ways of being in and through its urban wanderings. In another context, Benjamin describes the unusual effects of city life on autobiographical writing as follows: "For autobiography has to do with time, with sequence and what makes up the continuous flow of life. Here, I am talking of space, of moments and discontinuities."[31] Writing about life in the city therefore resists the traditional autobiographical emphasis on time and sequence of events that collectively form the "flow of life." Instead, what we find in the city is a life of discontinuous moments and spatial dislocations that cannot be cobbled together into a narrative story. Bearing this in mind, Benjamin plays with the idea of "setting out the sphere of life—bios—graphically on a map."[32] In his construction of a cartographic sense of self, the self only discovers itself tracing its steps through a cityscape. Hence the strangeness of Benjamin's "autobiographical" writings of cities. Instead of dwelling on the familiar *personal* dramas of the bourgeois family that take place inside of homes between parents and children, what we find instead are a series of increasingly *impersonal* moments scattered throughout the city. Interior spaces fold into exterior spaces, interpersonal relationships give way to relationships mediated through parks, beer gardens, zoos, and streets; Oedipal particularization swells up with a polymorphous perversity that pervades the labyrinth of the city as such.

There are several important points to make about these reflections on childhood in the city. First, Benjamin emphasizes that getting lost can turn into an art of straying. As such, the dawdling of a child cannot be reduced to a disreputable behavior to be punished, but rather contains the potentiality to *achieve* a new mode of self (de)formation—an urban self that is not beholden to predetermined roles or rituals or behaviors, that finds itself outside itself in the cityscape. The straying self is an aesthetic reconfiguration of the relationship between body and environment that is not beholden to the dichotomies of public and private, interior and exterior that define the subjectivity of the average, everyday adult. Of course, the potentiality of this kind of unregulated and unsanctioned movement is disconcerting for those interested in social, political, or educational control (through colonial pedagogy, for instance). And no one was more aware of this than Benjamin, a German Jew who also happened to be a Marxist (of some kind). The straying of a child contains an emergent political dimension concerning which bodies can do what, when, and where.

Second, in yielding to distraction—to the phantasmagoria of the city—Benjamin does not merely fall into a deep dream state of intoxication from which he cannot awaken (from which adults must save him). Rather, by delving further into the labyrinth of the city a new a sudden awakening occurs—one that presents its own, profane (if not perverse) and dispersed form of alertness and openness to facets of the city that would otherwise remain completely insignificant. This awakening is affectively charged with a strong erotic potentiality. Note that the erotic pleasure is not the reinforcing of existing habits, nor is it the arrival of a new set of habits (in this case, sexual preferences and mores). The erotic has yet to be fully wedded to certain ends, and in this state of awakening, is full of creative possibilities that have yet to be channeled into specific forms. The public city becomes knowable in the precise moment it folds into and enlarges the personal sensorium through erotic swellings. What leaves an imprint on Benjamin is not the fulfillment or deferral of pleasure, but rather the appearance of the erotic as a possibility for reconfiguring life.

We could break down this educational moment of distraction into the following steps (granted this is a gross reduction):

1. There is a prescribed duty to perform a certain social or religious function dictated by an adult (as the embodiment of tradition).

2. Walking the streets of the city distracts the child from this duty (profanation), suspending internalized habits (disorientation).

3. The ensuing distraction of the mind from specific ends (indifference) creates the preconditions for something different and unexpected to potentially emerge (the potentiality of new habits swells up).

4. The sensation of such potentiality produces its own kind of (erotic) pleasure.

5. Such pleasure lacks a ground to unify it, synthesize it, and give it meaning and thus produces a new sense of an urban self as open and alert (rather than attentive). The city becomes knowable through this innervated and extended sensorium.

In short, distraction renders inoperative the work of apperception. There is no longer a perceptual faculty capable of uniting experiences under a single, stable, and transcendental "I." Instead, the self mimetically folds into the city. A new kind of educational experience becomes possible: one that does not have foundations in apperception and that does not follow the educational path of self-cultivation or self-formation through attentiveness. Rather, what we find is self-dispersal (a giving away of the self) through new, unanticipated encounters and pleasures that swell up as the child becomes increasingly open and alert to what the city offers.

But there is also a danger here—remember cities are battlefields!—that the child's erotic swellings will ultimately topple over into forms of Oedipalized hedonism. In his early writings, Benjamin warns against the eroticism of youth being co-opted by prostitution.[33] Likewise, in his writings on cities, he highlights how the emergence of big cities enabled prostitution to take on a "new arcana" arising from within the "labyrinthine character of the city itself."[34] It would therefore seem that the unique potentiality of the city is also a problem. The art of straying is found in cultivating a youthful sense of erotic possibility that undermines preexisting hierarchies and authority predicated on child/adult dichotomies that nevertheless does not regress into a fetishized and commodified form of sexuality.

For the adult, a similar experience of distraction can happen when he or she enters a city for the first time as a newcomer. Between 1925 and 1930, Walter Benjamin wrote a series of city portraits that included descriptions of his travels to Naples, Moscow, and Marseilles. These brief sketches of foreign cities were able to capture the particular nature of each city. But there was more at stake in these portraits—something that comes through only when they are put in constellation with one another. Read together, they can be seen as reflections on the unique potentiality of cities to provide a perceptual education in the art of straying. Such an art is uniquely accessible to the newcomer. Indeed, Benjamin writes, "Emigration is the key to the big city."[35] It is the key precisely because the emigrant is maximally distractible by the city as it swells up with various potentialities unnoticed by local residents deeply habituated into fixed patterns.

Concerning Moscow, Benjamin writes,

> The city [Moscow] seems already to deliver itself at the train station. Kiosks, arc lamps, buildings crystallize into figures that will never return. Yet this impression is dispelled as soon as I seek words. I must be on my way. . . . The instant you arrive, the childhood stage beings. On the thick sheet ice of the streets, walking has to be relearned. . . . Now the city turns into a labyrinth for the newcomer. Streets that he had located far apart are yoked together by a corner like a pair

of horses in a coachman's fist. The whole exciting sequence of topographical deceptions to which he falls prey could be shown only by a film: the city is on its guard against him, masks itself, flees, intrigues, lures him to wander its circles to the point of exhaustion.[36]

In this excerpt, Benjamin draws together several themes into a distilled image: the city, education, childhood, film, and distraction. For Benjamin, experiencing a city for the first time induces a childlike state. This state is characterized by both mental and physical forms of distraction. The unified sense of self—with its purposes, orientations, and destinations, in mind—seems to be abruptly suspended by the "impression" of the city as it "crystallizes" in a momentary flair. Without knowing what is more or less important, the whole panorama of the city fills up with potentially exciting and interesting things and events. The result is an absentminded listing of random objects (kiosks, arc lamps, buildings, etc.) that might otherwise have faded into the background of one's intentionally directed experience. What ought to be a focus of attention is neutralized, producing an all-over effect, or a flattening of background and foreground. Furthermore, the body must adjust itself to the possibility of taking on new habits of walking. Benjamin refers to this as a special kind of embodied "relearning" that breaks down old habits in anticipation of new, yet undefined ones. The city presents itself as a "labyrinth for the newcomer." The experience of this labyrinth comes through phenomenological changes in the feel of the connection between body and ground that displaces set habituations. In this manner, the adult's body reexperiences a certain kind of childlike potentiality for developing new habits without knowing what these new habits might be in advance. Benjamin also links his experience of city life with the experience of film, both of which are, in some ways, distracting. As several noted authors have pointed out,[37] for Benjamin, there are unique connections between the city and childhood, spatial and temporal distances, wandering and remembering, city shock and film shock that form important themes in his urban portraits, but what I would add here is that *distraction* is often the phenomenological bridge between these pairs.

In a description of his arrival at the island of Ibiza, Benjamin makes similar claims concerning the interconnection between seeing a city for the first time and the sudden opportunity to deform the relation between the self and its habits. He writes,

In any case, toward six o-clock in the evening I stood on the empty promenade deck next to the wheelhouse [of the ship *Ciudad de Valencia*], piecing together all the parts of the incomparable picture that large towns present to an observer gazing down from the heights of a ship. The sun was setting over the city, which seemed to have fallen silent. All life had retreated to the imperceptible transitions between the foliage on the trees, the cement of the buildings, and the rocks of the distant mountains. I stood and thought of Horace's famous truism, "What exile fleeing from his native land would ever flee his own mind?"—and how questionable it is. For isn't traveling a purification, the overcoming of settled passions that are attached to one's accustomed environment, and hence an opportunity to develop new ones—something that in fact amounts to a metamorphosis?[38]

Benjamin arrives with his habituated patterns, learned skills, dispositions, and predefined interests that orient him in certain directions and not others. Yet, gazing out at an "incomparable picture" of a new city, his sense of self gives way to a new passion that causes the mind to flee from its former self. Predetermined orientations are suddenly left idle. The "I" that unifies the self is interrupted by the upsurge, which itself is the precondition for a metamorphosis into something/someone else. It is important to note that this passion emerged at the precise moment of mental lapse in the face of a sprawling city that could not be easily synthesized or conceptualized but had to be "pieced together" by a diffuse, nondirected, scattered form of attunement.

This positive result is far from guaranteed as wandering and wayfaring can easily lead to mere diversion. Benjamin warns,

> The labyrinth is the habitat of the dawdler. The path followed by someone reluctant to reach his [sic] goal easily becomes labyrinthine. A drive, in the stages leading to its satisfaction, acts likewise. But so, too, does a humanity (a class) which does not want to know where its destiny is taking it.[39]

In other words, the newcomer who is shocked upon arrival in a foreign city can be the key to unlocking its hidden potentiality for new ways of life, or can end up being absorbed into mere distraction as an avoidance strategy. We can think here of the fate of the flaneur as, in some sense, the opposite of the newcomer: a dawdler whose class privilege allows him or her to avoid the knowability of his or her historical fate by turning to the all-too-familiar amusements of the city. Indeed, Benjamin argues that the flaneur is never truly absentminded in the same way as the newcomer. He writes, "In the flaneur, the joy of watching prevails over all. It can concentrate on observation; the result is the amateur detective. Or it can stagnate in the rubbernecker; then the flaneur has turned into a *badaud*. The revealing representations of the big city have come from neither. They are the work of those who have traversed the city absently, as it were, lost in thought or worry."[40] In other words, the flaneur is captivated by particular acts of looking. Captivation narrows attunement down to a highly individuated, atomized level of a single observer and his or her private pleasure in the sheer power of the gaze. Subsequently, the flaneur takes on the traits of a detective whose single-minded focus is on "solving" specific crimes (crimes of property) at the expense of the latent knowability of the city as such—latent yet somehow distorted in its various dream particles. The concentration implied by the behavior of the flaneur-as-detective prevents him or her from ever producing a "revealing representation of the big city" in its knowability as it is first felt in the innervated and extended sensorium of the newcomer. While the newcomer might also gaze on the city (and thus appear to privilege sight as an access point), it is precisely the city *as a whole* that lights up from this kind of looking rather than this or that particular feature of the city. The gaze fills itself with the city, yielding to it, and thus, vision itself is touched by the city down to its nerves and tissues. A global *sense* of the city—its dreamscape as something knowable—only arrives when the mind strays as the unsupervised body (de)forms its habits. While the flaneur might learn about specific crimes against the implicit background of the city, the newcomer studies this background as such, transposing it into the foreground of a momentary, first encounter.

The artfulness of straying only emerges *after* the interruption and dispersal of preset habits and orientations—including the habituation of seeing found in the flaneur. The leveling effect induced by the newcomer's experience of Moscow, for instance, is a necessary though not sufficient condition for fending off the temptations of mere diversion. In addition, the open alertness of distraction must yield to what is *most swollen and grotesque* in a cityscape (even if it at first appears irrelevant). The emigrant and the newcomer have a distinct advantage in achieving this kind of attunement. As a newcomer himself, Benjamin was often receptive in just the right way to the points of foreign cities visited—points where their logic was most exposed and thus most knowable. The Paris arcades were perfect examples. The city arcades of Paris were the maximal swelling point of bourgeois subjectivity externalizing itself in architectural form, and this is why they contained more educational potential to be studied than other examples of Parisian architecture. The arcades were swollen with the dreamscape of the bourgeoisie to a state where they inadvertently expressed the knowability of this condition. Paris, on this reading, was the capital of the nineteenth century because its cityscape *was the most swollen* and thus the most studious for revealing the dream world of that century. The arcades, in turn, expressed this exaggeration of the city's formal elements—and as such, made palpable the century's implicit secrets to those distracted enough to yield to it. This means that swollenness is not always found in the most fashionable or up-to-date elements in a city. There is something untimely about a swelling—it either arrives too late or too early, not unlike the child or the newcomer who are also out-of-synch with the spatial and temporal rhythms of a city. Swelling points meet up with these wanderers precisely because they are equally discordant with the "contemporary."

Or we might think of Benjamin's reflections on Naples, coauthored with Asja Lacis. The knowability of the city—its "porosity"—swells up to become visible (and thus knowable) only through a diffuse, distracted form of open alertness. The lack of specific attentiveness and focus enables a global attunement to what the city offers up about itself as knowable. Benjamin and Lacis write, "Porosity is the inexhaustible law of life in this city, reappearing everywhere."[41] Global alertness to this "everywhere" quality enables the authors to trip over porosity in all its variegated forms and manifestations, from the permeability of the stone architecture to the migration of street life into interior living spaces (and vice versa) to the "true laboratories of this great process of intermingling"[42] at the cafés. Straying through the city leads to a temporary suspension of mental and motor habits. The self becomes porous, mimetically folding city and sensorium. But this enables the newcomer to study the knowability that swell up in the seemingly inconsequential details of city life as it courses throughout his or her own body. When swells meet—as waves in an ocean of experience suddenly surge—then straying becomes artful.

These descriptions highlight how one must mimetically absorb the distractedness of the cityscape through the art of straying in order to study the city's truth. For the child and the newcomer, cities reconfigure life by working on the most basic senses and forms of motor attunement. Children and newcomers are harbingers of a postapperceptive, thoroughly distracted, alert, urban educational experience. In straying into the allure of the pandering streets, the preconditions for an aesthetic, perceptual transformation take hold of the body—a transformation that disrupts developmental narratives, educational narratives, and political narratives concerning *who* can do *what*, *where*, and *when*. Thus, there is something radically democratic and anarchistic in the art of straying. But even more importantly, the paradox of this educational experience should not be glossed over: it is only through nondurational, fragmentary, and distracted innervation of the body that the durational truth of the city as a whole (and, at the most extreme point of engorgement, the nineteenth century as such) can become knowable. Truth (what persists) is not antithetical to study (what is nondurational). Rather, truth can only be experienced as an inflation or exaggeration of the implicit, fleeting nature of study to a point where it becomes visible (knowable) as a determinate phenomenon. The wave of study crests as swells meet, intensifying one another to express a truth that is inexpressible in any one studious moment, encounter, or touch.

Perfecting the Art of Straying Against Fascism

In conclusion, we can formulate the politics of this art more concretely by turning once again to fascism. Fascists never have much good to say about cities. Nazis Party leaders in Germany thought that cities were ruled by Jews and that urban life in general diluted consciousness of race, the folk, and soil. Hitler once told Hermann Rauschning that the "empty urban masses" were susceptible to the "stupid godless propaganda" of Marxism.[43] In fact, Hitler even suggested that German peasants who were intuitively connected to the land be sent to cities as missionaries to save the urban masses. In this sense, cities were places to be conquered and occupied so as to mitigate against the contaminating influences of Jews and Marxists. Cities were threats to the hegemonic power of Nazism so they occupied the streets. The mixing of races, ideas, and the potentiality for distraction all undermined the absolute rule that the fascists aspired to attain. Given this background, it is not surprising that in the 2016 election, Trump lost in most of the large, densely populated metropolitan centers in the United States. Political analyses of the data point toward the typical list of factors to explain these results, including a concentration of the nation's more affluent, tech-savvy, and highly educated population in urban areas. Further, metropolitan centers that are predominately white went to Trump, while those with higher numbers of Latino/as, immigrants, and LGBTQ populations went to Hillary Clinton.[44] Certainly these data are important to highlight, but it is also possible to place these results in relation to broader historical trends within the struggle against fascism. Why is it that Trump's rhetorical style did not trigger fascist psychological or bodily expressions in these large, American urban centers? It has been my contention throughout this chapter that cities themselves—and their extended and intensified opportunities for distraction—are antifascist educational forms. This does not mean that cities guarantee anything—no awakening is ever guaranteed by any educational form.

For instance, we must heed Benjamin's warning that wandering in the city can lead to the intoxicating sleep of mere diversion. If this is the case, what lessons can we glean for navigating the city? If his radio broadcasts offer one possible resource for thinking through this question, here I would suggest that the *form* of Benjamin's writings might be another. As Graeme Gilloch and David Kishik both argue,[45] Benjamin presents us not simply with a philosophy of the city but with philosophy *as* a city—philosophy takes on the features of city life in its compositional form so that the global condition of the twentieth century in general can be thrown into light. At this point, we can quote Eduard Devrient, whom Benjamin cites in *The Arcades Project*, "Rainshowers annoy me, so I gave one the slip in an arcade. There are a great many of these glass-covered walkways, which often cross through the blocks of buildings and make several branchings, thus affording welcome shortcuts."[46] Most important is Devrient's observation that the arcades are composed of branchings and shortcuts that provide multiple connections between different points. Benjamin's formal appropriation of such branchings and shortcuts in his style of writing enters into the commodity-driven, distractive dream of the arcades so as to throw it into high relief, provoking an awakening. The collections of notes and reflections that make up the labyrinthian body of *The Arcades Project* therefore aid against mere diversion by carefully building up constellational branchings that indirectly express the epoch of nineteenth-century Paris—its past and its unrealized future(s)—in a form that is both parts mimetic semblance and play. Benjamin's writings re-present or re-collect the nondurational study of the city experienced through straying, making it free through heightened visibility. As such, awakening to the image of the city through evocative writing by scholars such as Benjamin (but also poets such as Baudelaire) can help make wandering more artful. This does not mean that writing about the city can present us with a manual on how to stray or a model to be exemplified (and merely repeated). Instead such writings can act as teacherly invitations to encounter the (de)forming powers of the city once again, and as a result, learn a new way to learn (study by straying and straying through study). This might be particularly important for those of us who are long-time residents of cities, and thus not children or newcomers. It might help us fall *out of sync* with the habituated constraints of our daily milieus.

Extrapolating from Benjamin's writings, we might pose the following "study guide" to help wanderers avoid the traps of both fascist hardening and divertive dawdling. In other words, I would like to end by further unpacking the "how" of Benjamin's artful teachings in *The Arcades Project*.

1. As argued above, to avoid mere diversion, wanderers ought to cultivate high alertness to the maximal swelling points of a city, or those points at which the city reveals its knowability. Such swelling points are not likely the most timely or fashionable or trendy aspects of a city. Instead, if Benjamin is correct, they are to be found in that which is somewhat untimely. That which is fading away reveals itself with uncanny clarity, providing unique opportunities for awakening. Fascist attunement would miss such swelling points, opting instead for the most spectacular and grandiose totems of power. The hardness, coldness, and manipulative qualities of the authoritarian personality resist the kind of openness to swelling points offered up by the ruins of cities. These swelling points are points of maximal yield, maximal exposure, and thus are vulnerable points where the dream of past generations shows itself, making its dream logic knowable. Yet the defensive walls constructed around the fascist psyche do not allow for any "illegal immigration" of ideas, sensations, or contacts. The result is a crusting over of habits of mind and body that is antithetical to the educational life of experimentation encouraged and necessitated by the multitude of encounters one has in a city, especially in moments when one strays off the main avenues and into the backstreets and ruins.

2. Be open to the plasticity of educational times and places. In his theory of knowledge buried in *The Arcades Project* Benjamin states, "On the differentials of time (which for others, disturb the main lines of the inquiry), I base my reckoning."[47] The city is one vast inlay of differential temporalities, moving forward and backward simultaneously. Benjamin is concerned with excavating the layers of history buried within this cityscape. It is no longer a chronologically coherent story, but rather a multiplicity of intersecting and diverging moments that, when brought into contact, can momentarily swell up into a thought image or thought sound. Fascist history is not plastic in this sense. It is instead rigid and highly codified to reinforce a single, definitive narrative of blood and soil. As such, the multiplicity of differential times emerging from within the city are politically destabilizing for any construction of history as a unified myth.

3. Open the self up to collectivization. The body of the wanderer of the city is a nondenumberable, massive, swollen entity. As it gives itself away by yielding to the city through autocartography (an exterior mapping of the self as wandering away from itself), this body exposes itself to the potentiality for collective massification. A massive collective is not reducible to either the atomized, bourgeois flaneur or the crowd. For Benjamin, the flaneur "reflects the fluctuations of commodities"[48] through his or her flanerie. Such wandering is therefore caught up in the phantasmagoric dreamscape of the city which remains unknowable in its familiarity. Likewise, the crowd is perpetually intoxicated, and this intoxication induces a perpetual sleep. Drawing on Edgar Allan, Baudelaire, and other writers, Benjamin describes the crowd as emerging between "the figure of shock and contact with the metropolitan masses."[49] Benjamin continues: "They do not stand for classes or any sort of collective; rather, they are nothing but the amorphous crowd of passers-by, the people in the street."[50] The crowd has no sense of its collectivity. It is merely a conglomerate of flaneurs passing, absentmindedly

down the street. Yet the crowd is also highly susceptible to fascist, charismatic leaders. He summarizes this dark turn as follows: "This 'crowd' on which the flâneur takes delight, is just the empty mold with which, seventy years later, the *Volksgemeinschaft* [People's Community] was cast."[51] Benjamin thus suggests that fascism is, in some sense, a response to the problems of the bourgeois individual (epitomized by the flaneur) as he or she confronts the crowd (with equal parts shock and pleasure). Instead of a crowd, a pluralized student body would be a multitude, and thus a diasporic, swarm. Whereas fascist crowds are cold, hard, and unified by blood and soil, this alternative, massive collective runs hot to the point of swelling over into divergent strands of alterity that cannot be reunified in terms of a nation or a people.

4. Artful straying through the city inspired by Benjamin's teachings enables one to be (1) shocked by what swells up to become knowable and (2) to leverage this shock in order to open up a space and time of potentiality that exists when habits are disturbed, allowing apperception to *learn how to learn*. Learning how to learn is a short-circuiting of one's apperceptive apparatus through a full-bodied alter-shock, exaggerating apperception to the point of its dissolve. The result is an innervative massification and dispersal of the self into the city—an urban form of study without end or particular destination (a learning how to learn that continually repotentializes itself as study). To live a life outside of fascist collectivity, there needs to be a return to the potentiality found between existing habits and future habits—a youthful, threshold existence where city and self swell together to form monstrous (de)formations. When all previous coordinates defining the who, what, when, and where of learning are suspended, then one can learn how to learn anew by giving one's self over to artful straying. It has been my contention that Benjamin can provide unique tools for thinking through the perceptual, embodied, erotic, and collective dimensions of such a political and aesthetic education

as it exists in the circulating bodies, images, and events of cities, especially at particular pressure points in cities where swellings occur with most frequency and intensity. When we turn to the city for educational inspiration, we might find a small yet important political force awaiting us when we are most absentminded: a force that does not have a clear name but signals the arrival of a coming community—diasporic, open, alert, massive, and most importantly, artfully distracted.

CINEMA

If I have argued that radio serves an important educational use in early childhood education, swelling children into a youthful sense of historical consciousness, such swelling is certainly more acute in cinematic experience, which for Benjamin, produces multiple sensorial innervations beyond mere vision. Whereas some see film as nothing more than mere diversion, Benjamin argues that in film we find a medium in which "educational value and consumer value converge, thus making possible a new kind of learning."[1] This chapter is an attempt to unpack this phrase in order to understand how film is within, yet in some senses resists, mere commodity status or ideological manipulation. This means finding in film resources for an antifascist education. To do so is to enlarge the scope of the notion of the "art of straying" introduced in the last chapter. It is my contention that film is a distracted medium par excellence in three senses. First, it is distracting in terms of its technical qualities. Second, these qualities are exemplified in the slapstick comedy, which itself folds the human body into the mechanical through the mimesis of these technical qualities. And third, the audience itself absorbs this new kind of inhuman *physis* through their collective laughter. Laughter on this reading is an education of the bodily sensorium to a new kind of life that is neither reducible to existing habits nor correlated with future habits. The laughing body is a body in potential. This means that laughter is not merely a temporary diversion or form of escapism. Instead, it must be taken seriously as a nondestructive shock or innervating awakening. These three dimensions—technical distraction, slapstick comedy, and laughter—converge in the work of Charlie Chaplin, whose films will be offered as an acme of an antifascist form of informal education. In short, film makes the conditions of modern, technologically infused life tactile, with comedy being the genre that makes this tactility optimally free. Thus, comedy is the most educational form film can take (no joke!). But to tap into the educational dimension of comedic film, one has to take into account the cinematic experience as a whole, which includes the film's own logic, the collective setting of the cinema, and the embodied response. As such, in this chapter I will discuss films while also situating these films in the particular phenomenological context of the cinema as a place where bodies and comedic images on screen can mimetically fold into one another through both an optical unconscious and laughter.

Agreeing with Miriam Bratu Hansen, Benjamin's reflections on film cannot be easily dismissed as antiquated relics of another, bygone era. Instead, Hansen persuasively argues, Benjamin's "speculation on film and mass-mediated culture still speak to our concerns because the problems he articulated and the antinomies in which his thinking moved persist in the globalized media societies of today—in different forms and on a different scale, to be sure, but with no less urgency and no more hope for easy solutions."[2] In particular, Hansen finds Benjamin's analysis of innervation, mimetic displacement, optical unconscious, and *Spiel* (play) found in his commentary on film to be highly relevant to present questions related to art and politics in a digital age. In this chapter, I expand on this analysis by foregrounding the importance of film as an antifascist educational form—one that is exemplified in comedic slapstick and the collective, laughing body of the audience.

A Distracted Medium

As quoted above, Benjamin argues that film is unique in the modern era in that it offers an opportunity to balance out commercial and educational values. Such a balancing act is essential for understanding the possible educational effects of film on an audience. For instance, if a film only had educational value, it would be nothing more than a didactic lesson that would not take advantage of the uniqueness of the medium so much as repress it. Benjamin's description of Russian films, written in 1927, offers up such an assessment. The introduction of film and radio to the rural Russian population was, for Benjamin, one of "the most grandiose mass-psychological experiments ever undertaken in the gigantic laboratory that Russia has become."[3] It was an experiment in perceptual-cognitive reception precisely because film produces new ways of seeing and feeling the world. As proof of the potentially radical redistribution of the sensible offered up by film, Benjamin cites a curious example of Russian peasants who were unable to follow two simultaneous narratives in a film. Furthermore, they did not exhibit anticipated emotional reactions to scenes of drama or comedy. For this reason, Benjamin reports that Russian filmmakers began to make educational films for an explicitly rural population lacking access to city life and/or more advanced technologies. These films were purely didactic in nature, focusing on lessons concerning the evils of alcoholism or how to cope with insect infestation. Paradigmatic examples had a single narrative, and the scenes were arranged in chronological order so as not to cause confusion. In short, their didacticism was an attempt to focus attention while minimizing the possibility for perceptual distraction. Although there might be some educational value to such didacticism (enabling the learning of specific, utilitarian lessons to improve life for rural peasants), Benjamin is clearly concerned that something in the medium itself had been lost. The result was an impoverished notion of cinema that was lacking in both formal and technical experimentation. The possibilities for a positive acclimatization to distraction were foreclosed on by a retreat back to the primacy of attentiveness. By isolating the educational value of film over and above those technical features that granted it commercial value, the resulting notion of a cinematic experience was seriously limited. Indeed, commercially distracting genres such as comedy were denied to the Russian filmmaker. Benjamin concludes with a suggestion: "The Russian film can reestablish itself on firm ground only when Bolshevist society (and not just the state!) has become sufficiently stable to enable a new 'social comedy' to thrive, with new characters and typical situations."[4] In other words, cinema can thrive if and only if new comedic forms are invented that do not simply reproduce bourgeois life, but rather tap into the aesthetic fermentation of the Russian revolution itself. Such a move would not shy away from the kinds of technical playfulness that the educational films guarded against and commercial films indulged in. Instead, there would be an embrace of film as a playful space capable of pushing the faculties to their inflated points of rupture. At stake here is a cinema that shifts education from conservative attentiveness toward experimental distraction.

On the other hand, rejecting all educational value, we find the crass consumerism of the American culture industry, which stands as a kind of inversion of the Russian cultural films described by Benjamin. Here one can recall the rather pessimistic assessment of film offered up by Max Horkheimer and Theodor W. Adorno in their classic *Dialectic of Enlightenment*. According to the authors, "film seeks strictly to reproduce the world of everyday perception" to the point that it "denies its audience any dimension in which they might roam freely in imagination; thus it trains those exposed to it to identify film directly with reality."[5] To watch a film is to watch an image of everyday perception perceiving itself. The result is a naturalization and universalization of the status quo without the space for critical reflection. As Horkheimer and Adorno aptly summarize, ". . . the simple reproduction of mind does not lead on to the expansion of mind."[6] The true political consequences of this are found in their example of Donald Duck cartoons, in which the audience comes to see the beating of the working class as amusing, and by extension, as a natural and necessary part of the order of society. The perverse joy in beating the oppressed reserved for the oppressor becomes a shared amusement, further universalizing class-specific passions. In sum, film is nothing more than a consumer value, produced to lull the masses into a perpetual feedback loop of the same, so that they do not reflect critically on the exploitation of their labor power by capitalists. In this sense, it accelerates what I have referred to previously as mere distraction or distraction as diversion. And it does so through the kinds of cinematic techniques that the Russian films minimized: multiple narratives, complex film editing, image montage, advanced camera movements, the emotive use of sound and music, flashbacks, and so forth—all of which are castigated by Horkheimer and Adorno as standardized forms of ideological manipulation.

If film as pure educational value focused on cultivating attentiveness through a minimization of technical experimentation, then film as pure consumer value heightens certain forms of technical experimentation in order to create increased diversions. Missed in both cases is what Benjamin refers to as a *new type of learning* that emerges when film brings together both education and consumer values, throwing into high relief an alternative perceptual system that is on high alert—open and attuned to the marginal, obscure, and different details of life lost in the phantasmagoria of images that define the culture industry. It is my wager that the new type of learning found in film takes hold over the body itself, shocking the sensorium and dislodging the faculties from their sedimented roles in the construction and maintenance of a bourgeois sense of a possessive self. This experience would utilize the dialectic between educational and consumer values to produce a nondurational moment of embodied study.

One might think that I am explicitly talking about avant-garde filmmaking outside the Hollywood system. It would seem that Adorno suggests as much. In the essay "Transparencies on Film," Adorno argues that realist aesthetics are "inseparable from [the] commodity form"[7] and ought to be replaced by certain progressive aesthetic experimentation emerging from within the most vanguard of autonomous art. If films "incite the viewers and listeners to fall into step as if in a parade,"[8] then radical aesthetics (especially in relation to montage) is the only possibility for regaining some kind of critical distance from consumer value. While Adorno criticized Benjamin for focusing on the progressive possibilities of commercial film, then the work of Andrew Hewitt calls into question the assumed correspondence between avant-gardism and leftist politics found in Adorno's writings. For Hewitt, modernity's avant-garde art overlaps with fascism in that both "result in a certain 'false sublation' of art and life."[9] While Hewitt focuses on Italian Futurism in his analysis, Mark Antliff proposes a similar thesis, this time in relation to the appropriation of the avant-garde by fascists in France between 1909 and 1939. In both cases, the authors reveal a certain naivete at work in Adorno's own approach to film, and in particular his overestimation of the progressive political potentials of montage, fragmentation, and collage-based aesthetics.[10] What is missing in Adorno's analysis is precisely what is compelling in Benjamin's. For Benjamin, film is uniquely capable of a dialectical synthesis of consumer and educational value that is not merely the negation of its consumer status but rather its extension to a maximal point of potentiality where it touches educational value. Certain avant-garde artistic movements such as Dada might have anticipated the aesthetics of film, yet Dadaism, for Benjamin, could not fulfill the demands that it created. This task was passed on to film.[11] In opposition to Adorno, Benjamin writes, "At no point in time, no matter how utopian, will anyone win the masses over to a higher art; they can be won over only to one nearer to them."[12] Instead of dismissing it, Benjamin opts for radical experimentation with the kitsch that defines both the decadence of the culture industry and the philistinism of fascism. Granting that kitsch is "100 percent, absolute and instantaneous availability for consumption," he nevertheless suggests that artists "take kitsch dialectically up into themselves, and hence bring themselves near to the masses while yet surmounting the kitsch. Today, perhaps, film alone is equal to this task."[13]

This does not mean that Benjamin is overly utopian. Indeed, he understands the business of filmmaking: "Film capital uses the revolutionary opportunities implied by this control for counterrevolutionary purposes. Not only does the cult of the movie star which it fosters preserve that magic of the personality which has long been no more than the putrid magic of its own commodity character, but its counterpart, the cult of the audience, reinforces the corruption by which fascism is seeking to supplant the class consciousness of the masses."[14] Benjamin makes a parallel argument for film under fascist dictatorships. In both cases, the opportunities for film to produce a new type of collective is exploited and turned against itself. If film can achieve a balance between educational and consumer value (thereby becoming a studious form), this is indeed a precious and precarious achievement, one that all too easily topples over into the kitschy barbarism of capitalism and/or fascism. Below I will explore in some detail how the technology of film and its filmic techniques offer up an image of cinematic straying that is antifascist. This is not the reproduction of what is, as Horkheimer and Adorno feared, but rather the repotentalization of what is precisely through a cinematic process that engages the body in a new kind of learning.

Innervation through Experimentation

In a telling note, Benjamin makes clear the connections between the experience of the city by the crowd and the experience of film by an audience: film "corresponds to profound changes in the apperceptive apparatus—changes that are experienced on the scale of private existence by each passerby in big-city traffic, and on the scale of world history by each fighter against the present social order."[15] What binds these together is a certain form of reception in distraction that unsettles the work of the apperceptive apparatus, disconnects the faculties, and produces a state of high alertness. But unlike the mere citizen walking down the street, Benjamin's description of the film audience has an important, added dimension that supplements this perceptual shock. Interestingly, Benjamin describes the film audience as an *absentminded examiner*. Such an examiner is not simply a consciously attentive examiner nor is he or she a passive, absentminded consumer. Something new is produced in the juncture of educational and consumer values—a new form of perception that is critical while simultaneously absentminded. Benjamin writes, "With regard to the cinema, the critical and uncritical attitudes of the public coincide. The decisive reason for this is that nowhere more than in the cinema are the reactions of individuals, which together make up the massive reception of the audience, determined by the imminent concentration of reactions into a mass. No sooner are these reactions manifest than they regulate one another."[16] The consumer attitude is uncritical (allowing the embodied self to be absorbed into the film through certain affective and perceptual lures), while the critical attitude is educational (shocking the self into a moment of judgment over this very same process). When in a collective, cinematic encounter between bodies and films, the two form an "imminent concentration" that "regulate" one another. This regulation is, importantly, not about mental oversight of one's personal reactions to watching a film. It does not concern critical interrogation of one's reactions. Instead, the audience is composed of absentminded examiners. This examination is thoroughly embodied, sensual, and intensive. Another way of putting this would be that the judgment at stake in cinematic experience is *distracted judgment*, or judgment that lacks a concept under which the experience could be assessed by a focused and autonomous "I." Instead, we find a sensorial form of judgment that is preconscious, instantaneous, and embodied. How does such judgment work? When watching a film, the audience swells up with affective intensities that then extend outward. The audience can gain an intuitive sense of its own collectivity through an affective moment. Alternatively, it can feel a certain discomfort or unease at moments when a certain affect does not intensify and spread or only intensifies for certain members of an audience (see my discussion of racist laughter below). In other words, when mass reaction is sensed, there is a critical, intuitive capacity to gage the status of a collective (unified or divided against itself). Distracted judgment *feels* this sense of equilibrium or division, extension or retraction in its own affective intensities as they link up with or separate from the mass. Importantly, this kind of intuitive, distracted judgment happens faster than conscious, critical reflection. As Benjamin emphasizes above, "No sooner are these reactions manifest than they regulate one another." *No sooner* implies an immediacy that can only come from an affective surge happening in the moment. There is no delay between perception and judgment. They merge into one another, forming the basis for nondurational study.

This form of distractedly critical perception is directly related to technical features of film. Benjamin quotes Duhamel, who described viewing a film as follows: "I can no longer think what I want to think. My thoughts have been replaced by moving images."[17] Duhamel indicates that he can no longer think what *he* wants to think. It is not simply that the speed of film leaves no time for thoughtful reflection but rather that it interrupts and suspends the distance and duration needed to reflect and judge. The bourgeois subject, and its purported psychological consistency, autonomy, and unity are critically undermined. Benjamin writes, ". . . the train of associations in the person contemplating these images is immediately interrupted by new images"[18] producing a shock effect to the perceptual-cognitive organization of the bourgeois self. But this does not signal, for Benjamin at least, the death of criticality. Instead, there is an "immediate, intimate fusion of pleasure—pleasure in seeing and experiencing—with an attitude of expert appraisal."[19] Whereas the bourgeois subject locates the critical capacity to appraise within reason and the mediated distance of contemplation, Benjamin seems to indicate that it can be more immediate and dispersed throughout the sensing body of the collective audience. Being critical here is *not* about a way of thinking, but rather concerns the arrival of a new way of *sensing* the world collectively. Stated differently, critique concerns sensory attunement instead of reflexive interpretation. It lodges itself within perceptual circuitry, sending a jolt of affective intensity surging through the system, fracturing the bourgeois "I," exposing it as radically expressive and public. Such a shock is not, as Hansen argues,[20] antithetical to playful innervation, but is rather part and parcel of it.

Film provides an example of what this new type of perception (absentminded yet critical) might feel like, while also acclimatizing the audience to its arrival. For instance, Benjamin describes film as "unfolding of all the forms of perception, the tempos and rhythms, which lie performed in today's machines."[21] Technical features of film unfold all forms of human perception, exaggerating them to the point where human perception becomes inhuman, machine-like. Film can accomplish that which is impossible for the naked, human eye. Take for instance the close-up, in which new aspects of our immediate experience are discovered; or slow motion, which reveals nuances of movement; or the pan shot, which widens the scope of the normal horizon line; or flashbacks and flash-forwards, which exploit the plasticity of time. Cameras enable the audience to discover an "optical unconscious" that lies below human perceptual capacities and yet is made tactile through the camera's "resources for sweeping and rising, disrupting and isolating, stretching or compressing a sequence, enlarging or reducing an object."[22] All of these examples reconfigure human perceptual rhythms and tempos, producing an innervated form of sensing the world that extends and intensifies the body's capacity for alertness and openness. Benjamin writes, film has the ability to "explode" the "prison-world" of the everyday "with the dynamite of its fractions of a second, so that now we can take extended journeys of adventure between their widely scattered ruins."[23] Film unfolds human perception, blasting open the organization of faculties so that new journeys can be undertaken, new discoveries made, and new sensations invented. While the conscious self might very well be indulging in the phantasmagoria of a typical narrative plot, the film audience's optical unconscious will swell with the movements of the camera that exceed narrative intent, developing unintended pleasures in that which emerges on the peripheries of consciously noted experience.

Another important feature of film is expressed in its dialectical structure. For Benjamin, the essential feature of film can be summarized as follows: "Discontinuous images replace one another in a continuous sequence."[24] While this continuous sequence binds film to the production and consumption process found in factories, there is something unique to cinema about the centrality of discontinuous images. On my reading, *discontinuity* speaks of the ever-present possibility to *rearrange* a contingent sequence. Thus, there is something revolutionary about the discontinuity of film that always threatens to undermine any given sense of linear sequence. Another way of putting this is that the discontinuity of images can undo the phantasmagoric illusion of continuity, while remaining immanent to the images that compose the illusion. If this is correct, then what is most important about film—not unlike the moment of waking up from a dream or the discontinuous moments of the art of straying in a city or the fragmentary citations and ephemera that compose *The Arcades Project*—is the educational function of discontinuity on the audience's sense of historical possibility. As Benjamin points out with reference to Chaplin's film *A Woman of Paris*, 125,000 meters of film were shot, while only 3,000 meters were used in the final cut. This suggests that film is "assembled from a very large number of images and image sequences that offer an array of choices to the editor; these images, moreover, can be improved in any desired way in the process leading form the initial take to the final cut."[25] Film is opposed to the traditional work of art precisely because of its plasticity. Its technical features thus embody an indeterminating process always open to various assemblages that do not follow teleologically determined, necessary pathways. "Improvement" cannot be read here in terms of progress culminating the realization of an essence or spirit, so much as in the sense of playing with variants through the allegorical experimentation with fragments (or, in this case, film stills). Indeed, for Benjamin, film is an ideal play-space (*Spielraum*) or a zone of indeterminate potentiality given over to chance and improvisational (de)formations.

Whereas the flaneur is famous for a certain voyeuristic contemplation of commodities through a detached gaze, the mass's mode of reception is fully embodied and immersive. As Benjamin writes, "the distracting element in film is also primarily tactile, being based on successive changes of scene and focus which have a percussive effect on the spectator." [26] One does not watch a film so much as allow the self to be touched by it, and by being touched, absorb the distracting medium into the self in the form of a mechanized optical unconscious. If possession presupposes a subject grasping an object, then touching indicates a yielding that passes through and into the body, exposing it to the potentiality for transformation beyond itself. Instead of a merely negative state of passive paralysis or mere shock (resulting in numbness), Benjamin sees a potentiality in the film for the construction of a different, crucial capability born out of the abrupt, percussive, dynamic, and contingent experience of cinematic discontinuity—a capability that arrives when apperceptual unity and continuity are laid to rest and a qualitatively different way of perceiving the self and world surges forth through haptic entanglement. In the moment of cinematic innervation, the tacit "I" that promotes a continuous sense of self suddenly is exposed to an underlying discontinuity that explodes its unity. The result is a complication of the stabilizing function of the "I." Its component perceptions can be rearranged, edited together in a new order, cut into a new sequence. There is no necessity here, only the contingencies introduced through the act of splicing together fragments. When film allows the self to touch and be touched by discontinuity, the self opens up to potentially infinite future articulations beyond the necessity of the present.

Consuming the unspooling, flickering, shuttering movement of images projected onto a screen into a palpitating body forms the circuit of critical education unique to film. Benjamin locates the "pedagogic side" of his work decisively as an intervention into what can and cannot be perceived. For instance, Benjamin quotes Rudolf Borchardt: "To educate the image-making medium with us, raising it to a stereoscopic and dimensional seeing into the depths of historical shadows."[27] Education concerns a "raising" of the image-making machinery (optical unconscious) within the human to the level of stereoscopic intensity and extension. This is a swelling of human, embodied perception to a point of mechanical reconstitution. The body becomes a body electric, stimulated by a current that jolts it to a new, stereoscopic level of alertness and openness to an amplified world of sights and sounds that would otherwise overwhelm and paralyze the bourgeois, contemplative subject. In short, raising the optical unconscious enables the mechanizability of bodily perception to become sensible and thus knowable, hence the study value of cinematic experience.

At its best—when it successfully balances consumer and educational value—cinematic experience is a thought image of *the art of straying*. It is the art form that embodies and induces perceptual straying/expansions/contractions/plasticities/multiplicities, thus mimetically reproducing the experience of the child or the newcomer in a city, but in a mediated form capable of showing its own showing. The straying here is sensorial in nature: cinematic alter-shock to the body throws the faculties off their allotted paths, producing unanticipated, passionate, collective configurations and critical, receptive capacities. The "I" wanders away from itself, while the human passes through the eye of the mechanical needle to come out on the other end swollen with an inhuman potentiality.

A small example can suffice to illustrate the disruptive effects of film on perceptual-cognitive conventions. I want to turn to Chaplin's work, in particular, and to comedy more broadly. It is my contention that comedic films—rather than avant-garde films—can act as paradigms for a cinema that has both consumer and educational values. Here it is important to recall how Benjamin explicitly stated that in Russia, the advent of a new kind of "social comedy" would be a truly revolutionary aesthetic gesture. The equivalent in Western, capitalist culture would certainly be Chaplin. Formally, Chaplin's comedy is not based on actions so much as "a theme and variations" or "elements of composition" that can be continually reshuffled and redeployed.[28]

This phenomenon is perfectly illustrated in Chaplin's *The Circus* (1928), which Benjamin describes as follows:

> The most wonderful part is the way the end of the film is structured. He strews confetti over the happy couple, and you think: This must be the end. Then you see him standing there when the circus procession starts off; he shuts the door behind everyone, and you think: This must be the end. Then you see him struck in the rut of the circle earlier drawn by poverty, and you think: This must be the

end. Then you see a close-up of his completely bedraggled form, sitting on a stone in the arena. Here you think the end is absolutely unavoidable, but then he gets up and you see him from behind, walking further and further away, with that gait peculiar to Charlie Chaplin; he is his own walking trademark, just like the company trademark you see at the end of other films. And now, at the only point where there's no break and you'd like to be able to follow him with your gaze forever—the film ends![29]

Instead of fulfilling commonsense assumptions about when a film might end, Chaplin subverts the audience's expectations. The result is twofold. First, the film undoes consumerist clichés, not through negation but rather by dialectically synthesizing them all into a sequence that defies the telos of film. By splicing together multiple endings, the film perpetually repotentialize itself. Each "ending" produces its own surplus, or a swell of alternative potentialities that suddenly burst onto the screen and insert themselves between events and their purported ends. The theme of "the end" makes itself visible and thus knowable through this repetition. In its knowability, "the end" displaces when and how something ought to end . . . or if their ought to be ends at all. The conventions of film offer up a new way to learn: one that makes ending stray from *an* end, thus opening up a messianic temporality between chronological time and its end. This is the time of maximal plasticity, where time can interrupt and suspend its own teleological destinations. And in this sense, repetition on a theme becomes educational precisely because it remains immanent to the very consumerist images and techniques so despised by Adorno while at the same time neutralizing the commonsense function of these images and techniques.

Straying means that the "hero" does not complete his or her actions, but rather repeats themes without end. Take Chaplin's short titled *One A.M.* from 1916. Chaplin arrives home early in the morning, clearly intoxicated. For almost ten full minutes he repeatedly attempts to walk up the staircase and go to bed. Yet he cannot succeed. He perpetually strays off-course until one is left with the deep sense of anxiety that he will never sleep. But this "failure" opens up the possibility for seemingly infinite potential repetitions of the same gestures over and over with increasing levels of comedic hilarity. By suspending the end of the action (by arriving in his bed and falling asleep), Chaplin shows the audience a way of being that is beyond the dialectic between action and consequence. Gestural repetition opens up actions to indefinite free use, not unlike a game of permutations, where each potentiality is examined, one after another, until a state of exhaustion is reached. Comedic film time exists in the drawing out of a surplus time betwixt and between an intention and its completion. This time is an interstitial time of minor, incidental gestures suddenly swelling up, exaggerating to a point of overtaking the action through thematic repetition. Chaplin's films are educational precisely because the repetition of the gesture allows these gestures to become sensible, and thus imbues them with knowability.

Yet it would be a mistake to assume that the gestures which swell to the surface in Chaplin's films are "human" in any strict sense of the term. Indeed, Chaplin's gestures are repetitions of stuttering stops and starts that mimetically reproduce cinematic rhythms. Benjamin states, "The innovation of Chaplin's gestures is that he dissects the expressive movements of human beings into a series of minute innervations. Each single movement he makes is composed of a succession of staccato bits of movement."[30] Heroic action is expressive of one's character, yet Chaplin's movements interrupt action and suspend character from expressing itself. Instead, he focuses on a micrological dissection of the innervative movements of the body. In these innervations, he discovers an inhuman substrate that swells to the surface to the point of merging the body's gestures with the staccato gestures of film as such. Benjamin observes that the "jerky sequence" of Chaplin's movements "applies the law of the cinematic image sequence to human motorial functions."[31] Instead of humanist, heroic action, we have a body that shows itself precisely at the point where it extends itself into a repetitive, mechanical gestures that lack heroic intention, control, or conclusion. Chaplin is an image of humanity exaggerating its body into a becoming-machine. Benjamin then asks the perplexing question, "What is it about this behavior that is distinctively comic?"[32] He does not answer the question, but I would venture to guess that the comical is precisely the moment when the body's ability to move interrupts the subject's actions, revealing a surplus of strange gestures that are familiar yet also alien—both self and other. These are neither reducible to existing habits nor do they exhibit future habits. Instead they are a potentiality for some new kind of life emerging within and against the conflagration of machine and human. Mimetically, the very same jerky sequence is reproduced in the laughter of the audience watching Chaplin.

Laughter

In a slightly different context, philosophers Joris Vlieghe, Maarten Simons, and Jan Masschelein argue that the educational logic of laughing should not be traced back to *e-ducare* (as the initiation of youth into an existing social system) but to *e-ducere*, meaning "leading out or an experience of moving us out of position, to expropriate us from the safe identity to which we are attached."[33] For these authors, education is a movement that leads the self beyond itself. Laughing is educational precisely because it deforms rather than informs the self (as in models of *e-ducare*). The impersonal, material dimensions of the body are publicly exposed in moments of laughter. In Benjamin's language, we might say that the body's presence swells forth, interrupting the control of the self over itself. This is an education in and of the body's mechanizable gesturality becoming sensible and thus knowable. In such moments, communal laughter produces an "unconditional equality"[34] of bodies, or a "democratic community-in-laughter,"[35] which undoes social norms separating bodies from one another.

If we position this interpretation of laughter as *e-ducere* within the space of the cinema, then we can expand on Vlieghe, Simons, and Masschelein's central claims in interesting ways. First, Vlieghe, Simons, and Masschelein's interpretation of laughter is located in the flesh, whereas Benjamin's interpretation of laughter fuses together flesh and machine. Laughter is how a body absorbs the sputtering, mechanical, repetitious, fluttering movement of film stills projected onto a screen into itself. Indeed, the laughing body is the *most* cinematic of bodies. Once full-bodied laughter beings, the subject cannot speak, complete an action, or even breathe. Thus, the symbolic and biological dimensions of the self are interrupted and suspended by a mechanical dimension surging forth. The laughing body gives itself over to mechanically reproducing a singular sound and a singular, repetitious gesture, as if it is caught in a loop. Most importantly, the laughing face is frozen into a mask. Unlike most forms of human communication, which utilize a subtle range of facial muscles to convey and emotion or an idea, laughter reduces the face to a singular grimace that is *not one's own making or doing*. What shines forth is an inhuman face—or, even better, a single *image* of an anonymous face that is caught in a repetition of its own grotesque gesturality. In short, laughter turns the subject into an inhuman, cinematic machine, and by doing so, enables this mechanizability to be studied *through the body*.

Importantly, the mimetic absorption of film into the body is described by Benjamin in terms of wave imagery. He writes, "Their [the audience's] waves lap around it [film]; they encompass it with their tide."[36] On my reading, waves of laughter best express the innervating properties of film as they are absorbed by an audience. For Benjamin, "Chaplin never allows the audience to smile while watching him. They must either double up laughing or be very sad."[37] Chaplin's films have consumer and educational value precisely because they produce laughter. A smile would not suffice as it speaks to a removed and discrete (perhaps ironic) distance from film's innervating impulse. In other words, a smile is not extended and intensified to the point of an intensive swelling up and an extensive spreading out of cinematic mechanization. Smiles are subjectively controlled, socially oriented responses. They lack the essential wave movement characteristic of *e-ducere*. Laughter is educational insofar as it makes sensible the presence of the potentiality of the body to be extended and intensified beyond itself through mechanization. On this interpretation, laughing is a form of nondurational, embodied study of the mechanizability of the body electric and its potentiality for producing a new, inhuman form of collective life. To laugh is to enter a threshold state between what the body was and what it might become as an inhuman, cinematic machine. On this reading, laughter becomes the art of the individual body straying from its assumed limitations as a *human* body controlled by a rational subject.

Second, for Vlieghe, Simons, and Masschelein, *collective* laughing can disrupt the hierarchical ordering of bodies and their socialized habits, producing an embodied sense of democracy. Benjamin would agree with these authors. But he would more forcefully emphasize the antifascist nature of this kind of massified study. Whereas the fascist body is precisely cold and hard, the laughing body described by Benjamin is swollen, hot, grotesque, and plastic (e.g., open, flexible, expansive). One is withdrawn behind boundaries and borders (hiding itself), whereas the other is radically vulnerable, exposed, made public (and thus made sensible and knowable). When laughing together, an audience produces a new kind of sonic, jolty, spasmatic collectivity that spreads outward, connecting individuals through laughter. This particular form of collectivity is not easily equated with either a class or a people. In fact, Benjamin refers to the audience as a "matrix"[38] of human and inhuman elements—a kind of composite creature that is born out of an electric infusion. This matrix of bodies and innervating forces takes up what has been made visible (the potentiality of the body) and makes it free (through the contagion of laughter). It is important to note that this contagion is not necessarily based on a shared sense of humor. Laughter in a theater can spread *regardless* of whether or not individuals find the content of the particular film funny. In other words, laughter can become relatively autonomous from its source. And in doing so, it becomes capable of distracting audience members from their preexisting preferences in order to draw them into the wave of laughter. Laughter can grip the body even if individuals do not know what they are laughing at! Laughter can take hold even across ideologically fixed lines. In moments of unbridled hilarity, we receive the first glimpse of an ecstatic, massive, elastic, mechanic body that inflates itself to a maximal point of plasticity above and beyond any rigid or hard boundaries defining what a body ought to do, how it ought to act, or where it ought to appear in a social order.

In the moment of yielding to the plastic, massive body through laughter, the individual body's capacity to swell beyond its assumed limitations becomes a special kind of *absentminded* criticism. This is not a criticism that is rational so much as sensorial, busting apart cold and hard boundaries that separate inside and outside, self and other. Do to the critical force of laughter, Benjamin is able to write that it is the "most revolutionary emotion of the masses."[39] Benjamin further speculates, "Only when in technology body and image space so interpenetrate that all revolutionary tension becomes bodily collective innervation, and all bodily innervations of the collective become revolutionary discharge, has reality transcended itself to the extent demanded by the *Communist Manifesto*."[40] The "bodily collective innervation" of which he speaks in this passage might be none other than the "revolutionary discharge" of collective laughter of a film audience swelling up and spreading out, claiming life's inhuman, mechanic potentiality.

This is not to deny that there is a certain violence inherent in laughing. Indeed, Benjamin places comedy and horror, laughing and crying close together. Yet I would venture that laughter is a *nondestructive* violence, or an educational violence that unleashes potentialities contained in yet restrained by the present social and economic management of bodies. Another way of putting this might be to phenomenologically connect the spasm of laughter as it reverberates through the body to the unique sensation of jolting awake (as if suddenly falling out of a dream into one's body). In both cases, the body undergoes an abrupt shock that dislodges certain rhythms, opening up space and time for alternatives to emerge. Processes of laughing and awakening are threshold conditions poised between states, and therefore contain an educational violence that might hurt but only insofar as it also provokes the untimely eruption of a potentiality for being otherwise. In this sense, laughter is the opposite of the fascist abuse and murder of bodies. While in both cases bodies fuse with technology, one produces awakenings while the other merely reproduces devastation. Whereas fascisms thrive on the "development of sadistic fantasies or masochistic delusions," the awakening of laughter can be a "preemptive and healing outbreak[s] of mass psychosis."[41] Notice that the psychosis does not disappear. Rather, it is healed from within itself by awakening to its own knowability as an illness. Thus, laughter is not outside of violence. Instead, it is violence turning against its own destructive impulses in order to make an alternative potential visible, audible, and free.

This positive, educational, and curative portrayal of laughter stands in stark contrast to that offered up by Horkheimer and Adorno. "Fun," they warn, "is a medicinal bath which the entertainment industry never ceases to prescribe" and which "makes laughter the instrument for cheating happiness." They go so far as to state that "To moments of happiness laughter is foreign; only operettas, and now films, present sex amid peals of merriment."[42] In a broken, fractured society, laughter becomes an index for that which is precisely impossible: happiness. But even worse, the authors suggest that laughter is the abnegation of critical thought, and therefore signifies an "irruption of barbarity"[43] through which each abandons the self to pleasure. The horizon of both capitalist standardization and fascist conformity co-opt the body so as to abruptly freeze the mental capacity for critical thought. Speaking specifically of Chaplin's comedic films, Adorno once wrote to Benjamin, "The idea that a reactionary individual can be transformed into a member of the avant-garde through an intimate acquaintance with the films of Chaplin, strikes me as simple romanticization; for I cannot count Kracauer's favourite film director, even after *Modern Times,* as an avant-garde artist . . . and I cannot believe that the valuable elements in this piece of work will attract the slightest attention anyway. You need only have heard that laughter of the audience at the screening of this film to realize what is going on."[44] There are several important points to make concerning this note to Benjamin.

First, Adorno, true to form, locates revolutionary potential squarely in the corner of the rare, autonomous avant-garde artist. Thus, he denies that art with consumer value could have educational value. Second, he misses how the lack of attention paid to the overtly political dimensions of the film (such as Chaplin's impassioned speech at the end) might very well be the precise condition for a political awakening. If Benjamin is correct, then comedy is educational because it is a form that innervates the optical unconscious. This lesson does not hold the attention of the audience. Instead, it covertly grips the perceptual apparatus of the audience as it becomes swollen with the speed, intensity, and dynamism of modern life in ways that destabilize the organization of the self. Third, Adorno dismisses laughter as a symptom of the film's complicity with the barbarism of the culture industry and thus the demise of the autonomous, rational subject. Missed here is an opportunity to think through the educational meaning of laughter as *e-ducere* or as a swelling point full of potentiality beyond the immunized bourgeois body and the hardness and coldness of the fascist body.

Instead, Horkheimer and Adorno reduce laughter to a "a caricature of solidarity" or a "parody" of reconciliation.[45] Laughter for them can only be *wrong* laughter, the paradigm of which would be racist laughter. I do not deny that racist laughter exists and that it poses a problem for the theory developed thus far. Racist laughter produces coldness and hardness toward otherness, and in this sense, is an exclusive form of laugher that never gives itself away. It sets clear boundaries concerning *who* can laugh, thus interrupting the diasporic movement of laughter. For this reason, racist laughter consolidates inside and outside groups. Further, racist laughter can be a form of domination over and against a targeted minority. From a position of superiority and exteriority, racist laughter embodies fascist irony. Recall that irony distances itself from its object, and as such can destroy both itself and the object through a cold and hard form of detachment. Laugher here becomes *weaponized* as law enforcing or law creating violence that must sacrifice someone or something in order to constitute a closed community in defense of its identity. Instead of overcoming sadistic fantasies or masochistic delusions, such laughter repeats them. It therefore proves that fascist pleasure is predicated on destruction rather than playfulness, on exclusion rather than openness, and attentiveness to its own boundaries rather than distraction in haptic zones of contact. Returning to the theme of distracted judgment introduced above, I argue that in the collective experience of laughing, a mass can study its own fascist tendencies as they express themselves. Fascism can come to make itself known through a form of laughter that is *not cinematic enough*, meaning it does not intensify and extend a sense of mechanizability so much as attempt to control and police its cold and hard boundaries. It prevents waves of laughter from breaching certain restrictions on who counts as part of a community.

We might think that Benjamin's response to such a critique would refute the charge of barbarism, but we would be wrong. Instead, Benjamin agrees with Horkheimer and Adorno's essential claim, but with a redemptive twist. "Barbarism?" asks Benjamin. "Yes, indeed. We say this in order to introduce a new, positive concept of barbarism."[46] Laughter is barbaric in the sense that it is violent. As I have argued above, such violence does not inevitably lead to fascist hardness and coldness. Rather, it can also release the body's potentiality for radical, democratic equality from within the very barbarism that Horkheimer and Adorno criticize. The grotesque gesticulations of the laughing body can extend and exaggerate beyond rigid boundaries into zones of contact with an emergent inhuman life that cannot be named or controlled or co-opted by any fascist form of organization or capitalist form of fetishization. Benjamin summarizes: "And the main thing is that [this swell of inhuman potentiality] does so with a laugh. This laughter may occasionally sound barbaric. Well and good."[47]

Auratic Laughter

Perhaps the most (in)famous part of Benjamin's essay "The Work of Art in the Age of Its Reproducibility" is his description of aura. The simple if not superficial reading of the essay can be quickly summarized as follows: the aura of the traditional work of art is liquidated by technical reproduction that replaces the uniqueness, authority, permanence, and distance implied in aura with the standardized, massified, ephemeral, reproducible nearness of media culture writ large, which is accessible to anyone at any time for multiple purposes (beyond the regulation of the church or the expert opinion of the art connoisseur). The most "powerful agent" in this process is, for Benjamin, none other than film, which demands a new set of concepts and a new theory of perception to account for its main technological features.[48] Rather than lament the waning of traditional aesthetic experience, Benjamin argues that art can now enter the political realm in new ways, unfettered by the constraints of aura. Summarizing his thesis, Benjamin writes that cinematic experience contains within itself a political potentiality that is "completely useless for the purposes of fascism."[49] In this sense, the essay sets up a series of dichotomies with film acting as the fulcrum. Yet, as Hansen points out, this initial division between pre- and post-auratic art betrays the complexity of Benjamin's engagement with the concept of aura throughout the rest of his writings. In an attempt to salvage aura, Hansen then argues that the concept is preserved yet displaced into the optical unconscious. This transformation redeems it for new collective use.

I would also like to "displace" aura—not through the optical unconscious but through laughter. If collecting preserves some hint of aura in suspended animation as a trace, then comedic film also "preserves" aura but in its own, mechanical way. My starting point for this reading rests in Benjamin's rather lyrical depiction of aura offered in the reproduction essay: "To follow with the eye—while resting on a summer afternoon—a mountain range on the horizon or a branch that casts its shadow on the beholder is to breathe the aura of those mountains, of that branch."[50] The passage then makes reference to the Greek origin of the word *aura* as "breath" or "breeze," complicating readings of Benjamin's concept of aura as distinctly scopophilic. It is important to note in this description how vision *alchemically turns into* breath. It is this *moment* of translation between seeing and breathing that is the location of aura. The implied distance that comes from detached viewing is exchanged for the intimacy and nearness of breathing something inside the body. Thus, seeing innervates or expands into breath as if swelling its perceptual capacity to envelop that which it would otherwise keep at a discrete distance. And with the folding of distance into nearness, so too subject and object seem to dissolve. On this reading, aura moves the senses (reconfiguring them) and the body animates aura producing mimetic similitude through breathing.

Furthermore, Benjamin emphasizes the pastoral mood of auratic movement as relaxed and tranquil. While the subject is immersed in contemplation and reverie, the speed and intensity of bodily innervation are low, peaceful, and languid. Interestingly, in writing about meditation, Benjamin observes that "breathing" is innervation's "most delicate regulator," with the sounds of yogic meditation acting as a "canon of such breathing."[51] The pastoral connoisseur of the mountains is able to surmount the initial distance of vision through a delicate breath not unlike the yogic master who breaths in the cosmos through an even and regulated breath controlled by chanting special, secret sounds. In both cases, there is a sense of the peacefulness of esoteric and/or private ritual that simultaneously grants aura its atmosphere of detachment and the possibility (through a certain practice of breathing) of nearness and proximity (if not merger). The delicacy of breathing means that it is silent, internal, and contemplative.

Film disrupts aura not by negating it but rather by *changing the tempo and rhythm* of how it is breathed in and the *sound* of how it is breathed out. In Benjamin's depiction of the primal scene of aura, the pacing is slow and languid. It concerns the romantic leisure time of the bourgeoisie, lost in contemplative or meditative reflection. The fast tempo of film swells forth from the rush of urban living, capitalist production, and technological reproduction. The mimetic absorption of speed through laughter means that slow breath turns into a rapid gulp and the tranquil breeze into a mighty, thunderous exhale. The isolated individual is exchanged for the collective audience—auratic movement is massified. Laughter, in other words, is not the delicate, quiet, contemplative breath of traditional auratic experience. Laughter is loud. And this loudness turns breath outward, toward the public. Aura thus shifts synesthetically from vision, to touch (through breath), to audibility. And in so doing, aura becomes radically free in its spasmatically diasporic movement outward. We could even say that the laugher is the loudest and most absentminded kind of teacher: the most grotesque, the most innervated, the most swollen. And because the laugher has no control over this laugh, cannot keep it secret, cannot keep it to him- or herself, he or she is radically poor as well—yielding a yield that cannot be possessed, or rather can only be possessed at the moment of subjective dispossession.

This aesthetic point concerning aura is crucial for understanding the consumer and educational value of film. While arguing that aura in the arts might be in decline, Benjamin nevertheless saw it return in the form of educational occultism surrounding figures such as Rudolf Steiner.[52] We might also see it return in the form of the false halo surrounding the radio conductor Walter Damrosch, whom I discussed in an early chapter. Thus, there is an interesting inverse argument at stake when we compare Benjamin's educational and aesthetic critiques. While aura declines in the arts, it expands in educational theory. Whereas the latter proclaims the arrival of new, political uses of art, the former proclaims the collapse of education into mere mysticism. What is lacking in both is the productive tension between educational and consumer values, best exemplified in comedic films and auratic laughter.

Antifascist Comedy

In the concluding aphorism to *One-Way Street* titled "To the Planetarium," Benjamin describes a historical shift in the relationship between human beings and the cosmos. The ancient version of this relationship focused on an "ecstatic contact" that could only be felt "collectively" through a kind of synesthetic innervation of the whole body that could propel it outside of itself. The result was an "ecstatic trance" [*Rausch*] that offered a "certain knowledge of what is nearest to us and what is remotest from us, and never of one without the other."[53] With the advent of the modern world, the ancient relationship to the cosmos was replaced with an "optical connection"[54] that lacked any ecstatic dimension. This optical detachment led to the objectification and rationalization of the cosmos and a subsequent desire to dominate it through technological means. The ancient, full-bodied, collective experience of the cosmos was subsequently deemed unimportant or something to be avoided. Yet it did not simply disappear. Instead, Benjamin warns that the repressed returns in the form of war fueled by a lust for "cosmic power."[55] While this might seem to be a nihilistic assessment of the modern era—most certainly manifest in the fascist embrace of war and its destructive potency—Benjamin nevertheless finds redemptive potential waiting to be explored in technology. He speculates that "In technology, a *physis* is being organized through which mankind's contact with the cosmos takes a new and different form from that which it had in nations and families."[56] This new *physis* is beyond the bourgeois family or the fascist nation. It is beyond the imperialist use of technology to dominate and destroy nature. When film embodies the art of straying (by intensifying and extending both consumer and educational values throughout the masses), it is a technology capable of producing this new kind of *physis*. To be more precise, film produces a comedic, laughing collective life that is deeply antifascist insofar as its sensorial apparatus is innervated by a stereoscopic image-making potentiality that unhinges the senses, disorganizes bodies, and creates diasporic swells open to anyone at all.

Fascist film is all about heroic action oriented toward the ultimate purpose of world domination and racial purity. Think of Leni Reifenstal's

Triumph of the Will (1935)—the quintessential Nazi propaganda film. It is full of images of the health, strength, and vitality of the chosen race as it embraces its world-historical task. And it includes images and sounds of the master race laughing at its own exuberance, its own self-congratulatory exaltation. Yet, it is important to point out that while it includes images of laughing youth, it is a *humorless* film. Thus, laughter is absorbed into the film so that the audience *will not have to laugh*. If there is any laughter here, it is wrong laughter in the sense that it merely consumes an image of itself and thus lacks any critical, educational value. Such laughter does not allow for absentminded judgment. In Benjamin's model, such judgment is predicated on an inflation and extension of mechanizability to such a degree that it becomes sensible and knowable in its massiveness. As Horkheimer and Adorno argue, fascism offers the "reverse of genuine mimesis." For if "mimesis makes itself resemble its surroundings, false projection makes its surroundings resemble itself."[57] Mimesis is the art of straying, of diasporically dispersing the self through mechanical gestures that transgress boundaries of race, class, and gender. False projection, on the other hand, resists such straying by creating a closed feedback loop where the image projected (by film) is internalized and then projected back onto a self-same world. In this model, the self becomes reified.

Juxtapose this next to Chaplin's *The Great Dictator* (1940). Here the tropes of fascist iconography are suspended and then played with as if they were toys. Although written before the film's release, Benjamin was sensitive to Chaplin's ability to "show up the comedy of Hitler's gravity."[58] And in so doing, Chaplin was both a symptom of destructive barbarism and its positive redemption—the laughter he induced was always close to toppling into profound horror. In a beautiful scene that illustrates this point, Chaplin as the great dictator suddenly takes a globe and turns it into a bouncing balloon. Plans for world supremacy are suddenly left idle through a prolongation of a moment of childlike ballet. The camera poetically lingers and savors these strange gestures, so out of place in the dictator's office. The scene stretches out time, entranced by a new comedic ethic of suspension that neutralizes the murderous, grave machinery of fascism. War becomes a dance, the will to possess the world becomes an experiment with movement. The resulting gestural repetitions yield to a temporality that is uniquely cinematic and comical—inserted into the film just at the moment when action was supposed to arrive. The result is not a "humanized" dictator made "less frightening" as George Potter suggests,[59] but rather an inhumanized dictator who gives himself over to a new rhythm and tempo that only emerges when action is decompleted and character suspended. An alternative potentiality is suddenly made concrete wherein destruction becomes playfulness. Chaplin has spliced into the film sequence a gestural discontinuity in which the innervated body breaks free from action to merge with music and dance in such a way as to produce a laugh at precisely the saddest and most horrifying moment of world domination—right before the world-as-balloon bursts. For Burkhardt Linder, such moments embody an educational form in which "the masses are alienated from their leaders."[60] But this alienation redoubles and becomes an intimacy with the potentiality for a new collective beyond the cult of fascistic leadership—one that is composed of de-composing, laughing bodies. Benjamin's notion of a "vision of the natural innocence of man"[61] could not be more visible and auditory for study—swelling up from within the mechanical barbarism that at first would appear to signal its ultimate demise.

RIDDLES

If we anchor Benjamin's theory of language in his early essays, including "The Role of Language in *Trauerspiel* and Tragedy" and "On Language as Such and on the Language of Man," we get a particular picture that focuses on the disintegration of a pure, creative language of names, and its potential redemption through translation. In this chapter, I want to take a somewhat different path, a neglected, poor, and marginal one that does not start from language in the *Trauerspiel* but from Benjamin's interest in children's word games, and in particular riddles. My argument is that the riddle is a particularly apt educational form for studying the dialectics of language that Benjamin's more esoteric writings articulate. Riddling is a unique educational experience that captures the complexity of language which can only be spoken in its dispersive, uncommunicative, and diasporic forking. In short, in the riddle, a secret to language is made visible (or audible) and thus opened up for free use beyond communicative instrumentality. Rather than dismissing riddles as mere diversions from the truth, I want to look more closely at how riddling offers a momentary, nondurational glimpse into the power of language that swells to its fullness in other activities (such as translation).

In this sense, I will privilege the strayings of children's language as important educational forms to reflect on. First, these are expressions of a certain potentiality within language to be more than mere communication. They communicate the noncommunicable excess of language within language, or the point at which language swells beyond itself from within itself. This is not a return to a paradisal language of pure, creative naming before the split between signifier and signified. But it is an opening to the potentiality that remains in language for new uses. Such uses escape the fetishization of language in capitalism, especially the communicative capitalism of neofascism, and therefore contain a radical political core needing to be redeemed.

Riddle Me This

What is a riddle? We might think of it as a special literary form that presents a secret. According to Daniel Heller-Roazen, a secret is something that must be concealed, but also transmitted in such a way that the secret can remain secretive. Heller-Roazen writes, "There must be some mechanism capable of establishing and maintaining the division that results from the existence of a secret: a test of sorts, which will determine where certain individuals stand with respect to what has been 'discerned' and 'separated.'"[1] The paradox of a secret is that it must be equal measures hidden and transmissible. Because of this, secrets often take the form of puzzles that can be passed down, inherited, and transmitted in a format that only a select few will be able to solve. Only the initiated have the knowledge needed to find the answer to a puzzle.

Riddles, as one possible manifestation of such puzzles, are poised on the cusp between esoteric knowledge and exoteric knowledge. Although there are a wide variety of puzzles, we can, for Heller-Roazen, pinpoint a particular form that the majority share in common. Citing Heller-Roazen, riddles "move from a collection of distinct and apparently contradictory characteristics toward a single subject."[2] The solution rests in discovering the underlying similarities between apparently dissimilar images or concepts. They are linguistic formulations that offer up comparisons between disparate yet connected elements. More often than not the descriptive elements in the riddle might be in opposition to one another, one positive and one negative or one figurative and one literal. Take for instance the riddle "What has eyes, but cannot see?" The answer is a potato. The two phrases in the riddle are exact opposites of one another. And yet, the phrases refer to the same object. The trick here is being able to see similarities across differences in appearance. It is also the case that the riddle seems to contain its answer within its paradoxical form. A true riddle would therefore not simply be solvable through the importation of preexisting knowledge from the outside. Instead, the answer unfolds from inside the structure of the riddle itself. The riddle makes something knowable . . . it exhibits the knowability of its secret in its very form.

In this sense, riddles exhibit two features: (1) opacity and (2) a hidden principle of their interpretation. Without opacity the riddle would lose its enigmatic character. When the enigma can be solved with reference to external knowledge, then it also cannot be called a true enigma (it is instead merely a scientific question). Thus, there must be a principle within its construction—hidden in plain sight—that contains the key to unlocking it. But this knowability is only accessible to those who have special knowledge.

For this reason, riddles—as a specific manifestation of what Heller-Roazen refers to as rogue tongues that include slang, jargon and cant—have often been associated with robbers, thieves, secret societies, and poets. The speech of these various groups often exhibits a hermetic characteristic that makes it impenetrable to outsiders yet also guarantees internal transmission and dissemination amongst a select few. This means that rogue tongues pose unique educational challenges. To learn their rules, one must be an initiate, but to be initiated means that one must know their rules. In this sense, the riddle is poised on the razor's edge between inclusion and exclusion, esoteric and exoteric forms of education. It holds onto its secret but in such a way that this secret is always threatened and made vulnerable to someone who might crack the code and expose the secret to the uninitiated, thus dissolving the secret entirely. Stated differently, if rogue tongues divide speech into two camps (exclusive vs. inclusive, opaque vs. transparent), then the riddle simultaneously reinforces this division and, potentially undoes it. In this sense, trying to crack a riddle is an unusual kind of educational experience, as one who is not supposed to know and who does not belong is given a clue that can undo the secret the riddle purportedly protects. The uninitiated initiate themselves—perhaps without ritual sanctification—into a society of secrets. Such an educational formula might best be summarized in the equally paradoxical notion of *esoteric democracy*. By this I mean a form of education that simultaneously speaks to a private world while also making this world virtually public through the challenge of the word game (which anyone might take up and study).

The paradox of a literary form that speaks to the general public but only in the form of a dark tongue haunts Marx's *Capital, Volume One* in interesting ways. As Fredric Jameson aptly points out, Marx's analysis of capitalism is poised as a riddle. Or perhaps better stated, a series of riddles that grow out of Marx's preliminary dissection of the commodity form. This expanding series of riddles culminates in what Jameson calls the "riddle of riddles,"³ which is capitalism itself. Jameson's literary interpretation of *Capital, Volume One* pinpoints the centrality of the riddle as a particularly dialectical form for presenting the paradoxes that always underlie the surface stability of capitalism. Because of the dialectical nature of the riddle, it stands in stark contrast to what Jameson refers to as the enemy of the first part of *Capital, Volume One*: the equation. Of course, "enemy" is merely figurative, for while the equation appears to be an abstract, static, mathematical formulation of equivalences, on closer inspection, it also contains a strange paradox that can also be rewritten as a riddle: how is it that a mathematical structure can, at the same time, contain a temporal dimension, a movement that destabilizes itself? The totality of interrelated riddles that emerge through Marx's representational schema are multiple and complex, as Jameson points out. But for our purposes here, I would like to highlight the very first appearance of the riddle in *Capital, Volume One*: "Name a sensuous thing that is at the same time suprasensible?" and several of the riddles that follow suite.

Of course, the answer to this enigmatic riddle is the commodity, which is both a sensuous use-value and an abstract and undifferentiated exchange-value. But what I want to highlight here is how Marx's first *pedagogical* move in *Capital, Volume One* is to transform this banal feature of everyday exchange *into* a riddle. In other words, the commodity does *not*, at first, appear to be a riddle. Yet, Marx came to see the commodity as *the* riddle of capitalism. The trivial and the banal existence of the commodity swelled up with an excess of meaning that condensed into the form of a riddle. Out of this fundamental riddle, Marx proceeds to extract a series of subsequent riddles that revolve around the "metaphysical subtleties"⁴ of the commodity. For instance, Marx posits the "riddle of the equivalent form."⁵ In the equivalent form of value, x commodity A is worth y commodity B. The A in this equation is the relative value, or the commodity whose value is expressed in relation to commodity B. The equivalent, B, is the product of concrete labor practices yet comes to embody the abstract, undifferentiated labor of commodity A. Stated differently, a private form of concrete labor takes on the appearance of social, abstract labor. This process of abstraction enables it to act as an equivalent for another commodity. Isolated equivalents can be expanded almost infinitely to the point where one commodity can come to express the value of all other commodities, becoming what Marx calls a "universal equivalent."⁶ The world therefore inherits a general social relative form of value in the form of commodity B—now only recognized as an exchange-value. And another name for B commodity is none other than money.

Money contains within itself another series of riddles. To cite Marx directly, "The riddle of the money fetish is therefore the riddle of the commodity fetish, now become visible and dazzling to our eyes."[7] Money, as a type of commodity, is defined like all commodities by a dual life: it is a sensuous thing that nevertheless has suprasensible features that allow it to stand in for the value of all other commodities as a universal equivalent. But this time there is an added enigma built in. Marx points out that a universal equivalent is "excluded from the ranks of all other commodities."[8] As the *paradigm* of all commodities money must exclude itself from all other commodities. It is a commodity that is included only insofar as it is excluded from the rank and file of all other commodities. Here we find a historical materialist origin of the enigma of the paradigm which Giorgio Agamben has written so eloquently about.[9] According to Agamben, the paradigm's paradoxical status makes intelligible the class of objects which it comes to represent. And indeed, Marx argues that the riddle of money is precisely why it is the quintessential commodity making the enigma of the commodity form "visible" and "dazzling" but also all the more mysterious.

Returning to the form of the riddle, one can instantly recognize how the commodity expresses itself as the riddle of political economic theory—something seemingly trivial which Marx had to riddle in order to create a comprehensive theory of capital. Like all riddles, the commodity form juxtaposes two opposing and seemingly dissimilar features: it is abstract and particular, it is material and immaterial, it is a use-value and an exchange-value, it is sensuous and suprasensuous. And like the riddle, underlying these dissimilarities is a hidden, secret substrate that binds them together: abstract human labor. This answer is not something that is imported from outside the formal structure of the riddle. Rather, it is Marx's careful analysis of the commodity itself and its riddle that makes visible that which political economists had thus far failed to see, falling prey to a certain kind of commodity fetishism. One cannot see the labor behind the material object, giving the illusion that commodities create their own value spontaneously. Money as a common value form takes on the appearance of "making the world go around," obscuring the more fundamental role of labor in this process. Marx, as a careful reader of political economic theory, realized that a theory of labor could be riddled out of commodity fetishism.

In a sense, *Capital, Volume One* reconstructs the riddle of the commodity form as Marx discovered it in Ricardo, Smith, and other political economists. Marx is a riddler whose figurative work produces the paradox of the equation from *within* the equation. The reader encounters the "riddle of the commodity fetish" with fresh eyes and is asked to solve it along with Marx. For the reader, the form of the riddle enables the exoteric jargon of political economic theory to swell with a new kind of knowability. Yet, like all riddles, this hidden secret of labor power remains on the razor's edge between opacity and transparency. Although *Capital, Volume One* is therefore a book meant for revolutionary education, it is also a text written in and through a dark tongue that withdraws itself in its very presentation. The knowability of labor power (now visible in the form of a riddle) has not fully made itself free (as a teaching). Of course, Marx was concerned with this educational issue. In the preface to the French edition of *Capital, Volume One*, Marx himself posed the question of education. To the French citizens he wrote, "I applaud your idea of publishing the translation of *Capital* as a serial. In this form the book will be more accessible to the working class, a consideration which to me outweighs everything else."[10] Here Marx enthusiastically endorses the French translators' attempt to make his book a public event. Yet Marx is also hesitant, and in the following paragraph he demonstrates more reserve. "The method of analysis which I have employed, and which had not previously been applied to economic subjects, makes the reading of the first chapters rather arduous, and it is to be feared that the French public, always impatient to come to a conclusion, eager to know the connection between the general principles and the immediate questions that have aroused their passions, may be disheartened because they will be unable to move on at once."[11] Thus Marx reaches an educational standstill. He emphatically emphasizes the need for raising the class consciousness of the workers, yet at the same time recognizes the difficulties of teaching his own text to these workers. In an overtly Hegelian moment, Marx concludes that the only solution is to teach the workers "not to dread the fatiguing climb" toward the "luminous summits"[12] of the dialectic. As such, the difficult labor of the concept is largely left to the intellectual labor of the workers themselves as part of the historical struggle to attain class consciousness. At stake here is the transmissibility of that which has made itself visible through the riddle of the commodity.

This quandary is symptomatic of the literary form of the riddle as such which is always halfway between the public and the private spheres. *Capital, Volume One* is not a mistaken educational experiment. In its material approach to history, it embodies in concrete form the riddle it tries to solve, and in so doing, always risks the alienating *and* democratizing effects of the riddle. To write riddles is to simultaneously reinforce the insularity of a dark tongue while also and in the same gesture proposing the hypothesis that all thinking and speaking human beings can, in principle, answer it—especially the working class.

If Marx's riddle rides on the razor's edge between alienating and empowering its purported audience, the fate of riddle in critical theory does not easily dissolve with the publishing of *Capital, Volume One*. Instead, the riddle remains as a kind of subaltern literary form within critical theory. The pedagogical strategy of Marxism is to rewrite liberal economic thought as a riddle that no longer addresses expert theorists so much as the masses, who *live* the riddle (and thus already know its answer on an intuitive level). It is my argument that Benjamin's theory of riddles and his interest in children's games furthers this project in interesting ways. Here the children invent the jargon that educates the adults in the potentiality of language to communicate not this or that message but rather communicability itself. Thus the riddle continues to speak in a secret tongue, but it is a secret that flashes from the indeterminate future and thus is not owned by any experts or any secret society (but rather the coming generation). There are no initiates who can answer this riddle, and for this reason, its sparks are truly revolutionary.

Benjamin's Riddles

Benjamin takes up the riddle of riddles in his own particular way, further developing the educational dimension of this most paradoxical of literary forms. Importantly, Benjamin cites a critical distinction between solving a riddle and redeeming it. The first approach attempts to discover the hidden solution to the riddle for good, putting the riddle to rest. In this approach, the "mystery" of the riddle is only an appearance that disappears the minute which the riddle is resolved. As such, solving a riddle brings with it a certain level of disappointment precisely because the excitement of the riddle rests not so much in the solution as it does in the elevation of something that appears to contain nothing to the realm of the mysterious. Not unlike Heller-Roazen cited above, Benjamin seems to focus on the precariousness of the riddle as betwixt and between a constitutive opacity (mystery) and the intimation of a solution that would dissolve the opacity.

But Benjamin is keen to point out that redemption is something else entirely. Instead of assuming that the mystery of a riddle can be abolished through a witty solution, one can instead see that the mystery remains—not in the object of the riddle per se but in the language of the riddle as such. Benjamin writes, the "disappointment [in solving the riddle so easily] is not total, since in the last analysis there is an objective reason for the subjective appearance of the mystery inherent in an artifact or event," and this objective reason lies "in the fact that they, like all beings, have a share in mystery." Benjamin continues, "For precisely as word all being exists in a state of mystery by virtue of the symbolic force of the word."[13] The word is not only what solves the riddle and dissolves the mystery but is also the precondition or foundation of the puzzle to begin with. These words are not reducible to a communicative function, and contain within them a mysterious core. This core is not the content of what is communicated (as a solution to a riddle), but rather a *potentiality* not to communicate anything at all, or what Benjamin refers to as "noncommunicability."[14] Redemption concerns the noncommunicability within the communicable. Indeed, in a letter to Martin Buber, Benjamin clarifies, "[M]y concept of objective and, at the same time, highly political style of writing is this: to awaken interest in what was denied to the word; only where this sphere of speechlessness reveals itself in unutterably pure power can the magic spark leap between the word and the motivating deed. . . . Only the intensive aiming of words into the core of intrinsic silence is truly effective."[15] Language transcends its communicative function when it somehow conveys the limits of the unsayable within the sayable. This limit is not external to language but rather is its most enigmatic power. The noncommunicability within language is its nonconceptual content or the content within it that cannot pass into meaning. On this reading, a solution is a communication that fails to communicate the noncommunicabilty of words. Redeeming the riddle is really redeeming its noncommunicability, or that excessive swelling point within language that makes itself audible at the precise moment it falls silent.

The distinction between solving and redeeming the mystery of the riddle is reminiscent of Benjamin's discussion of the difference between knowledge and truth in *The Origin of German Tragic Drama*. "Knowledge," as Benjamin formulates it, "is possession."[16] It is akin to a solution to a riddle, which can be owned. Such possession negates the mystery of that which is possessed or grasped by a subject-supposed-to-know. Knowledge therefore sacrifices the sense of mystery for a sense of mastery over the opacity of the riddle. To extract knowledge from the riddle is to negate its noncommunicable opacity for communicable ends. Instead of yielding to the mystery of language expressed in the form of the riddle, knowledge destroys it in the name of solving. While such a method might very well lead to desirable outcomes, it also leads to disappointment.

Truth, on the other hand, lacks this sense of possessiveness. Instead of merely studying the content of the riddle, truth takes a different path—swelling up from within the nondurational in order to suddenly crash into the wave of that which remains noncommunicable. To express this point more directly, it is useful to reconceptualize the riddle as a *constellation*. Constellations, Benjamin speculates, "do not contribute to the knowledge of phenomena, and in no way can the latter be criteria with which to judge the existence of ideas."[17] Constellations concern ideas (truth) rather than knowledge. But what is a constellation? It is a representation of ideas, or the nonsensuous surplus beyond sensuous phenomena. These ideas only emerge through the juxtaposition of extreme and unique concepts, which are themselves the mediating points between phenomena and ideas. In a constellation, concepts have to be extreme, meaning that they have to be paradigms of a certain class, making that class intelligible. As such, it is only in the extreme, grotesque form of the concept that the concept shines forth as truly unique and singular. Also important to note is that the extreme form pushes the concept to its outer edge, to the point where it no longer equals itself. The paradigm is, after all, able to represent a class but only because it no longer belongs to that class. Paradoxically, the more a concept is pushed to its extreme, the more it opens itself up to the nonidentical within itself. This otherness makes the concept, in its uniqueness, capable of being put into relation with other dissimilar concepts in a constellation. The constellation hangs these extreme and unique concepts together precisely because they are extreme and unique. The truth (idea) only emerges out of the arrangement of disparate concepts strung together to form the outline of that which is immanent to the arrangement yet somehow transcends it as well. Truth is therefore not reducible to knowledge because it is only present as a suprasensible excess arising *across* concepts (rather than within any given concept). It cannot be apprehended from primary phenomena, but only from the configuration of concepts that the constellation harmonizes. Because we cannot know ideas, we cannot teach them. This is why, according to Benjamin, they "do not enter into the history of literature [or other forms of history]."[18] Ideas resist classification, which is an essential tool in teaching. Instead of communicating a lesson, ideas communicate noncommunicability, or the excessive mystery that redeems the word from its functional, instrumental use. What is transmitted via a constellation is the nontransmissibility of ideas—hence the paradoxical form of the riddle. If teaching makes something free, this paradox of the riddle means that it can never be a teaching, it can never offer up a lesson. It is always a dark tongue that retreats from opening itself up fully and passing itself on.

Here we have to be careful. Benjamin is clear that such noncommunicability has to be distinct from the play of mere allegorical distraction found within capitalism. Of course, we can find juxtapositions of seemingly dissimilar things throughout capitalism, but this should not lead us to the conclusion that Benjamin's theory rehashes this logic in a literary form. Marx seems to revel in the strange, surrealistic pairings that the market generates. He lists exchanges such as "20 yards of linen = 1 coat"[19] or "5 beds = 1 house."[20] Certainly there is a riddle here (Marx's riddle of labor), but what I want to emphasize is how these equations are precisely that, equations which always push the particular toward the average and the generalizable, resisting the unique and the extreme. The uniqueness of commodities (their use-values) must be negated in order for exchange to happen. And exchange, by definition, also negates uniqueness. The particular features of a bed that make it *a bed* and not a chair must be extracted, leaving behind nothing but abstract human labor. In this sense, riddles are the antithesis of capitalist equations. Like constellations, they do not negate particulars, rather they push them to an extreme point of swelling where they become knowable (in their truth). Indeed, without the particulars coming into contact with one another, then the mystery or enigmatic kernel of the riddle would disappear. The riddle functions only insofar as the uniqueness of concepts is felt as a tipping point.

Let me put it this way: when entering into exchange relationships in the market, one is not struck by the equation 5 beds = 1 house. Indeed, the exchange could not happen if one were distracted by the strangeness of this equation. The equation is both predicated on and produces anew reification and fetishization. Also, it invokes continuing allegorical chains of arbitrary relations. Here we can think of Marx's list of equivalences "20 yards of linen = 1 coat or 10 lb tea or = 40 lb. coffee or 1 quarter of corn or = 2 ounces of gold or ½ ton of iron or = etc."[21] Such allegorical shifting signifiers only come to a halt with the advent of money which takes on the universal form of value. Marx's educational wager was to transform the equation *into* a riddle and thus see within the knowledge of the market the enigma of the truth of capital. Such work was exhausting, but yielded an expansive theory, one which, as Jameson is quick to point out, is not a positivistic representation of capital so much as "partial" vision composed of "heterogeneous modes of construction or expression, wholly different types of articulation that cannot but, incommensurable with each other, remain a mixture of approaches that signals the multiple perspectives from which one must approach such a totality and none of which exhaust it."[22] The truth of capital that the equation resists can only be captured obliquely through an opaque riddle, whose form does not solve the problem of capitalism so much as continually reassert it in ever new (higher order) expressions. The history of Marxism can in turn be thought of as a rehashing of the enigmas of production and consumption over and over again in relation to specific historical or theoretical contexts. This would be the historical materialist equivalent of Benjamin's intonations of a "struggle for the representation of ideas,"[23] which, of course, can only come through a certain inflation of the noncommunicable within the communicable. The struggle to wrestle ideas from within a capitalist, reified language (the equation) is embodied in the riddle, which is a kind of constellational thinking in miniature. For Marx this would mean that the riddle of the commodity is "solved" only in a parodic sense: it reveals that the "secret" was always already there in most trivial detail of the system: the commodity.

Given this background, we can begin to appreciate the educational nature of the riddle with new eyes. For Susan Buck-Morss, Benjamin's dialectical image offers an alternative to either the Baroque dramatists that simply resign themselves to allegorical fragmentation or to the Christian theologians who deny fragmentation in the name of a transcendent, otherworldly unity. Both turn their backs on materiality. But not Benjamin, who finds another notion of redemption in Kabalistic traditions—a notion of redemption that is historical, materialist, and collective, and thus squares nicely with his Marxist tendencies. Buck-Morss summarizes as follows:

The truth thus revealed was expressed in the Kabbalist writings inventively, indirectly, in riddles, providing an antiauthoritarian form of pedagogy. . . . In their interpretation of the material world the Kabbalists did not deny its fallen state, and the consequent 'abysmal multiplicity of things' when compared to the unity of Divine Reality. Here they agreed with the Baroque allegoricists. But their texts describe 'with an infinite complexity' the ten 'Sefiroth,' the spheres and stages of God's attributes as these appear within nature *despite* that broken unity.[24]

In this way, a philosophical problem is "solved" through an educational form, the riddle, which indirectly reveals a truth that lies *within* the fractured, allegorical world of the commodity.

Theodor Adorno, like Benjamin, also emphasizes the connections between riddles and constellational thinking. For Adorno, philosophy cannot simply retreat into either idealism or empiricism. Instead it must confront the riddle of reality as it expresses itself in unintentional ways within philosophy's own tradition. This means there is no position of security from which philosophy might stake out first principles uncontaminated by the residue of historical struggle. He writes, "[P]hilosophy persistently and with the claim of truth, must proceed interpretively without ever possessing a sure key to interpretation; nothing more is given to it than fleeting, disappearing traces within the riddle figures of that which exists and their astonishing entwinings."[25] The "riddle figure" of a broken reality does not mean that there is a deeper, hidden, more authentic reality behind the facade that must be discovered and made present through interpretation. Adorno warns, "He who interprets by searching behind the phenomenal world for a world-in-itself [*Welt an sich*] which forms its foundation and support, acts mistakenly like someone who wants to find in the riddle the reflection of a being which lies behind it, a being mirrored in the riddle, in which it is contained."[26] Opposed to this strategy, Adorno suggests that "the function of riddle-solving is to light up the riddle-Gestalt like lightning and to negate it [*aufzuheben*], not to persist behind the riddle and imitate it."[27] In short, the secret of the riddle is not external to the form of the riddle. There is nothing behind the appearance of the riddle. Instead, the fragmentation of reality is expressed directly in the confrontation of opposing elements found on the riddle's constellational surface. Adorno rejects the search for hidden meaning to the riddle. This argument bears a striking resemblance to Benjamin's own emphasis on the noncommunicability of the riddle. Both resist tagging the riddle's purported solution to single, positivistic answers lurking behind a linguistic prompt. Instead, the lesson here is that the problem and the solution dissolve into one another, or even better, swell up into a state of indistinction. Like Marx and Benjamin before him, Adorno argues that the role of philosophy is to bring singular and dispersed elements together "so close" that "the solution springs forth"[28] in the very formulation of the problem. Another way of expressing this might be that the knowability of reality swells to the surface of the riddle that makes it visible.

Perhaps Adorno's most famous aphorism is "The whole is the false."[29] Instead of giving up on the truth because of the dominance of the false, the false, read from the perspective of messianic redemption, becomes the truth of a corrupt, exploitative system. Thus, truth is redeemed from within the very system that denies that the truth exists. The riddle, as an educational form, exists within the false as part of its linguistic practice; yet it also points to the truth within this falsehood that the falsehood refuses to recognize (that capitalism contains within it a noncommunicable excess known as revolution). In this way, the riddle is immanent to the very problem that it solves. Marx, for instance, could only posit the riddle of capitalism through the lies of the political theorists of the day. He used the falseness of the equation to pole-vault the truth into existence. And Benjamin could only express the fragmentation of life and of experience in the odd formulation of the riddle whose parts exist in a disjunctive synthesis.

But why is the riddle a preferable educational form for Benjamin, and how does it fit within the larger constellational curriculum posited in this book? Although Benjamin highlights film as an art form that embodies "perception in distraction," we might also highlight riddles as a linguist form of such distraction.

1. The riddle shocks, it interrupts our thinking patterns by presenting a surreal constellation which we are unaccustomed to. This causes a moment of disorientation, or absentmindedness, which is not so much the absence of thinking as it is thinking in potentiality, on the cusp of a thought beyond common sense habits.

2. The riddle opens up a space for which we do not yet have new habits of thinking. It forces certain kinds of dialectical habits to form and herein lies the pleasure of the riddle. To redeem the truth embedded in the riddle, one must not rely on existing habits. The puzzle is an educational form for disrupting assumed patterns of meaning found in language and the habits of language use. Because of this, it demands experimentation with a realm between existing habits of mind and new habits of mind. This is an unfamiliar, liminal zone that speaks equally to the passing away of what is and the arrival of something new and unforeseen. It is a kind of conceptual awakening from within the sleep of common sense—a learning to learn differently through the seemingly inconsequential and ephemeral act of studying a simple riddle.

3. If Benjamin once argued that in film "educational value and consumer value converge, thus making possible a new kind of learning,"[30] I would argue that the riddle can be similarly described. While Benjamin's *Origins of German Tragic Drama* might have high educational value, it has very little appeal to a wide audience of novices or children. Yet in riddles, we find a condensed, informal, and approachable form that is educational while also easy to consume. The kind of shocking confrontation (or boxing of the ears) caused by the riddle is not reducible to diversion. Instead, it offers a space of contact wherein educational value is transformed through the riddle and vice versa.

4. One might argue that the riddle is caught in an elitist circle described by Heller-Roazen. It is for initiates only, secret societies, experts with esoteric knowledge capable of cracking the code. It is therefore exclusive rather than inclusive. Its mysteries are reserved for the few not the many. But I want to suggest that Buck-Morss is correct and that in Benjamin's hands, the riddle becomes an antiauthoritarian educational form—or at least its antiauthoritarian educational potential is maximized while not,

thereby, reducing the mystery. Why is this so? Because for Benjamin, truth does not rest within the sphere of knowledge. Instead, the truth is the enigma itself; it is the noncommunicable excess that the riddle makes manifest as the potentiality of language as such. The "solution" no longer rests on the specific skills of a particular, informed and learned audience (of criminals, poets, or scholars). Instead, this truth is open to anyone—anyone who can be distracted by the dimension of language that resists being instrumentalized. Especially children.

Children's Riddles

For Benjamin, the language of children is full of riddles and word games that speak the noncommunicable excess of language (language beyond instrumental use). Thus, the most marginalized, excluded, and therefore powerless population—children—becomes the motor for generating a jargon that lacks all specialization. Perhaps we could call it the jargon of truth. Adults are put at the disadvantage by the little rogues with their dark tongues precisely because adults are focused on using language in a purely communicative way to solve problems or acquire knowledge. On the contrary, the "solution" to children's riddles is the noncommunicable signals ushered from a future that is present in the excess of their games. For adults, to confront such riddles is to return to the indeterminate potentiality of youth, and for children, making up riddles is akin to experimenting with a life yet-to-come.

In this sense, children's riddles and word games can be compared to sacred texts. In an interesting thought image titled "Pretzel, Feather, Pause, Lament, Clowning," Benjamin recalls a game that children used to play where you link up disconnected, random words to form a sentence. He recalls how "this game produced the most wonderful discoveries, especially among children."[31] This is because "to children, words are still like caverns, with the strangest corridors connecting them."[32] The sentences they produced surpassed the everyday language of adults in their ability to redeem language from communicative instrumentality. This redemption of language takes us back to Benjamin's fundamental observation about language as such: all language first and foremost "communicates itself."³³ Language neither serves a communicative function nor transmits meaning in such texts; instead it is a space for expressing a potentiality for language to take place. This place is also the place of a pure capacity (communicability) that is also and equality an incapacity (noncommunicability). Both children's word games and sacred texts express this truth, and therefore resist simple communicative transparency and immediacy. Yet, unlike sacred texts, children's word games (riddles included) need no specific expertise, no specific knowledge, and one need not be a member of a secret society to have access to the key. The mystery of language's communicability is made fully democratic.

Returning to the odd set of words "pretzel, feather, pause, lament, clowning," Benjamin ends his thought image with the following sentences produced by a child: "Time sweeps through nature like a pretzel. The feather paints the landscape, and if a pause ensues, it is filled with rain. No lament is heard, for there is no clowning around."³⁴ These sentences resist meaning. They do not point to an answer beyond or behind themselves. Instead, they present the idea of language (language's nonconceptual truth) through a constellation of displaced words. The game functions by distracting us from the denotative function of language long enough to illuminate a potentiality for language to manifest its own ineffable mystery now made visible.

According to Ursula Marx, Gudrun Schwarz, Michael Schwarz, and Ermut Wuzisla Benjamin's documentation of language games and riddles is "not directed toward a documentation of the acquisition of language, but rather toward specific aspects of infantile thinking and speaking—the detours in which it goes astray. Losing oneself in language. Benjamin latches onto the distorting effects of children's language. For him, linguistic blunders and misunderstandings do not find their meaning in being corrected."³⁵ Importantly, Benjamin was not interested in *developmental* models of children's language, where the goal is to move teleologically toward adult speech. Such would be the interest of psychology. Nor is he interested in correcting children's speech in order to discipline it into conforming with specific grammatical rules. Instead, he was interested in those moments of children's language that interrupted and suspended both development and grammatical discipline. Such interruptions were not errors or deficits so much as opportunities to enter into the mystery of language—not as something hidden behind the word, but rather on the surface of the word. The result is a word game that embraces the art of straying within language to its maximal point of swelling forth into visibility (knowability). The perfect example of how straying could lead to poetic illumination can be found in an odd story retold by Benjamin in *Berlin Childhood around 1900*. The story concerns his Auntie Lehmann, who used to live on Steglitzer Strasse. The child mistook the name of the street for the German word for goldfinch (*Stieglitz*). Yet this misrecognition of language actually provided insight into the life of the old woman who "lived like a talking bird in its tree."[36] The purely denotative language of the adult is transformed into a magical language capable of expressing language's potentiality for communicating its own noncommunicability.

From a short catalog of Benjamin's son's linguistic blunders, we can pinpoint six distinct methods for interrupting the rather impoverished notion of language as a utilitarian tool for communication. They return us to the appearance of the inoperative dimensions of words (noncommunicability).

1. "Fursity" (university) = miniaturization

2. "Unlibry" (university library) = condensation (portmanteau words)

3. "Taechers" (teachers) = distortion

4. "The warm and the cold outbacker" (meaning unknown, perhaps referring to the drainpipes, which he thought were the staircase to the kitchen) = invention

5. "Gratophoph" (photograph) = inversion

6. "Kiss" (his name not only for the actual kiss but also anything damp, fruit juice, etc. on his face) = semblance[37]

These methods—miniaturization, condensation, distortion, invention, inversion, and semblance—connect the uncommunicable excess of language to a potentiality for being otherwise than a communicative medium. Subaltern linguistic methods invented by rogue tongues that stray off the path of standard word usage and grammar are perpetually distracted by the plasticity of language to deform itself through noncommunicative swelling points. And in this sense, these methods can be seen as truly imaginative. As outlined in chapter 1 of this book, Benjamin argues that imagination is not creative per se. Rather it plays a game of dissolving forms. Children's word games are part of the unending dissolution of language as it transforms itself into a ruin (to be excavated, as in Benjamin's radio broadcasts) or a rune (of a future language yet to be born). As Benjamin writes, ". . . only language sometimes has the ability to incorporate the imagination, for only language is able, in the most fortunate case, to keep the de-forming powers under control."[38] In word games, language strays from itself, making manifest the deforming excess of noncommunicability that rests at its heart. To reduce the straying of children's word games to mere diversions from proper speech or to mere deficits needing developmental correction would therefore betray language itself!

In this sense, imaginative word play is not the same as translation. Translation moves between two languages in order to hit on language as such, or what Benjamin refers to as "pure language."[39] Pure language, on this model, emerges through intralinguistic relations. It is a dimension that is beyond communicational functionality, and could even be said to be the noncommunicable nucleus that is perpetually in exile *inside* of individual languages. Benjamin says as such when he describes the work of the translator as mining that which "cannot be communicated"[40] in what is communicated. Yet the tactics reviewed here do not shuttle between two languages so much as deform one language according to its own, internal noncommunicable excess. In this sense, translations and word games offer up different access points for a shared educational experience of the potentiality of language that only emerges when language prefers not to communicate.

In sum, children stray from grammatical rules and conventions of word usage. They are distracted by a feature within language that is perpetually beyond itself yet paradoxically within itself at is most extreme edge. And through these distracting appropriations, the noncommunicable essence of speaking makes an appearance. The fundamental riddle of language is therefore not a secret owned or policed by a certain interest group or by trained specialists. It is instead part of the commonwealth of which children are the gatekeepers. In children's riddles, we find a way to square the circle identified by Heller-Roazen and illustrated by Marx's educational paradox. Traditionally, the riddle must simultaneously (1) assert its opacity while (2) giving the secret key to its interpretation. The democracy of the riddle is esoteric in that only a select few have the knowledge, skills, and/or privilege to interpret the riddle even if the riddle is posed to everyone. The problem is precisely that if (1) is dissolved in the interpretation or solution, then the riddle ceases to exist. Or if (2) dissolves and the opacity remains without hope of positing a solution, then the riddle equally disappears. Yet if we take Benjamin's lead and turn toward children's riddles and word games, we find that the opacity of language is not dissolved in the solution nor is the solution dissolved into the opacity. Instead, the riddle's opacity (its noncommunicability) *becomes its enigmatic origin point and destiny*. In this way, the riddle can truly become an antiauthoritarian educational form (as Buck-Morss argued), as this secret is hidden in plain sight, open to anyone whatsoever . . . or at least anyone with childlike eyes and ears.

Noncommunicative Democracy against Neofascist Communicative Capitalism

The riddle, as a form of noncommunicative communication, is distinct from the equation of capitalism, but does it still have any power to resist the affective communication of a neofascist like Trump? While Marx's educational labor was to transform the banal existence of the commodity into a riddle in order to reveal the logic of capital, it would seem that Trump openly speaks in riddles. Indeed, riddles have become the common currency of Trumpian-style neofascism. A simple example of this is Trump's neologism "covfefe," which went viral. Instead of taking down the tweet that contained the word, Trump leaned in, tweeting to his followers: "Who can figure out the true meaning of 'covfefe'?? Enjoy!" Considering that Trump speaks at a third- to seventh-grade level, it is not surprising that he employs many of the methods for destabilizing language's communicative function outlined above, including the invention of *covfefe*. He sees language as a game, and often combines contradictory meanings within one statement, transforming what ought to be straightforward into a complex riddle whose meaning contradicts itself. Alternatively, he juxtaposes multiple images and meanings that seem unrelated into a single statement that then begs the question: What is the missing connection? While William E. Connolly focuses on Trump's Big Lies as a distinct feature of his rhetoric,[41] I would like to highlight the predominance of the logic of the riddle in Trump-speak. This enables him to communicate in an esoteric way to his base, which has the inside knowledge needed to hear the *real* message. Take for instance Trump's infamous tweet of Hillary Clinton next to a six-pointed star and the tagline "most corrupt candidate ever." The esoteric knowledge needed to solve this riddle would have been easily accessible to antisemitic, white supremacists familiar with various conspiracy theories focused on Jewish global power and wealth. While Trump's reference to the former director of his National Economic Council, Gary Cohn, as a "globalist," might have easily been passed over by the press as nothing more than a synonym for a supporter of free trade, the word would have been instantly recognizable to Trump's neofascist, antisemitic followers as pointing out Cohn as a member of an international Jewish conspiracy.[42] Trump's antisemitism is, in other words, hidden in plain sight. As a rogue tongue, Trump's strange patterns are simultaneously democratic—appealing to a wide base that is, as Trump himself proclaims, "poorly educated" and angry at an intellectual elite who talk over their heads—and exclusive, often coded in such a way that right-wing extremists and white nationalists, such as the former KKK leader David Duke, can effectively read between the lines. Thus, what might appear to be anticommunicative is actually a highly effective instrumentalization of the riddle as part of a neofascist equation of power.

If indeed the riddle has become the authoritarian pedagogy of neofascism, then is there any anti-authoritarian potentiality left, as Benjamin, Adorno, and Buck-Morss argue? Perhaps what is needed here is a return to Benjamin's distinction between solving the riddle and redeeming it. Advocates of critical media literacy on the left might attempt to solve Trump's riddles by finding out the key buried within his messages. The goal is thus to look for missing knowledge in order to destroy the riddle. Certainly, there is much good here, and I in no way want to undermine this work. But Benjamin might opt for another path, one that stays resolutely on the surface of the riddle itself in order to see its lie as the truth—the truth of an affective, visceral form of neofascism that reveals its flexible, pliable strength through its absolute fetishization of communication. This alternative, Benjaminian strategy suspends the function of the riddle as an equation of power in order to study its form and, in turn, learn its truth. It admits that the riddle is a powerful tool of neofascism, yet for this very reason, struggles to redeem the riddle from this fate. To do so would be to search for an awakening within yet against Trump's twittergoria. The redemption of the riddle would begin from a simple observation about Trump's brand of neofascism: anything *can and must* to be said, over and over again. Indeed, if there is a categorical imperative underlying neofascism of the Trump era it is: Never stop speaking/tweeting/blogging/communicating! No press is bad press, so keep talking so you can control the terms of the debate. Trump can confess to crimes out in the open, retract his admissions, and then, in a side comment, retract his retraction without impunity—all within one twenty-four-hour news cycle. All of this is part of the disorienting logic of riddling his way in and out of legal, political, and ethical discussions. It creates a never-ending, attention-grabbing spectacle of scandal after scandal after scandal; neofascism only thrives through this excessive, hyperbolic spread of riddles and contradictions.

What is needed here is a rewriting of the riddle of neofascism so that it swells up with its *noncommunicable* excess that cannot be so easily fetishized as an equation of power. Such a strategy recognizes the dominance of the riddle in current politics not only as a threat to democracy but as a potential opening for an awakening to that which is noncommunicable within communication. And this, more than anything else, exploits Trump's compulsion to communicate. Because of Trump's incessant stream of circulating memes and tweets, communicability as an ability to *and* not to communicate that resides within the riddle is sacrificed. The noncommunicable excess of communicability—a preferring not to repeat empty slogans or bully one's opponents or indulge in a vacuous and continual stream of idle talk or spread gossip—is resolutely foreclosed on by the twitter stream that Trump both unleashes and responds to. Given this context, the riddle, which is always poised at the cusp between the communicable and the noncommunicable, could become a preferred educational form for expressing a language that makes its ability to not communicate audible. Such a riddle must resolutely stay on the surface of tweets and memes in order to find a point of awakening within the circuits of what Jodi Dean might call the "communicative capitalism"[43] of neofascism. The riddle of our times ought to awaken us to the shocking gravity of our complicity with neofascist communicative capitalism's fetishization of communication, and in so doing offer the slightest of shifts toward another horizon: one that is silent, democratically open, childlike, yet swelling with potentiality for a new use of language beyond communication.

CONCLUSION

Education as Potentializability

Let us enter into a dream, one of Benjamin's own.

I see myself in the Wertheim department store in front of a flat little box with wooden figures, such as a little sheep, just like the animal that made up Noah's Ark. But this little sheep was much flatter and made of a rough, unpainted wood. This toy lured me. As I let the salesgirl show it to me, it transpires that it is constructed like a magic tile, as found in many magic boxes: these little panels are loose and shift, all turning blue or red, according to how the ribbons are pulled. The flat, magical wooden toy grows on me all the more after I realize this. I ask the salesgirl the price and am most astonished that it costs more than seven marks. Then I make a difficult decision not to buy. As I turn to go, my last glance at it falls on something unexpected. The construction has transformed. The flat panel rises steeply upwards as an inclined plane; at its end is a door. A mirror occupies it. In this mirror I see what is playing out on the inclined plane, which is a road: two children run on the left side. Otherwise it is empty. All this is under glass. The houses, however, and the children on the street are brightly colored. Now I can no longer resist; I pay the price and put it about my person. In the evening I intend to show it to friends. But there is unrest in Berlin. The Nazis are threatening to storm the café where we have met; in feverish consultation we survey all the other cafés, but none appear to offer protection. So we make an expedition into the desert. There it is night; tents are erected; lions are close by. I have not forgotten my precious treasure, which more than anything I want to show everyone. But the opportunity does not arise. Africa mesmerizes everyone too much. And I wake up before I can reveal the secret which has in the meantime been fully revealed to me: the three phases into which the toy falls. The first panel: that colourful street with the two children. The second: a web of fine little cogs, pistons and cylinders, rollers and transmissions, all of wood, whirling together in *one* plane, without person or noise. And finally the third panel: a view of the new order in Soviet Russia.[1]

To briefly summarize: The dream begins with a toy—a toy that transforms itself. Benjamin is lured in by the toy, but decides not to purchase it. He walks away. But then something happens to distract him from his plan to exit the department store—something peripheral and unexpected catches his glance. The toy appears to shape-shift. From the corner of Benjamin's distracted eye, the toy calls back to him, interrupting his "adult" and "pragmatic" plans to leave it behind and return to other business. He subsequently purchases the item and desires to show it to his friends. Yet this desire is once again interrupted by the threat of Nazi invasion and impending violence. The toy remains like a secret with Benjamin, as he travels into the desert. He never reveals the toy, instead, Africa "mesmerizes" everyone too much. They cannot be distracted like Benjamin by a trivial thing like a toy. Rather, they are caught up in the world-historical drama unfolding around them. Given the circumstances, who has time for toys?

At the end of the retelling of the dream sequence, Benjamin dissects the secret of the toy. The toy essentially has three dimensions. First, it produces an image of children. Second, its magical inner workings are somewhere between industrial commodification (hence, the department store setting) and artisanal craft (it is composed of wooden gears). Third, it pole-vaults from children playing to a new vision of revolution—shifting registers from play to politics, from children to the masses, from immersion in color to immersion in the sights and sounds of social upheaval. There is much that could be said about this dream, but I want to zero in on several important themes I have been articulating throughout this book.

In fact, I would like to offer this dream as a monad of the book as a whole—a crystalline condensation of many of its main arguments. First, the toy causes distraction. As opposed to contemporary philosophies of attentiveness, Benjamin finds something educational in moments when we are absentmindedly thrown off course. Distraction (as alert, open, and dispersed attunement to the marginal and peripheral aspects of experience that exist on the very edge of our intentionality) enables the mind to wander, but also opens the body up to the possibility of alternative ways of sensing, alternative forms of habituation. The toy is imbued with a power to interrupt attention toward "sensible" modes of action and thus to suspend normal ways of being in the world. The magic here is not so much the magic of sorcery, as it is of perception itself to be caught off guard, fall off line, and find the body yielding to unexpected secrets that might appear childish. While Benjamin's dream companions are mesmerized by Africa, he proclaims a small freedom in his defiant distractedness, orienting himself to a different horizon of possibility. Stated differently, distraction offers a break with the narrative of war, injecting contingency into a seemingly unavoidable historical trajectory. This perceptual disorientation and reorientation away from the drama of war is not a mere delusion. It is rather a very real sensorial opening to an alternative dimension of life, one that is not easily dismissed as frivolous.

Second, the toy itself is not simply the result of a precapitalist cottage economy or of capitalist industrialization. On the one hand, it is sold in a department store, thus it is a symptom of mass commodification under capitalism. Indeed, the magical sparkle of the toy recalls, at first, the fetishization of commodities highlighted throughout this book. On the other hand, it is made of wood and thus recalls, no matter how faintly, an artisanship that is quickly being lost in the age of mechanical reproduction. The toy is a trace of something vanishing, and as such is a precious reminder of an alternative way of life within the very heart of the department store. At the same time, its hand-crafted qualities are put in the service of a complex mechanism that pole-vaults into a strange future. The toy is therefore magical but in a completely technologically suffused manner. This is an *untimely* object that is not at home neither in a precapitalist society of hand-crafted wears nor in a capitalist society of mass production. Indeed, the magical call of the toy might very well be a *demand* on Benjamin to *liberate* it from the department store and thus carry it out into a world beyond its own commodification. The object's transformation is akin to a kind of transformation of its commodity status from within the very fetishism that capitalism expands and intensifies. In a very literal way, the toy swells up with an alternative potentiality, an unfulfilled promise of being otherwise than the world around it. The phantasmagoria of images, signs, advertisements, and objects that saturate the cityscape produce dreams and intoxications, but the way to wake up from these hallucinations is not through their destruction so much as through the production of another, surrealist image: children running.

The toy produces an image of children, not unlike a miniature, Technicolor film. It is important to note that the children are colorful. As discussed earlier, there is something special about a child's perception. Instead of seeing objects, they are submerged in a field of color. It is not so much that they perceive color—as a subject standing over an object. Rather they *are* colorful. Stated differently, there is no clear separation between the child and the perceived color. The color field submerges the viewing subject and disperses objects. Because there is no viewer to be attentive and no objects to attend to, the color field that Benjamin attributes to children is a kind of pure experience of *immersive distraction*. Vision transforms into the tactile sensation of color swelling and fanning out in infinite directions not unlike a rainbow. For a moment, Benjamin himself seems to get lost in the shimmer of color, thus, in a sense, becoming indistinct from the children in the street. The distinction between child and adult disappears, or at least is momentarily dispersed through the work of the dream image. A youthful sense of potentiality emerges.

It is important to note that in the dream, the image of two children running in the street is an image of the production of life *shared* within a colorful landscape. The color of the children and the color of the street bleed into one another, forming a dynamic image of collectivity. This contrasts sharply to the fragmented form of collectivity that emerges in the rest of the dream. Benjamin is incapable of sharing his secret with his friends in the café. And when they are forced to leave because of Nazi threats, the only form of collective life that is experienced is either driven by fear or by hypnosis. Thus, Benjamin's secret is not so much the toy itself as it is the memory of a potentiality for a colorful collective life that exists only in the fragmentary image of children playing together. This is not so much a romantic desire to return to an age of innocence. Rather, it is a memory of a potentiality *that never was* that thrusts Benjamin forward into the revolutionary possibilities of social and economic transformation happening in Russia. Importantly, the toy's cogs were "without person or noise." This world of immanent distraction is without sound. Yet sound cannot be foreclosed. As discussed earlier, thought sounds are precisely those sounds that are on the cusp of fantasy and history, childhood and adulthood, drawing out the temporality of the dreamscape to the point where it swells up with historical becoming. We can imagine the leap to the third phase of the dream as a kind of echo location that emanates through the dream like a sonic blast.

This finally leads to my third point. The toy opens up a fantastical space that is antifascist. Its form of distraction induces images of another form of collective life beyond either the mediation of the commodity form or the fear induced through fascist politics. This is nothing less than a democratizing memory of a potential future.

The revelation of the dream does not take place in a state of total wakefulness. Indeed, Benjamin writes, "And I wake up before I can reveal the secret which has in the meantime been fully revealed to me." The emphasis here is on the very last seconds before being awake. In these fleeting moments—moments so short that they cannot be counted—the dream logic exposes itself in full, simultaneously intertwining three dimensions: image, technology, history. At the point at which sleep gives way to being awake, the dream condenses itself into a tightly woven knot that binds together seemingly disconnected elements to produce illumination. The dream swells in its own knowability.

Compare this with a dream of the Reich Minister of Public Enlightenment and Propaganda, Joseph Goebbels, from an entry in his private diary dated December 17, 1929. In this entry, Goeddels recalls being back in school and being pursued down the corridors by Jews screaming, "Hate, hate, hate." Barely able to keep ahead of his pursuers, he turned around and repeated the taunt, "Hate, hate, hate."[2] This is the typical fascist nightmare. It contains no hope of awakening from a cycle of hate. Instead, it merely recursively turns back in on itself, as if trapped in a circle of coldness and hardness, fear and intimidation. The dream remains fixed, self-perpetuating, a cruel coil that constricts the dreamer to the point of suffocation. The school becomes a den of iniquity, a stark competition for survival of the fittest. Goebbels must test his strength to see if he can outrun the degenerate Jews of his own, unconscious invention. Whereas Benjamin's dream dialectically swells to the outer rim of itself through the intimation of a potentiality for another world beyond war, Goebbels's dream is a trap, a self-fulfilling prophesy of the soon-to-come destruction of life by the mythic violence of Nazism.

In one, "education" is foreclosed on (the school replaces learning and teaching with mere, brute survival), whereas in the other, the possibility for education expands as the dream deforms itself at its apex in order to imagine life beyond war. One can only lead to terror whereas the other can lead elsewhere. . . .

If the toy in Benjamin's dream educates, it educates the eye to be distracted by a flash of that which surprises and interrupts. It educates the individual through images, detours, and diversions that not only resist fascism but also promote experimentation in the organization of life beyond law-destroying or law-creating powers. This is one form that education can take for Benjamin—but there are other forms. Mimetic similarities that expose the subject to difference, the absentmindedness of perceptual straying, and bodily innervations that intensify and extend the sensorium underlie the educational forms in this book. Throughout, the self swells to an extreme point where it knows itself only in so far as it turns away from itself, entangling itself with difference. My basic argument has been that mimetic displacements, perceptual innervations, and distracted wayfaring are educational experiences of *potentiality*. In all cases, the very potentiality for being awake is felt, and this is *the* primordial educational experience. Stated differently, the educational question is as follows: What educational forms allow abilities (potentialities) to express themselves? In relation to children, how can teaching, learning, and study induce enlargements (swells of potentialities) so that they become knowable as youthful life? In relation to adults, how can various unanticipated experiences induce recollections of the unfulfilled potentialities of youth and bring them into the present (so as to redeem them)? All subsequent forms of educational life are derivative, or perhaps more strongly, parasitically dependent on this most basic recovery of potentiality that is always already there, waiting to swell up in its knowability and transmissibility. Such potentiality makes the inheritance of tradition (even in its ruins) visible and free, and thus always keeps open the contingencies of the world for other forms of collective being.

Making something visible and free demands an awakening. Awakening is not a change of state (from being asleep to being awake), but the potentiality for a change of state within an existing state. It is sleeping *as not* sleeping, or sleeping passing away without passing beyond itself. Such awakening is not merely a transitional point on the way to being awake. This sequence would reduce awakening to a means to an end beyond itself. Instead, I see awakening as an educational pure means that has to be rigorously thought in itself. To do so is to pinpoint the moments of swelling up and passing beyond: when color vibrates into sound waves, when gazing synesthetically transforms into touch, when nondurational moments are collected and organized to express the fate of objects, when communicability suddenly expresses its noncommunicable essence, and so on. Such points of dissolve and emergence are the phenomenological anchors of educational life, which first and foremost concern potentiality. In this sense, there is something educationally precious about awakening as such, in itself (even if such awakening takes the shape of distraction, perceptual disorientation, imaginative deformation, or mimetic displacements). To pay tribute to awakening is, at least on my view, the purpose of Benjamin's constellational curriculum. The role of an educational philosophy in this sense would be to blast awakening from teleological ends, so that it stands still, buzzing with a potentiality that is often absorbed into ends before it is even recognized.

In the blink of an eye, an educational awakening reveals the plastic nature of temporality. As Peter Fenves argues, temporality is "plastic" when it takes a shape that is "wholly without direction, hence without past, present, or future, as they are generally understood."[3] In awakening, past, present, and future implode into a condensed moment of supersaturation, wherein there is a maximal tension between forces. This moment is contingent in that it is uncertain what direction it will lead to—being awake and continuing the dream are equally viable possibilities contained within awakening. The wave of learning can swell to a crest or turn inward, creating a vortex. Youth can progress toward maturity or regress toward immaturity—each is equally a potentiality. As such, an awakening speaks to a certain unpredictable swerve in time that loops back rather than marches forward. The challenge of Benjamin's educational forms is that they fall within this plastic shape of time, and thus outside convenient narratives, linear teleologies, or unidirectional developmental models leading necessarily from children to adults or immaturity to maturity or deformation to formation. Children's theater, for instance, insists on holding onto and making visible the very indeterminacy of the Russian Revolution, which the revolution itself would have liked to have extinguished (in the form of scientific Marxism). Or, experiencing the city as a newcomer returns the adult to the potentiality for experiencing newness that was once the terrain of childhood. Or, collecting enables humans to touch the fleeting and ephemeral nature of touch as an eternal truth latent within contingent knowledge. Or, laughing exposes the body to mechanization as a common substratum of modern life, calling into question what a body can do and what it might become. The list goes on. . . .

In comparison, Goebbels's dream has no sense of potentiality within it. Instead, hate merely propagates hate, which propagates more hate. This is a closed economy, or an affective dead-end, leading nowhere except back to its own obsessive confirmation of stereotypes, fears, and threats. The plasticity of time takes on the features of an eternal return in the most vicious and most deterministic of senses. And it is precisely because of this circle of hate that there can be no awakening from the nightmare, only the abyss of genocide.

At stake throughout this book is rigorously outlining a constellation of educational wave-like forms that figure studying, learning, and teaching from within the sheer abundance of an indeterminating potentiality. Instead of defining what counts as education from a point outside of and over this wave-like plasticity of forces, intensifications, and extensions, we find in Benjamin's writings a curiosity geared into what emerges as knowable and transmissible from inside the pulsing of waves. Such an education means that there are no externally secured criteria for judging educational life. To do so would be to enact mythic, neofascist violence over educational life in the form of boundaries and limitations concerning blood and soil. How then does education add something to life? It does not simply reproduce what is nor does it suggest ends toward which education can be directed. Opposed to either of these options, Benjamin's educational forms induce awakenings that are indeterminate swellings within what is while extending what is to its extreme point where it touches its own potentiality for transformation (its capacity to become different by touching difference). Such swellings potentiate a situation, raising its knowability or, if it becomes a teaching, its transmissibility to the surface. This is the most basic educational experience: tradition being made visible and free in its potentiality. The emphasis on educational life as a distinct mode of existence in Benjamin's work is therefore poised between two competing readings of Benjamin as a scholar of immanence versus transcendence, knowledge (nondurational) versus truth (eternal). Education, as I have theorized it throughout this book, concerns -abilities or potentialities. Such potentialities are neither immanent nor transcendent, but rather exist within a *threshold* that separates and conjoins the two. Educational life lives here, in the paradox of the threshold. As such, it is important to theorize educational life in Benjamin's work in order to understand how learning, teaching, and also studying problematize binaries that often creep into the secondary literature.

In this sense, Benjamin rejects any transcendental model of education that would stand outside or over the studying and learning that emerge from within the movements of life. In fact, the hardness, coldness, and manipulative characteristics of the authoritarian personality that Adorno highlighted are precisely violence over potentiality from an ironically detached, judgmental distance. All three character traits resist swellings, or change points, and in turn, the potentiality to become otherwise. At stake here is a decisively democratic form of educational philosophy that massifies the potentialities of life through social, political, and technological entanglements by making them visible and free.

This book has been one attempt to observe and organize the educational forms explored by Benjamin throughout his scattered notes, essays, and books into a constellational curriculum capable of pole-vaulting out of the past into the present moment. While there are certainly new educational forms that could be added to this constellation (e.g., video games, blogs, tweets, and so forth), it has been my contention that the forms implicitly and explicitly discussed by Benjamin are still relevant. Even if certain forms are marginal and untimely, reviewing the ways in which Benjamin's constellation weaves together distracted moments of open alertness, perceptual and bodily innervation, and noncoercive, mimetic couplings can be a source of inspiration for reinventing antifascist education for the present. The resulting curriculum charts the echoes of educational awakenings through city streets, into collections muffled by stacks of books, through distant radio waves whose afterlives are still spinning out into deep space, into cluttered and chaotic performances on street corners, into the jittery movements of on-screen comedians, and encapsulated by silly riddles that might make us smile or shake our heads in disbelief. Instead of judging these seemingly errant daydreams, mishaps, and/or meanderings, I have yielded to them and followed them down the rabbit hole in order to get lost in strange places, marginalia, and junk. The rather unexpected text you have just read is a trace of this path—a teaching of my own, one that now makes visible and free its origins in various studies and learnings. Through absentminded examinations and imaginative deformations, I have discovered an oblique educational logic that redeems history, and in this sense, returns humanity to the unfulfilled potentiality of its youth yet to come.

Notes

Introduction

1. In particular, see the theory of "assaultive speech" in Mari J. Matsuda, Charles R. Lawrence III, Richard Delgado, and Kimberle Williams Crenshaw, *Words That Wound: Critical Race Theory, Assaultive Speech, and the First Amendment* (Boulder, CO: Westview Press, 1993).

2. During his lifetime, Benjamin only engaged in one overtly antifascist project: the ill-fated attempt for form the leftist literary journal *Krise und Kritik*. Planning for the journal started in the autumn of 1931, right at the beginning of the rise of National Socialism. The editors, including Bertolt Brecht, Benjamin, Bernard von Brentano, and Herbert Ihering saw the journal as a response to the Nazi Kampfbund für deutsche Kultur, founded in 1928 to battle the culture of leftist intellectuals. See Erdmut Wizisla, *Benjamin and Brecht: The Story of a Friendship* (London: Verso, 2016).

3. See, for example, Roger Griffin *The Nature of Fascism* (London: Routledge, 1993); Umberto Eco, "Ur-Fascism," *New York Review of Books*, June 22, 1995, https://www.nybooks.com/articles/1995/06/22/ur-fascism/; Lawrence Grossberg, *Under the Cover of Chaos: Trump and the Battle for the American Right* (London: Pluto Press, 2018) for examples of these different approaches.

4. Franz Neumann, *Behemoth: The Structure and Practice of National Socialism, 1933–1944* (Chicago: Ivan R. Dee, 2009), 39.

5. Ibid., 97.

6. Ibid., 103.

7. Eric Fromm, *Escape from Freedom* (New York: Henry Holt Company, 1994), 206.

8. Ibid., 276.

9. Ibid., 239–40.

10. Cited in "Disguised Fascism Seen as a Menace; Prof. Luccock Warns That It Will Bear the Misleading Label 'Americanism,'" *New York Times*, September 12 (1938): 15.

11. Theodor W. Adorno, "Types and Syndromes," in *The Authoritarian Personality: Abridged Edition*, ed. Theodor W. Adorno, Else Frenkel-Brunswik, Daniel J. Levinson, and R. Nevitt Sanford (New York: Norton, 1950), 355.

12. Theodor W. Adorno, "Freudian Theory and the Pattern of Fascist Propaganda," in *The Essential Frankfurt School Reader*, ed. Andrew Arato and Eirke Gebhardt (New York: Continuum, 2002), 134.

13. Theodor W. Adorno, Else Frenkel-Brunswik, Daniel J. Levinson, and R. Nevitt Sanford, "Introduction," *The Authoritarian Personality: The Abridged Edition*, ed. Theodor W. Adorno, Else Frenkel-Brunswik, Daniel J. Levinson, and R. Nevitt Sanford (New York: Norton, 1950), 1.

14. Adorno, "Freudian Theory and the Pattern of Fascist Propaganda," 119.

15. Theodor W. Adorno, *Critical Models: Interventions and Catchwords*, trans. Henry W. Pickford (New York: Columbia University Press, 1998), 198.

16. Hermann Rauschning, *The Voice of Destruction* (New York: G. P. Putnam's Sons, 1940), 247.

17. Adorno, *Critical Models*, 201.

18. Adolf Hitler, *Mein Kampf*, trans. Dorothy Thompson (New York: Reynal and Hitchcock, 1940), 618.

19. Adorno, "Freudian Theory and the Pattern of Fascist Propaganda," 133.

20. Theodor W. Adorno, "Prejudice in Interview Material," in *The Authoritarian Personality: Abridged Edition*, ed. Theodor W. Adorno, Else Frenkel-Brunswik, Daniel J. Levinson, and R. Nevitt Sanford (New York: Norton, 1950), 309.

21. Adorno, Frenkel-Brunswik, Levinson, and Sanford, *The Authoritarian Personality*, 6.

22. Adorno, *Critical Models*, 192.

23. Ibid., 190.

24. Ibid., 182.

25. Ibid., 183.

26. Theodor W. Adorno, *Minima Moralia: Reflections on a Damaged Life*, trans. E. F. N. Jephcott (London: Verso, 2005), 192–93.

27. Adorno, *Critical Models*, 193.

28. Ibid., 195.

29. Adorno, "Freudian Theory and the Pattern of Fascist Propaganda," 137.

30. Theodor W. Adorno and Hellmut Becker, "Education for Maturity and Responsibility," *History of the Human Sciences*, 12, no. 1 (1999): 22–34.

31. Adorno, "Prejudice in Interview Material," *The Authoritarian Personality*, 336.

32. A point confirmed by historical analyses of educational reform in Germany and Italy. See Gilmer W. Blackburn, *Education in the Third Reich: A Study of Race and History in Nazi Textbooks* (Albany: State University of New York, 1985); Heinz Sünker and Hans-Uwe Otto, eds. *Education and Fascism: Political Identity and Social Education in Nazi Germany* (London: Falmer Press,

1997); Eden K. McLean, *Mussolini's Children: Race and Elementary Education in Fascist Italy* (Lincoln: University of Nebraska Press, 2018).

33. See K. Daniel Cho, "Adorno on Education or, Can Critical Self-Reflection Prevent the Next Auschwitz?" *Historical Materialism* 17 (2009): 74–97; Henry Giroux, "Education after Abu Ghraib: Revisiting Adorno's Politics of Education," *Cultural Studies* 18, no. 6 (2004): 779–815; Volker Heins, "Saying Things that Hurt: Adorno as Educator," *Thesis Eleven* 101, no. 1 (2012): 68–82; Shannon Mariotti, *Adorno and Democracy: The American Years* (Lexington, KY: University of Kentucky Press, 2016).

34. Peter E. Gordon, "The Authoritarian Personality Revisited: Reading Adorno in the Age of Trump," *boundary 2* 44, no. 2 (2017): 31–56.

35. While beyond the scope of the present volume, it is interesting to speculate that Trumpism might very well be a sublation of both the cartel economic structure outlined by Neumann and the more or less diffuse, social and technological forms of domination outlined by Adorno.

36. William E. Connolly, *Aspirational Fascism: The Struggle for Multifaceted Democracy Under Trumpism* (Minneapolis: University of Minnesota Press, 2017).

37. Clarissa Ward, "Anti-Semitism Never Disappeared in Europe: It's Alive and Kicking," accessed December 2, 2018. https://www.cnn.com/2018/11/27/europe/anti-semitism-analysis-ward-intl/index.html.

38. Anti-Defamation League, "Audit of Anti-Semitic Incidents: Year in Review 2017," accessed November 6, 2018, https://www.adl.org/media/11174/download.

39. Peter Beinart, "What Trump Means When He Calls Gary Cohn a 'Globalist,'" *The Atlantic*, March 9, 2018, https://www.theatlantic.com/politics/archive/2018/03/trump-globalist-cohn/555269/.

40. Connolly, *Aspirational Fascism*, 44.

41. Lia Haro and Romand Coles, "Eleven Theses on Neo-Fascism and the Fight to Defeat It," *Theory and Event* 20, no. 1 (2017): 106, 108.

42. Walter Benjamin, *Selected Writings, Volume 2, Part 1, 1927–1930*, ed. Michael W. Jennings, Howard Eiland, and Gary Smith (Cambridge, MA: Harvard University Press, 2005), 319.

43. Ibid., 321.

44. Ibid. 313.

45. Ibid., 315.

46. Ibid., 319.

47. Ibid., 320.

48. Allison Ross, *Walter Benjamin's Concept of the Image* (New York: Routledge, 2015).

49. See both Susan Buck-Morss, *The Origin of Negative Dialectics: Theodor W. Adorno, Walter Benjamin, and the Frankfurt Institute* (New York: The Free Press, 1977) and Miriam Bratu Hansen, *Cinema and Experience: Siegfried Kracauer,*

Walter Benjamin, and Theodor W. Adorno (Berkeley: University of California Press, 2012) for detailed discussions of this concept in Benjamin's work.

50. Hansen, *Cinema and Experience*, 137.

51. Walter Benjamin, *The Origin of German Tragic Drama*, trans. John Osborne (London: Verso, 2009), 34–35.

51. Walter Benjamin, *Gesammelte Briefe, Volume 1*, ed. Christoph Gödde and Henri Lonitz (Frankfurt am Main: Suhrkamp, 1995), 382–83.

52. Ibid.

53. Ibid.

54. Walter Benjamin, *The Arcades Project*, trans. Howard Eiland and Kevin McLaughlin (Cambridge, MA: Belknap Press, 1999), Konvolut N (N3, 1), 463.

55. Adorno and Becker, "Education for Maturity and Responsibility," 29.

56. Adorno, "Types and Syndromes," *The Authoritarian Personality*, 383.

57. Walter Benjamin, *Gesammelte Schriften, Volume 4, Part 1*, ed. Tillman Rexroth (Frankfurt am Main: Suhrkamp Verlag, 1991), 87.

58. Walter Benjamin, *Selected Writings, Volume 1, 1913–1926*, eds. Marcus Bullock and Michael W. Jennings (Cambridge, MA: Belknap Press, 2004), 466.

59. Ibid., 480.

60. Walter Benjamin, *Selected Writings, Volume 2, Part 2, 1931–1934*, eds. Michael W. Jennings, Howard Eiland, and Cary Smith (Cambridge, MA: Belknap Press, 2005), 732.

61. Ibid.

62. Ibid.

63. Adorno, "Types and Syndromes," *The Authoritarian Personality*, 348.

64. Winfried Menninghaus, *Schwellenkunde: Walter Benjamin's Passage des Mythos* (Frankfurt am Main: Surhkamp Verlag, 1986).

65. Jane O. Newman, *Benjamin's Library: Modernity, Nation, and the Baroque* (Ithaca, NY: Cornell University Press, 2011).

66. Jack Zipes, "Building a Children's Theater: 2 Documents: Introduction," *Performance*, 1 (1973): 12–32.

67. Walter Benjamin, *Selected Writings: Volume 4, 1938–1940*, eds. Howard Eiland and Michael W. Jennings (Cambridge, MA: Belknap Press, 2003), 389–400.

Instruction

1. See Howard Eiland, "Translators Introduction," in *Walter Benjamin: Early Writings: 1910–1917*, ed. Howard Eiland (Cambridge, MA: Belknap Press, 2011) for an overview of this period of Benjamin's life.

2. For criticisms of these trends see Gert J. J. Biesta, *The Beautiful Risk of Teaching* (New York: Routledge, 2014) and also Tyson E. Lewis, *Inoperative*

Learning: A Radical Rewriting of Educational Potentialities (New York: Routledge, 2017).

3. Gerhard Richter, *Inheriting Walter Benjamin* (London: Bloomsbury, 2016), 30.

4. Ibid., 5.

5. Susan Buck-Morss, *The Dialectics of Seeing: Walter Benjamin and the Arcades Project* (London: Verso, 1991), 337.

6. Howard Eiland, "Education as Awakening," *boundary 2*, 45, no. 2 (2018): 203–19.

7. Walter Benjamin, *The Arcades Project*, eds. Howard Eiland and Kevin McLaughlin (Cambridge, MA: Harvard University Press, 1999), Konvolut K (K1a, 2), 390.

8. Ibid., Konvolut N (N4, 4), 464.

9. Ibid., Konvolut N (N18, 4), 486.

10. Margaret Cohen, *Profane Illuminations: Walter Benjamin and the Paris of Surrealist Revolution* (Berkeley, CA: University of California Press, 1993), 53.

11. Benjamin, "Paris, the Capital of the Nineteenth Century," in *The Arcades Project*, 13.

12. Walter Benjamin, *Selected Writings: Volume 2, Part 2, 1927–1934*, eds. Michael W. Jennings, Howard Eiland, and Gary Smith (Cambridge, MA: Harvard University Press, 2005), 664.

13. Benjamin, *The Arcades Project*, Konvolut O (O2a, 1), 494.

14. Ibid.

15. Ibid.

16. Others, such as Karin Burk, have highlighted the educational significance of this notion of swelling, but I want to make it a hallmark of Benjamin's theory of education. See Burk, *Kindertheater als Möglichkeitsraum: Untersuchungen zu Walter Benjamins, "Programm eines proletarischen Kindertheaters"* (Bielefeld, Germany: transcript Verlag, 2015).

17. Benjamin, *The Arcades Project*, Konvolut N (N3a, 3), 463.

18. Samuel Weber, *Benjamin's -abilities* (Cambridge, MA: Harvard University Press, 2008).

19. Walter Benjamin, *Gesammelte Briefe, Volume 1*, ed. Christoph Gödde and Henri Lonitz (Frankfurt am Main: Suhrkamp, 1995), 382–83.

20. Walter Benjamin, *Selected Writings, Volume 1, 1913–1926*, eds. Marcus Bullock and Michael W. Jennings (Cambridge, MA: Belknap Press, 2004), 463.

21. Ibid., 465.

22. Ibid., 464.

23. Benjamin, *Early Writings*, 101.

24. Ibid., 116.

25. Ibid.

26. Ibid., 123.

27. Benjamin, *Gesammelte Briefe*, Volume 1, 382–83.
28. Which has been heavily criticized by Gert J. J. Biesta in *The Rediscovery of Teaching* (New York: Routledge, 2017).
29. Benjamin, *Gesammelte Briefe*, Volume 1, 382–83.
30. Ibid.
31. Walter Benjamin, *The Origin of German Tragic Drama*, trans. John Osborne (London: Verso, 2009), 45.
32. Interestingly, this sheds new light on the nature of homework. The teacher demands that students produce evidence of their learning through the production of written work. Such work cannot be considered a teaching precisely because it has not necessarily swelled from within the learning at its maximum point of saturation. Instead, it is prompted by an external command to verify a process that does not yet have the capacity to verify itself.
33. Benjamin, *Gesammelte Briefe*, Volume 1, 382–83.
34. See, for instance, the essays collected in Charles Bingham and Alexander M. Sidorkin's edited volume *No Education without Relation* (New York: Peter Lang, 2004) for examples of teaching as always already relational.
35. Benjamin, *Gesammelte Briefe*, Volume 1, 382–83.
36. Alternatively, we might argue that although Benjamin rejects the example in his early writings on the academy, he does want to retain some notion of the example that *shows* its own showing, that shows itself in its transmissibility. This logic is further explored by Giorgio Agamben's insightful comments on the example in *The Signature of All Things: On Method* (London, Zone Books: 2009).
37. Benjamin, *Selected Writings, Volume 1, 1913–1926*, 327.
38. Ibid.
39. Sami Khatib, "Barbaric Salvage: Benjamin and the Dialectic of Destruction," *Parallax* 24, no. 2 (2018): 135–58.
40. Benjamin, *Gesammelte Briefe*, Volume 1, 382–83.
41. Walter Benjamin, *Selected Writings: Volume 3, 1935–1938*, eds. Howard Eiland and Michael W. Jennings (Cambridge, MA: Belknap Press, 2006), 162.
42. Whereas educational scholars have returned to Aristotle to argue for virtue ethics or character ethics, Benjamin would argue that they are missing an opportunity *within* the poverty of the new barbarism of the modern world to think through a new ethics of teaching. See, for instance, David Carr and Jan Steutel (eds.), *Virtue Ethics and Moral Education* (London: Routledge, 2005).
43. Benjamin, *Selected Writings: Volume 2, Part 2, 1931–1934*, 732.
44. Walter Benjamin, *Selected Writings: Volume 2, Part 1, 1927–1930*, eds. Michael W. Jennings, Howard Eiland, Gary Smith (Cambridge, MA: Belknap Press, 2005), 370.
45. Benjamin, *Selected Writings, Volume 1, 1913–1926*, 308.
46. Benjamin, *Selected Writings: Volume 2, Part 2, 1931–1934*, 812.
47. Howard Eiland, "Reception in Distraction," *boundary 2* 30, no. 1 (2002), 60.

48. Carolin Duttlinger, "Between Contemplation and Distraction: Configurations of Attention in Walter Benjamin," *German Studies Review*, 30, no. 1 (2007), 45.

49. Martin Heidegger, *Being and Time*, trans. John Macquarrie and Edward Robinson (New York: Harper Perennial, 2008).

50. Benjamin, *Selected Writings: Volume 2, Part 2, 1927–1934*, 643.

51. Ibid.

52. Benjamin, *Selected Writings: Volume 1, 1913–1926*, 280.

53. Ibid.

54. Ibid., 281.

55. Ibid.

56. Ibid.

57. Ibid.

58. Ibid.

59. Matthew Charles, "Pedagogy as 'Cryptic Politics': Benjamin, Nietzsche, and the End of Education," *boundary 2* 41, no. 3 (2018): 35–62.

60. Sean Frazel, "Toward an Anti-Monumental Literary-Critical Style: Notes on Walter Benjamin and Jean Paul," *Telos*, 159 (2012): 35–48.

61. Ibid., 38.

62. Benjamin, *Gesammelte Briefe, Volume 1*, 382–83.

63. Paul North, *The Yield: Kafka's Atheological Reformation* (Stanford, CA: University of Stanford Press, 2015), 29.

64. Ibid., 239.

65. Benjamin, *Selected Writings: Volume 1, 1913–1926*, 38.

66. Benjamin, *The Correspondence of Walter Benjamin, 1910–1940*, 74.

67. Benjamin, *Selected Writings: Volume 2, Part 2, 1927–1934*, 589–90.

68. Ibid., 590.

69. Ibid., 587.

70. Ibid.

71. Ibid., 588.

72. Ibid.

73. Ibid.

74. See Matthew Carlin, "In the Blink of an Eye: The Augenblick of Sudden Change and Transformative Learning in Lukács and Benjamin," *Culture, Theory, and Critique* 51, no. 3 (2010): 239–56; Matthew Charles, "Towards a Critique of Educative Violence: Walter Benjamin and 'Second Education,'" *Pedagogy, Culture & Society*, 24, no. 4 (2016): 525–36.

75. Walter Benjamin, *The Correspondence of Walter Benjamin, 1910–1940*, ed. Gershom Scholem and Theodor W. Adorno, trans. Manfred R. Jacobson and Evelyn M. Jacobson (Chicago: University of Chicago Press, 2012), 295.

76. Irving Wohlfarth, "Resentment Begins at Home: Nietzsche, Benjamin, and the University," in *On Walter Benjamin: Critical Essays and Recollections*, ed. Gary Smith (Cambridge, MA: MIT Press, 1988), 233–34.

77. Benjamin, *The Correspondence of Walter Benjamin, 1910–1940*, 293.

78. Hans-Erhard Haverkampf has provided us with an important historical correction concerning Benjamin's infamous habilitation. Although Benjamin blamed his committee, Haverkampf makes the case that Benjamin is largely responsible for not having his habilitation accepted, and that, had he only played the game, he would have succeeded. Whatever the case might be, I would argue that the fairy tale is still a persuasive criticism of the academy and its rather restricted hold over what counts as "truth." See Hans-Erhard Haverkampf, *Benjamin in Frankfurt: Die zentralen Jahre 1923–1932* (Frankfurt: Societäts-Verlag, 2016).

79. Axel Honneth, *Pathologies of Reason: On the Legacy of Critical Theory*, trans. James Ingram (New York: Columbia University Press, 2009), 88–125.

80. Walter Benjamin. *Gesammelte Schriften, Volume 3*, eds. Rolf Tiedemann and Herman Schweppenhäuser (Frankfurt am Main: Suhrkamp Verlag, 1991), 272–74.

81. Benjamin, *Selected Writings: Volume 1, 1913–1926*, 487.

82. Ibid., 281.

83. Ibid., 249.

84. Ibid., 245.

85. Ibid., 250.

86. Here I am careful not to equate divine and educational violence as identical. Like James Martel, I see the two as overlapping in several respects: (1) both are nonbloody and (2) both suggest a form of human action not defined by myth or fetishism. Yet they are different in that educational violence does not enact transcendental authority over children. At the same time, what is missed by Martel is that divine violence is not immanent to children's lives either. I suggest that it is most properly located in the paradoxical position of potentiality, which cuts across the distinction between immanence and transcendence (see the conclusion to this book for a further discussion of this topic). See James Martel, "A Divine Pedagogy? Benjamin's 'Educative Power' and the Subversion of Myth and Authority," *boundary 2* 45, no. 2 (2018): 171–86.

87. Benjamin, *Selected Writings: Volume 2, Part 1, 1927–1930*, 274.

88. Benjamin, *Selected Writings: Volume 2, Part 2, 1927–1934*, 425.

89. Jane O. Newman, *Benjamin's Library: Modernity, Nation, and the Baroque* (Ithaca, NY: Cornell University Press, 2011).

90. Granted that a precocious Benjamin was highly critical of the First German Youth Congress held in 1913 precisely because it devalued youth while privileging themes of "racial hygiene or agrarian reform or abstinence" (in *Walter Benjamin: Early Writings*, 136).

91. William E. Connolly, *Aspirational Fascism: The Struggle for Multifaceted Democracy Under Trumpism* (Minneapolis: University of Minnesota Press, 2017).

92. Leo Lowenthal and Norbert Guterman, *Prophets of Deceit: A Study of the Techniques of the American Agitator* (New York: Harper and Brothers, 1949), 4.

93. Connolly, *Aspirational Fascism*, 16.
94. Susan Sontag cited in Jill Krementz, *The Writer's Desk* (New York: Random House, 1996), 17.
95. Sandra L. Cepeda, Dean McKay, Sophie C. Schneider, et al., "Politically-Focused Intrusive Thoughts and Associated Ritualistic Behaviors in a Community Sample," *Journal of Anxiety Disorders* 56 (May, 2018): 35–42.
96. Marina Van Zuylen, *The Plenitude of Distraction* (New York: Sequence Press, 2017).
97. Alexander Garcia Düttmann, "Tradition and Destruction: Walter Benjamin's Politics of Language," in Andrew Benjamin and Peter Osborne (Eds.), *Walter Benjamin's Philosophy: Destruction and Experience* (London: Routledge, 1994), 32–58.
98. Gilmer W. Blackburn, *Education in the Third Reich: Race and History in Nazi Textbooks* (Albany: State University of New York, 1985).
99. Umberto Eco, "Ur-Fascism," *New York Review of Books*, June 22, 1995, https://www.nybooks.com/articles/1995/06/22/ur-fascism/.
100. Roger Griffin, *The Nature of Fascism* (London: Routledge, 1994).
101. Lowenthal and Guterman, *Prophets of Deceit*, 34.
102. Theodor Adorno, *The Psychological Technique of Martin Luther Thomas' Radio Addresses* (Stanford: Stanford University Press, 2000), 26.
103. Ibid., 131.
104. Connolly, *Aspirational Fascism*, 17.
105. Ibid.
106. Lowenthal and Guterman, *Prophets of Deceit*, 63.

Radio Broadcasts

1. Sabine Schiller-Lerg, "Walter Benjamin, Radio Journalist: Theory and Practice of Weimar Radio," *Journal of Communication Inquiry* 13, no. 1 (1989): 43–50; Jeffery Mehlman, *Walter Benjamin for Children: An Essay on His Radio Years* (Chicago: University of Chicago Press, 1993); Graeme Gilloch, *Walter Benjamin: Critical Constellations* (New York: Polity Press, 2002); Lecia Rosenthal, "Introduction," *Walter Benjamin on the Radio: An Introduction*, in *Radio Benjamin*, ed. Lecia Rosenthal (London: Verso, 2014): ix–xxix; Esther Leslie, "Playspaces of Anthropological Materialist Pedagogy: Film, Radio, Toys," *boundary 2* 45, no. 2 (2018): 139–56.
2. Klaus Doderer, "Walter Benjamin and Children's Literature," in *"With the Sharpened Axe of Reason": Approaches to Walter Benjamin*, ed. Gerhard Fisher (Oxford: Berg, 1996), 169–76.
3. Jaeho Kang, *Walter Benjamin and the Media: The Spectacle of Modernity* (Cambridge, UK: Polity Press, 2014).

4. Tadashi Dozono, "The Fascist Seduction of Narrative: Walter Benjamin's Historical Materialism beyond Counter-Narrative," *Studies in Philosophy and Education* 37 (2018): 513–27.

5. In this sense, the chapter is an attempt to intervene in current discussions of childhood in Benjamin's thought, only this time through a sonic lens. See for instance, Matthew Charles, "Towards a Critique of Educative Violence: Walter Benjamin and 'Second Education,'" *Pedagogy, Culture & Society* 24, no. 4 (2016): 525–36; Klaus Doderer, "Walter Benjamin and Children's Literature," in *"With the Sharpened Axe of Reason": Approaches to Walter Benjamin*, ed. Gerhard Fisher (Oxford: Berg, 1996), 169–76; Sam Dolbear, Esther Leslie, and Sebastian Truskolaski, "Introduction," in *The Storyteller: Short Stories*, eds. Sam Dolbear, Esther Leslie, and Sebastian Truskolaski (London: Verso, 2016), ix–xxxii; Sam Dolbear and Hannah Proctor, "'Cracking Open the Natural Teleology': Walter Benjamin, Charles Fourier and the Figure of the Child," *Pedagogy, Culture and Society* 24, no. 4 (2016): 495–503; Gerhard Fischer, "Benjamin's Utopia of Education as *Theatrum Mundi et Vitae*: On the *Programme of a Proletarian Children's Theatre*," in *'With the Sharpened Axe of Reason': Approaches to Walter Benjamin*, ed. Gerhard Fischer (Oxford: Berg, 1996), 201–17; Gillian Lathey, "Enlightening City Childhoods: Walter Benjamin's Berlin and Erich Kästner's Dresden," *Pedagogy, Culture and Society* 24, no. 4 (2016), 485–93; Hans-Thies Lehmann, "An Interrupted Performance: On Walter Benjamin's Idea of Children's Theatre," in *"With the Sharpened Axe of Reason": Approaches to Walter Benjamin*, ed. Gerhard Fischer (Oxford: Berg, 1996), 179–200; Esther Leslie, "Colonial and Communist Pedagogy," *Pedagogy, Culture and Society* 24, no. 4 (2016): 517–24; Tyson E. Lewis, *Inoperative Learning: A Radical Rewriting of Educational Potentiality* (New York: Routledge, 2017); Carlo Salzani, "Experience and Play: Walter Benjamin and the Prelapsarian Child," in *Walter Benjamin and the Architecture of Modernity*, eds. Andrew Benjamin and Charles Rice (Melbourne: re.press, 2009), 175–98; Eric L. Tribunella, "Benjamin, Benson, and the Child's Gaze: Childhood Desire and Pleasure in the David Blaize Books," *Pedagogy, Culture and Society* 24, no. 4 (2016): 505–15.

6. Cited in Susan Buck-Morss, *Dialectics of Seeing* (London: Verso, 1991), 345.

7. Walter Benjamin, *Selected Writings, Volume 2, Part 2, 1931–1934*, eds. Michael W. Jennings, Howard Eiland, and Gary Smith (Cambridge, MA: Belknap Press, 2005), 419.

8. Ibid.

9. Ibid., 420.

10. Walter Benjamin, *Selected Writings, Volume 1, 1913–1926*, eds. Marcus Bullock and Michael W. Jennings (Cambridge, MA: Belknap Press, 2004), 50.

11. Ibid., 51.

12. Walter Benjamin, *Selected Writings, Volume 3, 1935–1938*, eds. Howard Eiland and Michael W. Jennings (Cambridge, MA: Belknap Press, 2006), 380.
13. Walter Benjamin, *Early Writings, 1910–1917*, ed. Howard Eiland (Cambridge, MA: Belknap Press, 2011), 218.
14. Benjamin, *Selected Writings, Volume 1, 1913–1926*, 50.
15. Ibid.
16. Ibid.
17. Ibid., 51.
18. Ibid.
19. See Jack Zipes, "Walter Benjamin, Children's Literature, and the Children's Public Sphere: An Introduction to New Trends in West and East Germany," *The Germanic Review: Literature, Culture, Theory* 63, no. 1 (1988): 2–5; Klaus Doderer, "Walter Benjamin and Children's Literature," in *"With the Sharpened Axe of Reason": Approaches to Walter Benjamin*, ed. Gerhard Fischer (Oxford: Berg, 1996), 169–75; Eric L. Tribunella, "Benjamin, Benson, and the Child's Gaze: Childhood Desire and Pleasure in the David Blaize Books," *Pedagogy, Culture and Society* vol. 24, no. 4 (2016): 505–15.
20. Benjamin, *Selected Writings, Volume 1, 1913–1926*, 410.
21. Ibid.
22. Ibid., 412.
23. Ibid.
24. Theodor Adorno, Walter Benjamin, Ernst Bloch, Bertolt Brecht, and Georg Lukács, *The Aesthetics of Politics* (London: Verso, 2008), 140.
25. This claim is highly limited and not at all meant to underestimate the more complex philosophy of music developed elsewhere in Benjamin's work. See, for instance, essays in *Klang und Musik bei Walter Benjamin*, ed. Tobias Robert Klein (Paderborn, Germany: Wilhelm Fink Verlag, 2013).
26. Benjamin, *Selected Writings, Volume 1, 1913–1926*, 442.
27. Ibid.
28. Benjamin, *Selected Writings, Volume 3, 1935–1938*, 389.
29. Ibid.
30. Eli Friedlander, "Farben und Laute in der *Berliner Kindheit um neunzehnhundert*," in *Klang und Musik bei Walter Benjamin*, ed. Tobias Robert Klein (Paderborn: Wilhelm Fink Verlag, 2013), 54–67.
31. Uta Kornmeier, "Akustisches in der *Berliner Kindheit um neunzehnhundert*," in *Klang und Musik bei Walter Benjamin*, ed. Tobias Robert Klein (Paderborn, Germany: Wilhelm Fink Verlag, 2013), 46–53.
32. Benjamin, *Selected Writings, Volume 1, 1913–1926*, 50.
33. Ibid.
34. Ibid., 264.

35. See Peter Fenves, *The Messianic Reduction: Walter Benjamin and the Shape of Time* (Stanford, CA: Stanford University Press, 2011) for a full analysis of the plastic notion of time in Benjamin's work.

36. Walter Benjamin, *Radio Benjamin*, ed. Lecia Rosenthal (London: Verso, 2014), 70.

37. Ibid., 71.

38. Ibid., 72.

39. Walter Benjamin, *Early Writings 1910–1917*, 123.

40. Benjamin, *Radio Benjamin*, 30.

41. Richard Wolin, *Walter Benjamin: An Aesthetic of Redemption* (Los Angeles: University of California Press, 1994).

42. See also Kang, *Walter Benjamin and the Media: The Spectacle of Modernity*.

43. Walter Benjamin, *Selected Writings, Volume 3, 1935–1938*, 143.

44. Ibid., 146.

45. Ibid., 162.

46. Benjamin, *Selected Writings, Volume 2, Part 2, 1931–1934*, 774.

47. Benjamin, *Radio Benjamin*, 14.

48. Benjamin, *Selected Writings, Volume 3, 1935–1938*, 161.

49. Benjamin, *The Arcades Project*, Konvolut C (C1, 6), 83.

50. Ibid.

51. Benjamin, *Radio Benjamin*, 171.

52. Ibid.

53. Walter Benjamin, *Selected Writings, Volume 4, 1938–1940*, trans. Howard Eiland and Michael W. Jennings (Cambridge, MA: Belknap Press, 2003), 184.

54. Ibid., 185.

55. Benjamin, *Radio Benjamin*, 16.

56. Paul North, *The Problem of Distraction* (Stanford, CA: Stanford University Press, 2011).

57. Benjamin, *Radio Benjamin*, 27.

58. Ibid.

59. Ibid., 66.

60. Ibid., 119.

61. Ibid., 10.

62. See the chapter in this book on children's theater for another example of this same point.

63. Benjamin, *Radio Benjamin*, 15.

64. Ibid., 11.

65. Walter Benjamin, *Selected Writings, Volume 2, Part 1, 1927–1930*, eds. Michael W. Jennings, Howard Eiland, and Gary Smith (Cambridge, MA: Belknap Press, 2005), 27.

66. Benjamin, *Radio Benjamin*, 31.

67. Ibid., 201.

68. Benjamin, *Selected Works, Volume 2, Part 1, 1927–1930*, 101.
69. Ibid.
70. Carlo Salzani, "Experience and Play: Walter Benjamin and the Prelapsarian Child," in *Walter Benjamin and the Architecture of Modernity*, eds. Andrew Benjamin and Charles Rice (Melbourne: re.press, 2009), 175–98.
71. Walter Benjamin, *Walter Benjamin's Archive: Images, Texts, Signs*, eds. Ursula Marx, Gudrun Schwarz, Michael Schwarz, and Erdmut Wizisla (London: Verso, 2015), 107.
72. Benjamin, *Radio Benjamin*, 43.
73. Benjamin, *Selected Writings, Volume 2, Part 1, 1927–1930*, 114.
74. Theodor W. Adorno, *Current of Music: Elements of a Radio Theory*, ed. Robert Hullot-Kentor (New York: Polity Press, 2009), 148.
75. Theodor W. Adorno, "The Radio Symphony," in *Radio Research, 1941*, ed. Paul F. Lazarsfeld and Frank Stanton, 110–39 (New York: Duell, Sloan, and Pearce, 1941), 122–23.
76. Theodor W. Adorno, "Fetish Character in Music and Regression of Listening," in *The Essential Frankfurt School Reader*, eds. Andrew Arato and Eike Gebhardt (London: Continuum, 2002), 286.
77. Max Horkheimer and Theodor W. Adorno, *Dialectic of Enlightenment: Philosophical Fragments*, ed. Gunzelin Schmid Noerr, trans. Edmund Jephcott (Stanford, CA: University of Stanford Press, 2002), 129.
78. Ibid.
79. Theodor W. Adorno, "Analytical Study of the NBC 'Music Appreciation Hour,'" *The Musical Quarterly* 78, no. 2 (1994): 326.
80. Ibid., 328.
81. Ibid., 331.
82. Ibid.
83. Ibid.
84. Ibid., 355.
85. Ibid., 365.
86. Ibid., 337.
87. Ibid., 358.
88. Ibid.
89. Ibid., 358.
90. Ibid., 361.
91. Ibid., 353.
92. Ibid., 360.
93. Ibid., 370.
94. W. J. T. Mitchell, *Picture Theory: Essays on Verbal and Visual Representation* (Chicago: University of Chicago Press, 1995).
95. Vilém Flusser, *Toward a Philosophy of Photography* (London: Reaktion Books, 2000).

96. Fredric Jameson, *Postmodernism or, The Cultural Logic of Late Capitalism* (Durham, NC: Duke University Press, 1992), 54.

97. Katja Rothe, "Die Schule des Entzugs. Walter Benjamins Radio-Kasper," *Sinnhaft. Strategien des Entzugs* vol. 22, no. 1 (2009): 74–89.

Children's Theater

1. See Gerhard Fischer, "Benjamin's Utopia of Education as *Theatrum Mundi et Vitae: On the Programme of a Proletarian Children's Theatre*," in *"With the Sharpened Axe of Reason": Approaches to Walter Benjamin*, ed. Gerhard Fischer (Oxford: Berg, 1996), 201–17; Hans-Thies Lehmann, "An Interrupted Performance: On Walter Benjamin's Idea of Children's Theatre," in *"With the Sharpened Axe of Reason": Approaches to Walter Benjamin*, ed. Gerhard Fischer (Oxford: Berg, 1996), 179–200; Jack David Zipes, "Political Children's Theater in the Age of Globalization," *Theater* 33, no. 2 (2003): 3–25; Karin Burk, *Kindertheater als Möglichkeitsraum: Untersuchungen zu Walter Benjamins, "Programm eines proletarischen Kindertheaters"* (Bielefeld, Germany: transcript Verlag, 2015); Giulio Schiavoni, Giulio, "Zum Kinde: 'Programm eines proletarischen Kindertheaters' / 'Eine kommunistische Pädagogik' / 'Kinderbücher,'" in *Benjamin-Handbuch: Leben – Werk – Wirkung*, ed. Burkhardt Lindner, 373–85 (Stuttgart, Weimar: J. B. Metzler Verlag, 2006); Oded Zipory, "One Day Is a Whole World: On the Role of the Present in Education between Plan and Play," in *Philosophy of Education Society Yearbook, 2016*, ed. Natasha Levinson (Urbana-Champaign, IL: University of Illinois Press, 2016), 334–43.

2. Walter Benjamin, *The Origin of German Tragic Drama*, trans. John Osborne (London: Verso, 1998), 188.

3. Ibid., 124.

4. Jane O. Newman, *Benjamin's Library: Modernity, Nation, and the Baroque* (Ithaca, NY: Cornell University Press, 2011), 84.

5. Walter Benjamin, *Selected Writings: Volume 2, Part 2, 1931–1934*, eds. Michael W. Jennings, Howard Eiland, and Gary Smith (Cambridge, MA: Belknap Press, 2005), 721.

6. Ibid., 691.

7. Ibid., 800.

8. Ibid., 801.

9. Walter Benjamin, *Selected Writings: Volume 3, 1935–1938*, eds. Howard Eiland and Michael W. Jennings (Cambridge, MA: Belknap Press, 2006), 391.

10. Benjamin, *Selected Writings: Volume 2, Part 2, 1931–1934*, 693.

11. Benjamin, *Selected Writings: Volume 3, 1935–1938*, 392.

12. Ibid., 391.

13. Benjamin, *Selected Writings: Volume 2, Part 2, 1931–1934*, 515.

14. Ibid.
15. Walter Benjamin, *Selected Writings, Volume 1, 1913-1926*, eds. Marcus Bullock and Michael W. Jennings (Cambridge, MA: Belknap Press, 2004), 26.
16. Walter Benjamin, *Selected Writings: Volume 2, Part 1, 1927-1930*, eds. Michael W. Jennings, Howard Eiland, and Gary Smith (Cambridge, MA: Belknap Press, 2005), 273.
17. Ibid.
18. Ibid., 201.
19. Benjamin, *Selected Writings: Volume 3, 1935-1938*, 391.
20. Benjamin, *Selected Writings: Volume 2, Part 1, 1927-1930*, 205.
21. Ibid.
22. Ibid.
23. Ibid., 204.
24. Ibid., 274.
25. Walter Benjamin, *Selected Writings: Volume 4, 1938-1940*, eds. Howard Eiland and Michael W. Jennings (Cambridge, MA: Belknap Press, 2003), 338.
26. Benjamin, *Selected Writings: Volume 3, 1935-1938*, 390.
27. Benjamin, *Selected Writings: Volume 4, 1938-1940*, 305.
28. Benjamin, *Selected Writings: Volume 2, Part 1, 1927-1930*, 205.
29. Benjamin, *Selected Writings: Volume 3, 1935-1938*, 26.
30. Benjamin, *Selected Writings: Volume 2, Part 1, 1927-1930*, 206.
31. Ibid., 202.
32. Ibid., 204.
33. Ibid.
34. Ibid., 202.
35. Ibid., 203.
36. Ibid., 204.
37. Ibid., 203.
38. Burk, *Kindertheater als Möglichkeitsraum*, 10.
39. Benjamin, *Selected Writings: Volume 2, Part 1, 1927-1930*, 370.
40. Ibid., 203.
41. Ibid.
42. Ibid., 202.
43. See Miriam Bratu Hansen. *Cinema and Experience: Siegfried Kracauer, Walter Benjamin, and Theodor W. Adorno* (Los Angeles, CA: University of California Press, 2011).
44. Benjamin, *Selected Writings, Volume 3, 1935-1938*, 135.
45. Ibid., 134.
46. See Benjamin, *Selected Writings, Volume 2, Part 2 1931-1934*, 584. While this is an important updating of proletarian theater for a Western, bourgeois audience, Benjamin's analysis falls back on Aristotelian notions of action, identification, and character development. It is uncertain whether or not this

is a retreat from his early claims that Brecht ought to be placed in a subaltern genealogy with the mourning plays or if the Aristotelian dimension is the result of historical necessity brought about by bourgeois society itself.

47. Zipes, "Political Children's Theater in the Age of Globalization," 9.

Collections

1. Benjamin, *Selected Writings, Volume 1, 1913–1926*, eds. Marcus Bullock and Michael W. Jennings (Cambridge, MA: Belknap Press, 2004), 465.

2. Howard Eiland, "Translator's Forward," in Walter Benjamin, *Berlin Childhood Around 1900* (Cambridge, MA: Belknap Press, 2006), xiv.

3. Graeme Gilloch, *Myth and Metropolis: Walter Benjamin and the City* (Cambridge, UK: Polity Press, 1996), 92.

4. Walter Benjamin, *The Arcades Project*, trans. Howard Eiland and Kevin McLaughlin (Cambridge, MA: Belknap Press, 2002), Konvolut H (H4, 3), 210.

5. Walter Benjamin, *Selected Writings, Volume 4, 1938–1940*, eds. Howard Eiland and Michael W. Jennings (Cambridge, MA: Belknap Press, 2003), 190.

6. Walter Benjamin, *Selected Writings, Volume 2, Part 2, 1931–1934*, eds. Michael W. Jennings, Howard Eiland, and Gary Smith (Cambridge, MA: Belknap Press, 2005), 815.

7. Walter Benjamin, "The Flâneur's Return," in Franz Hessel *Walking in Berlin: A Flâneur in the Capital*, trans. Amanda De Marco (Cambridge, MA: MIT Press, 2017), xix.

8. Ibid.

9. Walter Benjamin, *Selected Writings, Volume 4, 1938–1940*, trans. Howard Eiland and Michael W. Jennings (Cambridge, MA: Belknap Press, 2003), 268.

10. Paul North, *The Problem of Distraction* (Stanford, CA: Stanford University Press, 2011), 162.

11. Ibid., 163.

12. Walter Benjamin, *The Arcades Project*, trans. Howard Eiland and Kevin McLaughlin (Cambridge, MA: Belknap Press, 2002), Konvolut M (M16a, 4), 447.

13. Walter Benjamin, *Selected Writings, Volume 3, 1935–1938*, eds. Howard Eiland and Michael W. Jennings (Cambridge, MA: Belknap Press, 2006), 275.

14. Benjamin, *The Arcades Project*, Konvolut H (H2, 5), 206–7.

15. Cited in Susan Buck-Morss, *The Dialectics of Seeing: Walter Benjamin and the Arcades Project* (Cambridge, MA: MIT Press, 1991), 346.

16. An emphasis on touch in relation to study and collecting helps give added specificity to Brendan Moran's emphasis on the physicality of study. See Moran, "Kafkan Study," *boundary 2* 45, no. 2 (2018), 87–110.

17. Walter Benjamin, *Selected Writings: Volume 2, Part 2, 1931–1934*, eds. Michael W. Jennings, Howard Eiland, and Gary Smith (Cambridge, MA: Belknap Press, 2005), 492.
18. Ibid., 487.
19. Ibid., 489.
20. Ibid., 491.
21. Benjamin, *Selected Writings, Volume 3, 1935–1938*, 275.
22. Benjamin, *Selected Writings, Volume 2, Part 2, 1931–1934*, 487.
23. Cited in *Walter Benjamin's Archive: Images, Texts, Signs*, eds. Ursula Marx, Gudrun Schwarz, Michael Schwarz, and Erdmut Wizisla (London: Verso, 2015), 25.
24. Benjamin, *Selected Writings, Volume 2, Part 2, 1931–1934*, 487.
25. Ibid.
26. Benjamin, *The Arcades Project*, Konvolut J (J80, 2), 368.
27. See Margaret Cohen, "Benjamin's Phantasmagoria: The *Arcades Project*," in *The Cambridge Companion to Walter Benjamin*, ed. David S. Ferris (Cambridge, UK: Cambridge University Press, 2004), 199–220.
28. Walter Benjamin, *The Origin of German Tragic Drama*, trans. John Osborne (London: Verso, 1998), 166.
29. Ibid., 175.
30. Ibid., 131.
31. Benjamin, *The Arcades Project*, Konvolut J (J80, 2), 369.
32. Ibid., Konvolut J (J55, 13), 328.
33. 182.
34. Benjamin, *The Origin of German Tragic Drama*, 182.
35. Benjamin, *Selected Writings, Volume 4, 1938–1940*, 173.
36. Benjamin, *Selected Writings, Volume 2, Part 2, 1931–1934*, 486–87.
37. Benjamin, *Selected Writings, Volume 3, 1935–1938*, 267.
38. Ibid., 282–83.
39. Ibid., 267.
40. Ibid., 268.
41. Ibid., 271.
42. Ibid., 282.
43. Ibid., 283.
44. Ibid., 284.
45. Ibid., 285.
46. Ibid., 400.
47. See Jan Masschelein and Maarten Simons, "School as Architecture for New Comers and Strangers: The Perfect School as Public School?" *Teachers College Record*, vol. 112 (2010): 535–55 for an analysis of pedagogical baptism.
48. Benjamin, *Selected Writings, Volume 3, 1935–1938*, 351.
49. Ibid.

50. Ibid., 350.
51. See Birgit Schwarz. *Hitlers Museum: Die Fotoalben Gemäldegalerie Linz:* Dokumente zum 'Führermuseum' (Vienna, Austria: Böhlau Verlag, 2004).
52. Benjamin, *Selected Writings, Volume 1, 1913–1926*, 319.
53. Ibid.
54. Deborah Azrael, Lisa Hepburn, David Hemenway, and Matthew Miller, "The Stock and Flow of U.S. Firearms: Results from the 2105 National Firearms Survey," *Russell Sage Foundation Journal of the Social Sciences* 3, no. 5 (2017), 38–57.

Cityscapes

1. Walter Benjamin, *Selected Writings: Volume 2, Part 2, 1931–1934*, eds. Michael W. Jennings, Howard Eiland, and Gary Smith (Cambridge, MA: Belknap Press, 2005), 598.
2. Stephen Dobson, "Urban Pedagogy: A Proposal for the Twenty-First Century," *London Review of Education* 4, no. 2 (2006), 99–114.
3. Jonathan Crary, *Suspensions of Perception: Attention, Spectacle, and Modern Culture* (Cambridge, MA: MIT Press, 1999), 33.
4. Timothy Campbell, *Improper Life: Technology and Biopolotics from Heidegger to Agamben* (Minneapolis: University of Minnesota Press, 2011).
5. Paul North, *The Problem of Distraction* (Stanford, CA: Stanford University Press, 2012).
6. Carolin Duttlinger, "Between contemplation and distraction: Configurations of attention in Walter Benjamin," *German Studies Review* 30, no. 1 (2007), 33–54.
7. Walter Benjamin, *Selected Writings: Volume 4, 1938–1940*, eds. Howard Eiland and Michael W. Jennings (Cambridge, MA: Belknap Press, 2003), 233.
8. Walter Benjamin, *The Arcades Project*, trans. Howard Eiland and Kevin McLaughlin (New York: Belknap Press, 2002), 16.
9. Ibid.
10. Ibid.
11. Jürgen Habermas, *The Structural Transformation of the Public Sphere: An Inquiry into a Category of Bourgeois Society*, trans. Thomas Burger (Cambridge, MA: MIT Press, 1991).
12. For a comprehensive overview of the phantasmagoria in Benjamin's work as well as its long history in Marxism as such, see Margaret Cohen, "Benjamin's phantasmagoria: The *Arcades Project*," in *The Cambridge Companion to Walter Benjamin*, ed. David S. Ferris (Cambridge, MA: Cambridge University Press, 2004), 199–220.
13. Karl Marx, *Capital Volume One: A Critique of Political Economy*, trans. Ben Fowkes (London: Penguin Classics, 1992).

14. Benjamin, *The Arcades Project*, 18.
15. Graeme Gilloch, *Walter Benjamin: Critical Constellations* (Malden, MA: Polity Press, 2013).
16. Benjamin, *Selected Writings, Volume 4*, 120.
17. Ibid.
18. Marina Van Zuylen, *The Plenitude of Distraction* (New York: Sequence Press, 2017).
19. Benjamin, *Selected Writings, Volume 4*, 120.
20. Immanuel Kant, *Critique of Pure Reason*, eds. and trans. Paul Guyer and Allen W. Wood (New York: St. Martin's, 1965), 138.
21. Howard Caygill, *Walter Benjamin: The Colour of Experience* (London: Routledge, 1998).
22. North, *Distraction*, 164.
23. See Peter Szondi, "Walter Benjamin's City Portraits," in *On Walter Benjamin: Critical Essays and Recollections*, ed. Gary Smith (Cambridge, MA: MIT Press, 1988), 18–32.
24. Benjamin, *Selected Writings, Volume 3, 1935–1938*, eds. Howard Eiland and Michael W. Jennings (Cambridge, MA: Belknap Press, 2002), 386.
25. Ibid.
26. Ibid.
27. Ibid.
28. Ibid., 404.
29. Ibid.
30. Ibid.
31. Walter Benjamin, *Selected Writings, Volume 2, Part 2, 1931–1934*, 612.
32. Ibid., 596.
33. See Walter Benjamin, "Life of Students," in *Selected Writings, Volume 1, 1913–1926*, trans. Marcus Bullock and Michael W. Jennings (Cambridge, MA: Belknap Press, 2004), 37–47.
34. Benjamin, *Selected Writings, Volume 4*, 189.
35. Ibid., 174.
36. Walter Benjamin, *Selected Writings: Volume 2, Part 1, 1927–1930*, eds. Michael W. Jennings, Howard Eiland, and Gary Smith (Cambridge, MA: Belknap Press, 2005), 23.
37. Carlo Salzani, "Experience and Play: Walter Benjamin and the Prelapsarian Child," in *Walter Benjamin and the Architecture of Modernity*, eds. Andrew Benjamin and Charles Rice (Melbourne: re.press, 2009), 175–98; Graeme Gilloch, *Myth & Metropolis: Walter Benjamin and the City* (Malden, MA: Polity Press, 1996); Burkhardt Lindner, "The *Passagen-Werk*, the Berliner Kindheit, and the Archaeology of the 'Recent Past,'" *New German Critique*, 39 (autumn 1986), 25–46.
38. Benjamin, *Selected Writings, Volume 2, Part 2, 1931–1934*, 645.

39. Benjamin, *Selected Writings, Volume 4*, 171.
40. Benjamin, *Selected Writings, Volume 4*, 41.
41. Benjamin, *Selected Writings: Volume 1, 1913–1926*, 417.
42. Ibid., 421.
43. Hermann Rauschning, *The Voice of Destruction* (New York: G. P. Putnam's Sons, 1940), 55–56.
44. Richard Florida, "How America's Metro Areas Voted," *CityLab*, November 29, 2016, https://www.citylab.com/equity/2016/11/how-americas-metro-areas-voted/508355/.
45. Gilloch, *Myth & Metropolis*; David Kishik, *The Manhattan Project: A Theory of a City* (Stanford, CA: Stanford University Press, 2015).
46. Benjamin, *The Arcades Project*, Konvolut A (A3a, 2), 42.
47. Ibid., Konvolut N (N1, 2), 456.
48. Ibid., Konvolut J (J79, 4), 367.
49. Walter Benjamin, *Selected Works, Volume 4, 1938–1940*, 320.
50. Ibid., 320–21.
51. Benjamin, *The Arcades Project*, Konvolut J (J66, 1), 345.

Cinema

1. Walter Benjamin, *Selected Works, Volume 3: 1935–1938*, eds. Howard Eiland and Michael W. Jennings (Cambridge, MA: Belknap Press, 2002), 142.
2. Miriam Bratu Hansen, *Cinema and Experience: Siegfried Kracauer, Walter Benjamin, and Theodor W. Adorno* (Berkeley: University of California Press, 2012), 80.
3. Walter Benjamin, *Selected Works, Volume 2, Part 1, 1927*–1930, eds. Michael W. Jennings, Howard Eiland, and Gary Smith. Cambridge, MA: Belknap Press, 14.
4. Ibid., 15.
5. Max Horkheimer and Theodor W. Adorno, *Dialectic of Enlightenment: Philosophical Fragments*, ed. Gunzelin Schmid Noerr, trans. Edmund Jephcott (Stanford, CA: Stanford University Press, 2002), 99–100.
6. Ibid., 100.
7. Theodor W. Adorno, "Transparencies on Film," *Culture Industry*, ed. J. M. Bernstein (London: Routledge, 2001), 182.
8. Ibid., 183.
9. Andrew Hewitt, *Fascist Modernism: Aesthetics, Politics, and the Avant-Garde* (Stanford, CA: Stanford University Press, 1993), 81.
10. See Mark Antliff, *Avant-Garde Fascism: The Mobilization of Myth, Art, and Culture in France, 1909–1939* (Durham, NC: Duke University Press, 2007). Antliff also questions Benjamin's own endorsement of avant-garde montage,

highlighting the role of futurism in Italian fascism. But what I would like to stress is that for Benjamin, montage in and of itself was not exactly antifascist. Read in relation to his comments on distraction and film, we might retort that montage was of interest to Benjamin if and only if it expressed both educational and consumer value.

11. Benjamin, *Selected Works, Volume 3: 1935–1938*, 119.
12. Walter Benjamin, *The Arcades Project*, trans. Howard Eiland and Kevin McLaughlin (Cambridge, MA: Belknap Press, 2002), Konvolut K (K3a, 1), 395.
13. Ibid.
14. Benjamin, *Selected Works, Volume 3: 1935–1938*, 113.
15. Ibid., 132.
16. Walter Benjamin, *Selected Writings, Volume 4, 1938–1940*, eds. Howard Eiland and Michael W. Jennings (Cambridge, MA: Belknap Press, 2003), 264.
17. Ibid., 267.
18. Ibid.
19. Ibid., 264.
20. Hansen, *Cinema and Experience*.
21. Benjamin, *The Arcades Project*, Konvolut K (K3, 3), 394.
22. Benjamin, *Selected Works, Volume 3: 1935–1938*, 117.
23. Ibid.
24. Ibid., 94.
25. Ibid., 109.
26. Benjamin, *Selected Writings, Volume 4, 1938–1940*, 267.
27. Benjamin, *The Arcades Project*, Konvolut N (N1, 8), 458.
28. Benjamin, *Selected Writings, Volume 2, Part 1, 1927–1930*, 223.
29. Ibid., 199–200.
30. Benjamin, *Selected Writings, Volume 3, 1935–1938*, 94.
31. Ibid.
32. Ibid.
33. Joris Vlieghe, Maarten Simons, and Jan Masschelein, "The Educational Meaning of Communal Laughter: On the Experience of Corporeal Democracy," *Educational Theory* 60, no. 6 (2010), 731.
34. Ibid., 721.
35. Ibid., 731.
36. Walter Benjamin, *Selected Writings, Volume 3, 1935–1938*, eds. Howard Eiland and Michael W. Jennings (Cambridge, MA: Belknap Press, 2006), 119.
37. Benjamin, *Selected Writings, Volume 2, Part 1, 1927–1930*, 199.
38. Benjamin, *Selected Writings, Volume 4, 1938–1940*, 267.
39. Ibid., 224.
40. Benjamin, *Selected Writings, Volume 2, Part 1, 1927–1930*, 217–18.
41. Benjamin, *Selected Writings, Volume 3, 1935–1938*, 118.
42. Horkheimer and Adorno, *Dialectic of Enlightenment*, 112.

43. Ibid.
44. Theodor W. Adorno, *The Complete Correspondences: 1928–1940*, ed. Henri Lonitz, trans. Nicholas Walker (Cambridge, MA: Harvard University Press, 1999), 130.
45. Horkheimer and Adorno, *Dialectic of Enlightenment*, 112.
46. Walter Benjamin, *Selected Writings, Volume 2, Part 2, 1931–1934*, eds. Michael W. Jennings, Howard Eiland, and Gary Smith (Cambridge, MA: Belknap Press, 2005), 732.
47. Ibid., 735.
48. Benjamin, *Selected Writings, Volume 3, 1935–1938*, 104.
49. Ibid., 102.
50. Ibid., 105.
51. Walter Benjamin, *Selected Writings, Volume 1, 1913–1926*, eds. Marcus Bullock and Michael W. Jennings (Cambridge, MA: Belknap Press, 2004), 466.
52. See Benjamin, "Light from Obscurantists," in *Selected Writings, Volume 2, Part 2, 1931–1934*, 653–57.
53. Benjamin, *Selected Writings, Volume 1, 1913–1926*, 486.
54. Ibid.
55. Ibid.
56. Ibid., 487.
57. Max Horkheimer and Theodor Adorno, *Dialectic of Enlightenment: Philosophical Fragments*, ed. Gunzelin Schmid Noerr, trans. Edmund Jephcott (Stanford, CA: Stanford University Press, 2002), 154.
58. Benjamin, *Selected Writings, Volume 2, Part 2, 1931–1934*, 792.
59. George Potter, "The Tramp & The Culture Industry: Adorno, Chaplin, and the Possibility of Progressive Comedy," *Arizona Quarterly: A Journal of American Literature, Culture, and Theory* 69, no. 1 (2013): 87.
60. Burckhardt Lindner, "Das Kunstwerk im Zeitalter seiner technischen Reproduzierbarkeit," in *Benjamin-Handbuch: Leben-Werk-Wirkung*, ed. Burckhardt Lindner (Stuttgart, Germany: J. B. Metzler Verlag, 2006), 247.
61. Benjamin, *Selected Writings, Volume 1, 1913–1926*, 206.
62. See Hansen, *Cinema and Experience* and R. L. Rutsky, "Walter Benjamin and the Dispersion of Cinema," *Symplokē* 15, no. 1–2 (2007), 8–23.

Riddles

1. Daniel Heller-Roazen, *Dark Tongues: The Art of Rogues and Riddlers* (New York: Zone Books, 2013), 65.
2. Ibid., 68.
3. Fredric Jameson, *Representing* Capital: *A Reading of Volume One* (London: Verso, 2011), 24.

4. Karl Marx, *Capital, Volume 1*, trans. Ben Fowkes (London: Penguin Books, 1990), 163.
5. Ibid., 150.
6. Ibid., 160.
7. Ibid., 187.
8. Ibid., 162.
9. Giorgio Agamben, *The Signature of All Things: On Method*, trans. Luca D'Isanto and Kevin Attell (New York: Zone Books, 2009).
10. Marx, *Capital*, 104.
11. Ibid.
12. Ibid.
13. Walter Benjamin, *Selected Writings, Volume 1, 1913–1926*, eds. Marcus Bullock and Michael W. Jennings (Cambridge, MA: Belknap Press, 2004), 267.
14. Ibid., 268.
15. Walter Benjamin, *The Correspondences of Walter Benjamin, 1910–1940*, eds. Gershom Scholem and Theodor W. Adorno, trans. Manfred R. Jacobson and Evelyn M. Jacobson (Chicago: University of Chicago Press, 2012), 80.
16. Walter Benjamin, *The Origin of German Tragic Drama*, trans. John Osborne (London: Verso, 2009), 29.
17. Ibid., 34.
18. Ibid., 38.
19. Marx, *Capital*, 157.
20. Ibid., 151.
21. Ibid., 155.
22. Jameson, *Representing* Capital, 6.
23. Benjamin, *Origin*, 37.
24. Susan Buck-Morss, *The Dialectics of Seeing: Walter Benjamin and the Arcades Project* (Cambridge, MA: MIT Press, 1991), 231.
25. Theodor Adorno, "The Actuality of Philosophy," trans. Benjamin Snow, *Telos*, 31 (Spring 1977), 126.
26. Ibid., 127.
27. Ibid.
28. Ibid.
29. Theodor Adorno, *Minima Moralia: Reflections on a Damaged Life*, trans. E. F. N. Jephcott (London: Verso, 2005), 50.
30. Walter Benjamin, *Selected Writings: Volume 3, 1935–1938*, eds. Howard Eiland and Michael W. Jennings (Cambridge MA: Belknap Press, 2006), 142.
31. Walter Benjamin, *Selected Writings: Volume 2, Part 2, 1931–1934*, eds. Michael W. Jennings, Howard Eiland, and Gary Smith (Cambridge, MA: Belknap Press, 2005), 726.
32. Ibid.
33. Benjamin, *Selected Writings, Volume 1, 1913–1926*, 63.

34. Walter Benjamin, *Selected Writings: Volume 2, Part 2, 1931–1934*, 727.
35. Ursula Marx, Gudrun Schwarz, Michael Schwarz, and Ermut Wuzisla (eds.), *Walter Benjamin's Archive: Images, Texts, Signs* (London: Verso Press, 2007), 110.
36. SW, 3, 358.
37. Listed in Marx, Schwarz, Schwarz, and Wuzisla, *Walter Benjamin's Archive: Images, Texts, Signs*, 119–20.
38. Benjamin, *Selected Writings, Volume 1, 1913–1926*, 281–82.
39. Ibid., 257.
40. Ibid., 261.
41. William E. Connolly, *Aspirational Fascism: The Struggle for Multifaceted Democracy Under Trumpism* (Minneapolis: University of Minnesota Press, 2017).
42. Peter Beinart, "What Trump Means When He Calls Gary Cohn a 'Globalist,'" *The Atlantic*, March 9, 2018, https://www.theatlantic.com/politics/archive/2018/03/trump-globalist-cohn/555269/.
43. Jodi Dean, *Democracy and Other Neoliberal Fantasies: Communicative Capitalism and Left Politics* (Durham, NC: Duke University Press, 2009). See also Derek R. Ford and Tyson E. Lewis, "On the Freedom to be Opaque Monsters: Communist Pedagogy, Aesthetics, and the Sublime," *Cultural Politics* 14, no. 1 (2018), 95–108.

Conclusion

1. Walter Benjamin, *The Storyteller*, eds. Sam Dolbear, Esther Leslie, and Sebastian Truskolaski (London: Verso, 2016), 40–41.
2. Cited in David Irving's article, "Revelations from Goebbels' Diary: Bringing to Light Secrets of Hitler's Propaganda Minister," *Journal of Historical Review* 15, no. 1 (1995), 2–17.
3. Peter Fenves, *The Messianic Reduction: Walter Benjamin and the Shape of Time* (Stanford, CA: Stanford University Press, 2011), 3.

Bibliography

Adorno, Theodor, W. "The Radio Symphony." In *Radio Research, 1941*, edited by Paul F. Lazarsfeld and Frank Stanton, 110–39. New York: Duell, Sloan, and Pearce, 1941.

———. "Prejudice in Interview Material." In *The Authoritarian Personality: Abridged Edition*, edited by Theodor W. Adorno, Else Frenkel-Brunswik, Daniel J. Levinson, and R. Nevitt Sanford, 297–345. New York: Norton, 1950.

———. "Types and Syndromes." In *The Authoritarian Personality: Abridged Edition*, edited by Theodor W. Adorno, Else Frenkel-Brunswik, Daniel J. Levinson, and R. Nevitt Sanford, 346–88. New York: Norton, 1950.

———. "The Actuality of Philosophy." *Telos* 31 (Spring, 1977): 120–33.

———. "Analytical Study of the NBC 'Music Appreciation Hour.'" *The Musical Quarterly* 78, no. 2 (1994): 125–377.

———. *Critical Models: Interventions and Catchwords*. Translated by Henry W. Pickford. New York: Columbia University Press, 1998.

———. *The Complete Correspondences: 1928–1940*. Edited by Henri Lonitz, translated by Nicholas Walker. Cambridge, MA: Harvard University Press, 1999.

———. *The Psychological Technique of Martin Luther Thomas' Radio Addresses*. Stanford: Stanford University Press, 2000.

———. *Culture Industry*. Edited by J. M. Bernstein. London: Routledge, 2001.

———. "Fetish Character in Music and Regression of Listening." In *The Essential Frankfurt School Reader*, editors Andrew Arato and Eike Gebhardt, 270–99. London: Continuum, 2002.

———. "Freudian Theory and the Pattern of Fascist Propaganda." In *The Essential Frankfurt School Reader*, edited by Andrew Arato and Eirke Gebhardt, 118–37. New York: Continuum, 2002.

———. *Minima Moralia: Reflections on a Damaged Life*. Translated by E. F. N. Jephcott. London: Verso, 2005.

———. *Current of Music*. Edited by Robert Hullot-Kentor. New York: Polity Press, 2009.

Adorno, Theodor, W. and Hellmut Becker. "Education for Maturity and Responsibility." *History of the Human Sciences* 12, no. 1 (1999): 22–34.

Adorno, Theodor, W., Else Frenkel-Brunswik, Daniel J. Levinson, and Nevitt R. Sanford. "Introduction." In *The Authoritarian Personality: Abridged Edition*, edited by Theodor W. Adorno, Else Frenkel-Brunswik, Daniel J. Levinson, and R. Nevitt Sanford, 1–30. New York: Norton, 1950.

Agamben, Giorgio. *The Signature of All Things: On Method*. Translated by Luca D'Isanto and Kevin Attell. New York: Zone Books, 2009.

Anti-Defamation League. "Audit of Anti-Semitic Incidents: Year in Review 2017." Accessed November 6, 2018. https://www.adl.org/media/11174/download.

Azrael, Deborah, Lisa Hepburn, David Hemenway, and Matthew Miller. "The Stock and Flow of U.S. Firearms: Results from the 2105 National Firearms Survey." *Russell Sage Foundation Journal of the Social Sciences* 3, no. 5 (2017): 38–57.

Beinart, Peter. "What Trump Means When He Calls Gary Cohn a 'Globalist,'" *The Atlantic*, March 9, 2018. https://www.theatlantic.com/politics/archive/2018/03/trump-globalist-cohn/555269/.

Benjamin, Walter. *Gesammelte Schriften, Volume 3*. Edited by Rolf Tiedemann and Herman Schweppenhäuser. Frankfurt am Main, Germany: Suhrkamp Verlag, 1991.

———. *Gesammelte Schriften, Volume 4, Part 1*. Edited by Tillman Rexroth. Frankfurt am Main, Germany: Suhrkamp Verlag, 1991.

———. *Gesammelte Briefe, Volume 1*. Edited by Christoph Gödde and Henri Lonitz. Frankfurt am Main, Germany: Suhrkamp Verlag, 1995.

———. *The Arcades Project*. Edited by Howard Eiland and Kevin McLaughlin. Cambridge, MA: Harvard University Press, 1999.

———. *Selected Writings: Volume 4, 1938–1940*. Edited by Howard Eiland and Michael W. Jennings. Cambridge, MA: Belknap Press, 2003.

———. *Selected Writings, Volume 1, 1913–1926*. Edited by Marcus Bullock and Michael W. Jennings. Cambridge, MA: Belknap Press, 2004.

———. *Selected Writings, Volume 2, Part 1, 1927–1930*. Edited by Michael W. Jennings, Howard Eiland, and Gary Smith. Cambridge, MA: Belknap Press, 2005.

———. *Selected Writings, Volume 2, Part 2, 1931–1934*. Edited by Michael W. Jennings, Howard Eiland, and Gary Smith. Cambridge, MA: Belknap Press, 2005.

———. *Selected Writings, Volume 3, 1935–1938*. Edited by Howard Eiland and Michael W. Jennings. Cambridge, MA: Belknap Press, 2006.

———. *The Origin of German Tragic Drama*. Translated by John Osborne. London: Verso, 2009.

———. *Early Writings (1910–1917)*. Edited by Howard Eiland. Cambridge, MA: Belknap Press, 2011.

———. *The Correspondence of Walter Benjamin, 1910–1940*. Edited by Gershom Scholem and Theodor W. Adorno. Translated by Manfred R. Jacobson and Evelyn M. Jacobson. Chicago: University of Chicago Press, 2012.

———. "The Flâneur's Return." In *Walking in Berlin: A Flâneur in the Capital* by Franz Hessel, xiii–xix. Translated by Adrian Nathan West. Cambridge, MA: MIT Press, 2017.

Biesta, Gert J. J. *The Beautiful Risk of Teaching*. New York: Routledge, 2014.

———. *The Rediscovery of Teaching*. New York: Routledge, 2017.

Bingham, Charles and Alexander Sidorkin, eds. *No Education without Relation*. New York: Peter Lang, 2004.

Blackburn, Gilmer W. *Education in the Third Reich: A Study of Race and History in Nazi Textbooks*. Albany: State University of New York, 1985.

Bloch, Ernst. "Walter Benjamin in the Internment Camp." In *On Walter Benjamin: Critical Essays and Recollections*, edited by Gary Smith. Cambridge, MA: MIT Press, 1988.

Buck-Morss, Susan. *The Dialectics of Seeing: Walter Benjamin and the Arcades Project*. London: Verso, 1991.

Burk, Karin. *Kindertheater als Möglichkeitsraum: Untersuchungen zu Walter Benjamins "Programm eines proletarischen Kindertheaters."* Bielefeld, Germany: transcript Verlag, 2015.

Carlin, Matthew. "In the Blink of an Eye: The Augenblick of Sudden Change and Transformative Learning in Lukács and Benjamin." *Culture, Theory, and Critique* 51, no. 3 (2010): 239–56.

Carr, David, and Jan Steutel, eds. *Virtue Ethics and Moral Education*. London: Routledge, 2005.

Charles, Matthew. "Towards a Critique of Educative Violence: Walter Benjamin and 'Second Education.'" *Pedagogy, Culture, and Society* 24, no. 4 (2016): 525–36.

———. "Pedagogy as 'Cryptic Politics': Benjamin, Nietzsche, and the End of Education." *boundary 2* 41, no. 3 (2018): 35–62.

Cepeda, Sandra L., Dean McKay, and Sophie Schneider, et al. "Politically-Focused Intrusive Thoughts and Associated Ritualistic Behaviors in a Community Sample." *Journal of Anxiety Disorders*, date of access March, 31, 2018.

Cho, K. Daniel. "Adorno on Education or, Can Critical Self-Reflection Prevent the Next Auschwitz?" *Historical Materialism*, 17 (2009): 74–97.

Cohen, Margaret. "Benjamin's Phantasmagoria: The *Arcades Project*." In *The Cambridge Companion to Walter Benjamin*, edited by David S. Ferris. Cambridge, UK: Cambridge University Press, 2004.

Connolly, William E. *Aspirational Fascism: The Struggle for Multifaceted Democracy Under Trumpism*. Minneapolis: University of Minnesota Press, 2017.

Dean, Jodi. *Democracy and Other Neoliberal Fantasies: Communicative Capitalism and Left Politics*. Durham: Duke University Press, 2009.

"Disguised Fascism Seen as a Menace; Prof. Luccock Warns That It Will Bear the Misleading Label 'Americanism.'" *New York Times*, September 12, 1938: 15.

Doderer, Klaus. "Walter Benjamin and Children's Literature." In *"With the Sharpened Axe of Reason": Approaches to Walter Benjamin*, edited by Gerhard Fisher, 169–76. Oxford: Berg, 1996.

Dolbear, Sam, Esther Leslie, and Sebastian Truskolaski. "Introduction." In *The Storyteller: Short Stories*, edited by Sam Dolbear, Esther Leslie, and Sebastian Truskolaski, xi–xxxii. London: Verso, 2016.

Dolbear, Sam, and Hannah Proctor. "'Cracking Open the Natural Teleology': Walter Benjamin, Charles Fourier and the Figure of the Child." *Pedagogy, Culture and Society* 24, no. 4 (2016): 495–503.

Dozono, Tadashi. "The Fascist Seduction of Narrative: Walter Benjamin's Historical Materialism Beyond Counter-Narrative." *Studies in Philosophy and Education*, 37 (2018): 513–27.

Duttlinger, Carolin. "Between Contemplation and Distraction: Configurations of Attention in Walter Benjamin." *German Studies Review* 30, no. 1 (2007): 33–54.

Düttmann, Alexander Garcia. "Tradition and Destruction: Walter Benjamin's Politics of Language." In *Walter Benjamin's Philosophy: Destruction and Experience*, edited by Andrew Benjamin and Peter Osborne, 32–58. London: Routledge, 1994.

Eco, Umberto. "Ur-Fascism." *The New York Review of Books*, June 22, 1995. https://www.nybooks.com/articles/1995/06/22/ur-fascism/.

Eiland, Howard. "Reception in Distraction." *boundary 2* 30, no. 1 (2002): 51–66.

———. "Translator's Forward." In Walter Benjamin, *Berlin Childhood around 1900*, vii–xvi. Cambridge, MA: Belknap Press, 2006.

———. "Education as Awakening." *boundary 2* 45, no. 2 (2018): 203–19.

Fenves, Peter. *The Messianic Reduction: Walter Benjamin and the Shape of Time*. Stanford, CA: Stanford University Press, 2011.

Ferber, Ilit. *Philosophy and Melancholy: Benjamin's Early Reflections on Theater and Language*. Stanford, CA: Stanford University Press, 2013.

Fischer, Gerhard. "Benjamin's Utopia of Education as *Theatrum Mundi et Vitae*: On the *Programme of a Proletarian Children's Theatre*." In *'With the Sharpened Axe of Reason': Approaches to Walter Benjamin*, edited by Gerhard Fischer, 201–18. Oxford: Berg, 1996.

Florida, Richard. "How America's Metro Areas Voted." *CityLab*, November 29, 2016. https://www.citylab.com/equity/2016/11/how-americas-metro-areas-voted/508355/.

Flusser, Vilém. *Toward a Philosophy of Photography*. Translated by Anthony Mathews. London: Reaktion Books, 2000.

Ford, Derek R., and Tyson E. Lewis. "On the Freedom to be Opaque Monsters: Communist Pedagogy, Aesthetics, and the Sublime." *Cultural Politics*, 14, no. 1 (2018): 95–108.

Frazel, Sean. "Toward an Anti-Monumental Literary-Critical Style: Notes on Walter Benjamin and Jean Paul." *Telos*, 159 (2012): 35–38.
Friedlander, Eli. "Farben und Laute in der *Berliner Kindheit um neunzehnhundert*." In *Klang und Musik bei Walter Benjamin*, edited by Tobias Robert Klein, 55–68. Paderborn, Germany: Wilhelm Fink Verlag, 2013.
Fromm, Eric. *Escape from Freedom*. New York: Henry Holt Company, 1994.
Gelley, Alexander. *Benjamin's Passages: Dreaming, Awakening*. New York: Fordham University Press, 2014.
Gilloch, Graeme. *Myth and Metropolis: Walter Benjamin and the City*. Cambridge, UK: Polity Press, 1996.
———. *Walter Benjamin: Critical Constellations*. New York: Polity Press, 2002.
Giroux, Henry. "Education After Abu Ghraib: Revisiting Adorno's Politics of Education." *Cultural Studies* 18, no. 6 (2004): 779–815.
Gordon, Peter E. "The Authoritarian Personality Revisited: Reading Adorno in the Age of Trump." *boundary 2* 44, no. 2 (2017): 31–56.
Griffin, Roger. *The Nature of Fascism*. London: Routledge, 1994.
Grossberg, Lawrence. *Under the Cover of Chaos: Trump and the Battle for the American Right*. London: Pluto Press, 2018.
Hanssen, Beatrice. *Walter Benjamin's Other History: Of Stones, Animals, Human Beings, and Angels*. Berkeley: University of California Press, 1998.
Hansen, Miriam Bratu. "Room-for-Play: Benjamin's Gamble with Cinema." *October* 109 (Summer 2004): 3–45.
———. *Cinema and Experience: Siegfried Kracauer, Walter Benjamin, and Theodor W. Adorno*. Berkley: University of California Press, 2012.
Haro, Lia, and Coles, Romand. "Eleven Theses on Neo-Fascism and the Fight to Defeat It." *Theory and Event* 20, no. 1 (2017): 100–12.
Haverkampf, Hans-Erhard. *Benjamin in Frankfurt: Die zentralen Jahre 1923–1932*. Frankfurt: Societäts-Verlag, 2016.
Heidegger, Martin. *Being and Time*. Translated by John Macquarrie and Edward Robinson. New York: Harper Perennial, 2008.
Heins, Volker. "Saying Things that Hurt: Adorno as Educator." *Thesis Eleven* 101, no. 1 (2012): 68–82.
Heller-Roazen, Daniel. *Dark Tongues: The Art of Rogues and Riddlers*. New York: Zone Books, 2013.
Hewitt, Andrew. *Fascist Modernism: Aesthetics, Politics, and the Avant-Garde*. Stanford, CA: Stanford University Press, 1993.
Hitler, Adolf. *Mein Kampf*. Translated by Dorothy Thompson. New York: Reynal and Hitchcock, 1940.
Honneth, Axel. *Pathologies of Reason: On the Legacy of Critical Theory*, translated by James Ingram. New York: Columbia University Press, 2009.
Horkheimer, Max, and Theodor W. Adorno. *Dialectic of Enlightenment: Philosophical Fragments*. Edited by Gunzelin Schmid Noerr, translated by Edmund Jephcott. Stanford, CA: Stanford University Press, 2002.

Irving, David. "Revelations from Goebbels' Diary: Bringing to Light Secrets of Hitler's Propaganda Minister." *The Journal of Historical Review* 15, no. 1 (1995): 2–17.

Jameson, Fredric. *Postmodernism or, The Cultural Logic of Late Capitalism*. Durham, NC: Duke University Press, 1992.

———. *Representing* Capital: *A Reading of Volume One*. London: Verso, 2011.

Kang, Jaeho. *Walter Benjamin and the Media: The Spectacle of Modernity*. Cambridge, UK: Polity Press, 2014.

Khatib, Sami. "Barbaric Salvage: Benjamin and the Dialectic of Destruction." *Parallax* 24, vol. 2 (2018): 135–58.

Kishik, David. *The Manhattan Project: A Theory of a City*. Stanford, CA: Stanford University Press, 2015.

Kornmeier, Uta. "Akustisches in der *Berliner Kindheit um neunzehnhundert*." In *Klang und Musik bei Walter Benjamin*, edited by Tobias Robert Klein, 47–54. Paderborn, Germany: Wilhelm Fink Verlag, 2013.

Krementz, Jill. *The Writer's Desk*. New York: Random House, 1996.

Lathey, Gillian. "Enlightening City Childhoods: Walter Benjamin's Berlin and Erich Kästner's Dresden." *Pedagogy, Culture and Society* 24, no. 4 (2016): 485–93.

Lehmann, Hans-Thies. "An Interrupted Performance: On Walter Benjamin's Idea of Children's Theatre." In *"With the Sharpened Axe of Reason": Approaches to Walter Benjamin*, edited by Gerhard Fischer, 179–200. Oxford: Berg, 1996.

Leslie, Esther. "Colonial and Communist Pedagogy." *Pedagogy, Culture and Society* 24, no. 4 (2016): 517–24.

———. "Playspaces of Anthropological Materialist Pedagogy: Film, Radio, Toys." *boundary 2* vol. 45, no. 2 (2018): 139–56.

Lewis, Tyson E. *On Studying: Giorgio Agamben and Educational Potentiality*. New York: Routledge, 2013.

———. *Inoperative Learning: A Radical Rethinking of Educational Potentialities*. New York: Routledge, 2017.

Lindner, Burckhardt. "Das Kunstwerk im Zeitalter seiner technischen Reproduzierbarkeit." In *Benjamin-Handbuch: Leben-Werk-Wirkung*, edited by Burckhardt Lindner, 229–50. Stuttgart: J. B. Metzler Verlag, 2006.

Lowenthal, Leo, and Norbert Guterman, *Prophets of Deceit: A Study of the Techniques of the American Agitator*. New York: Harper and Brothers, 1949.

Mariotti, Shannon. *Adorno and Democracy: The American Years*. Lexington: University of Kentucky Press, 2016.

Martel, James. "A Divine Pedagogy? Benjamin's 'Educative Power' and the Subversion of Myth and Authority." *boundary 2* 45, no. 2 (2018): 171–86.

Marx, Karl. *Capital, Volume 1*. Translated by Ben Fowkes. London: Penguin Books, 1990.

Marx, Ursula, Gudrun Schwarz, Michael Schwarz, and Erdmut Wizisla, eds. *Walter Benjamin's Archive: Images, Texts, Signs.* London: Verso, 2015.
Masschelein Jan, and Maarten Simons. "School as Architecture for New Comers and Strangers: The Perfect School as Public School?" *Teachers College Record*, 112 (2010): 535–55.
Matsuda, Mari J., Charles R. Lawrence III, Richard Delgado, and Kimberle Crenshaw. *Words That Wound: Critical Race Theory, Assaultive Speech, and the First Amendment.* Boulder, CO: Westview Press, 1993.
McLean, Eden K. *Mussolini's Children: Race and Elementary Education in Fascist Italy.* Lincoln: University of Nebraska Press, 2018.
McLuhan, Marshall. *Understanding Media.* New York: McGraw-Hill, 1964.
Mehlman, Jeffery. *Walter Benjamin for Children: An Essay on His Radio Years.* Chicago: University of Chicago Press, 1993.
Menninghaus, Winfried. *Schwellenkunde: Walter Benjamin's Passage des Mythos.* Frankfurt am Main: Surhkamp Verlag, 1986.
Mitchell, W. J. T. *Picture Theory: Essays on Verbal and Visual Representation.* Chicago: University of Chicago Press, 1995.
Moran, Brendan. "Kafkan Study." *boundary 2* 45, no. 2 (2018): 87–110.
Neumann, Franz. *Behemoth: The Structure and Practice of National Socialism, 1933–1944.* Chicago: Ivan R. Dee, 2009.
Newman, Jane O. *Benjamin's Library: Modernity, Nation, and the Baroque.* Ithaca, NY: Cornell University Press, 2011.
North, Paul. *The Problem of Distraction.* Stanford, CA: Stanford University Press, 2011.
———. *The Yield: Kafka's Atheological Reformation.* Stanford, CA: University of Stanford Press, 2015.
Rauschning, Hermann. *The Voice of Destruction.* New York: G. P. Putnam's Sons, 1940.
Richter, Gerhard. *Inheriting Walter Benjamin.* London: Bloomsbury, 2016.
Rochlitz, Rainer. *The Disenchantment of Art: The Philosophy of Walter Benjamin.* Translated by Jane Marie Todd. New York: Guilford, 1996.
Rosenthal, Lecia. "*Walter Benjamin on the Radio:* An Introduction." In *Radio Benjamin*, edited by Lecia Rosenthal, ix–xxix. London: Verso, 2014.
Ross, Allison. *Walter Benjamin's Concept of the Image* (New York: Routledge, 2015).
Rothe, Katja. "Die Schule des Entzugs. Walter Benjamins Radio-Kasper." *Sinnhaft. Strategien des Entzugs* 22, no. 1 (2009): 74–89.
Rutsky, R. L. "Walter Benjamin and the Dispersion of Cinema," *Symplokē* 15, no. 1–2 (2007): 8–23.
Salzani, Carlo. "Experience and Play: Walter Benjamin and the Prelapsarian Child." In *Walter Benjamin and the Architecture of Modernity*, edited by Andrew Benjamin and Charles Rice, 175–200. Melbourne, AU: re.press, 2009.

Sandlin, Jennifer A., Brian B. Schultz, and Jack Burdick, Jack, eds. *Handbook of Public Pedagogy: Education and Learning Beyond Schooling*. New York: Routledge, 2009.
Sanford, R. Nevitt. "Contrasting Ideologies of Two College Men." In *The Authoritarian Personality: Abridged Edition*, edited by Theodor W. Adorno, Else Frenkel-Brunswik, Daniel J. Levinson, and R. Nevitt Sanford, 31–56. New York: Norton, 1950.
Schiavoni, Giulio. "Zum Kinde: 'Programm eines proletarischen Kindertheaters' / 'Eine kommunistische Pädagogik' / 'Kinderbücher.'" In *Benjamin-Handbuch: Leben – Werk – Wirkung*, edited by Burkhardt Lindner, 373–85. Stuttgart, Weimar: J. B. Metzler Verlag, 2006.
Schiller-Lerg, Sabine. "Walter Benjamin, Radio Journalist: Theory and Practice of Weimar Radio." *Journal of Communication Inquiry* 13, no. 1 (1989): 43–50.
Schwarz, Birgit. *Hitlers Museum: Die Fotoalben Gemäldegalerie Linz:* Dokumente zum 'Führermuseum.' Vienna: Böhlau Verlag, 2004.
Sünker, Heinz, and Hans-Uwe Otto, eds. *Education and Fascism: Political Identity and Social Education in Nazi Germany*. London: Falmer Press, 1997.
Tribunella, Eric L. "Benjamin, Benson, and the Child's Gaze: Childhood Desire and Pleasure in the David Blaize Books." *Pedagogy, Culture and Society* 24, no. 4 (2016): 505–15.
Vlieghe, Joris, Maarten Simons, and Jan Masschelein. "The Educational Meaning of Communal Laughter: On the Experience of Corporeal Democracy." *Educational Theory* 60, no. 6 (2010): 719–34.
Ward, Clarissa. "Anti-Semitism Never Disappeared in Europe: It's Alive and Kicking." Accessed December 2, 2018. https://www.cnn.com/2018/11/27/europe/anti-semitism-analysis-ward-intl/index.html.
Weber, Samuel. *Benjamin's -abilities*. Cambridge, MA: Harvard University Press, 2008.
Wizisla, Erdmut. "Preface." In *Walter Benjamin's Archive: Images, Texts, Signs*, edited by Ursula Marx, Gudrun Schwarz, Michael Schwarz, and Erdmut Wizisla, 1–6. London: Verso, 2015.
———. *Benjamin and Brecht: The Story of a Friendship*. London: Verso, 2016.
Wohlfarth, Irving. "Resentment Begins at Home: Nietzsche, Benjamin, and the University." In *On Walter Benjamin: Critical Essays and Recollections*, edited by Gary Smith, 224–59. Cambridge, MA: MIT Press, 1988.
Wolin, Richard. *Walter Benjamin: An Aesthetic of Redemption*. Los Angeles: University of California Press, 1994.
Zipes, Jack. "Building a Children's Theater: 2 Documents: Introduction." *Performance*, 1 (1973): 12–32.
———. "Walter Benjamin, Children's Literature, and the Children's Public Sphere: An Introduction to New Trends in West and East Germany." *The Germanic Review: Literature, Culture, Theory* 63, no. 1 (1988): 2–5.

———. "Political Children's Theater in the Age of Globalization." *Theater* 33, no. 2 (2003): 3–25.

Zipory, Oded. "One Day Is a Whole World: On the Role of the Present in Education between Plan and Play." In *Philosophy of Education Society Yearbook, 2016*, edited by Natasha Levinson, 334–43. Urbana-Champaign, IL: University of Illinois Press, 2016.

Index

Absentminded examiner, 42, 44–45, 48, 49, 60–62, 103, 136–137, 160–161, 174, 209
   and criticality, 170
   See also distraction
Adorno, Theodor
   and mimesis, 177
   on anti–fascist education, 12–14
   on fascist subjectivity, 8–17
   on film, 158–159
   on laughter, 171–173
   on liberal ego, 21
   on listening, 64
   on nostalgia, 59
   on personality types, 23–24
   on radio, 86–91
   on riddles, 190–191
Agamben, Giorgio, 183
Allegory
   and collecting, 120–123
   and the commodity, 188–189
   as gaze, 124
   as touch, 124, 131
Arcades, 121, 148
Art of straying, 133
   and cinema, 155, 163, 177
   as wandering a city, 137, 142, 144, 149
   as word games/riddles, 194

Attention, 19, 23, 33, 42–44, 71, 103, 115, 134, 137–139, 145, 172, 203
   and fascism, 57, 199
   See also distraction
Aura, 74–75
   and examination value, 128
   and radio, 75, 90
   negative aura, 78
   versus trace, 117, 119–120
Awakening, 206–207
   and sound, 64, 68, 86
   and violence, 50–53
   as learning, 32–37
   as swelling/wave, 34, 207
   as threshold act, 25

Barbarism, 13, 22, 32, 49, 173, 177–178
Berlin, 63, 72, 75, 77–82, 84, 140–141, 201
Buck-Morss, Susan, 32, 189–190, 192, 197–198

Catastrophe, 59, 76–78, 81, 83, 89, 121
Caygill, Howard, 139
Chaplin, Charlie, 155, 163, 165–167, 169, 172, 177–178

Charles, Matthew, 46
Coldness, 9, 10–14, 16–18,
  20–25, 53, 57, 87, 89, 90,
  92, 107–108, 122, 130–131,
  152–153, 169, 170, 172–173,
  205, 209. *See also* hardness;
  manipulativeness; protofascist
  personality
Collectivizability, 26, 36, 96,
  104–109
Color, 65–73, 104, 204
Comedy, 46, 48, 61, 110, 155–157,
  165, 170, 172, 176–177
Commodity, 83–85, 89, 121–124,
  136, 150, 155, 159–160,
  181–184, 189–190, 197, 205.
  See also fetishism
Communicative capitalism, 180, 197,
  199
Connolly, William E., 14–16, 55–56,
  61, 197
Constellation, 19, 150, 187–190,
  194
  as curriculum, 19–21, 26–27, 31,
  44, 122, 191, 207–209
Crary, Jonathan, 134

Damrosch, Walter, 75, 88, 90, 92
(De)formation, 31, 45, 50, 139, 140,
  142, 154
  as grotesque, 61, 106
Democracy, 12, 14, 92, 169, 181,
  196–197, 199
  Liberal, 8
Dialectical images, 17, 20, 91, 189
  as thought image, 164
  See also thought sound
Discipline, 94–95, 97–101
Distraction, 18–19, 21–23, 27, 33,
  42–44, 57, 108, 116, 203–204
  and cinema, 155, 157–158, 160,
  172
  and riddles, 191
  and the city, 133–140, 142–145,
  147, 149–150
  as absentmindedness, 27, 31–32, 42
  versus diversion, 18, 42–43,
  56–57, 125, 133, 135–136, 139
  See also attention; absentminded
  examiner

Eiland, Howard, 32, 42–43, 113

Fairy tales, 32, 50, 52–55, 62, 74, 76
Fantasy, 69, 104
  and color, 67–68, 104
Fascism, 4–9, 11–16, 41, 55–56, 58,
  86–87, 89, 106–109, 131–132,
  149–153, 159–160, 171,
  173–174, 177, 206
  neofascism, 20–26, 55, 59, 92,
  131, 180, 197–199
  protofascistic personality type, 9,
  131
Fate, 115, 119–120, 124–125,
  128–129
Fenves, Peter, 207
Fetishism, 13, 16, 49, 60, 78, 88–90,
  92, 101, 124–125, 131, 136,
  144, 173, 180, 183–184, 188,
  198–199, 204
Flaneur, 24
  and the collective, 152–153
  and the gaze, 64, 117, 147
  as detective, 147
Friedlander, Eli, 68
Fromm, Eric, 7–8
Fuchs, Eduard, 117, 125–126

Gaze, 116–118, 121, 124, 127–128,
  130
  as grasping, 128
  in the city, 147
  See also flaneur

Gesture, 19, 45–46, 49, 53–54,
    75, 95, 100–101, 108–110,
    115–116, 177
  and Chaplin, 167
Gilloch, Graeme, 113, 137
Goeddels, Joseph, 205

Habit, 21–22, 44, 48, 67, 116, 124,
    137–139, 143, 145, 147–148,
    153, 167, 191–192
  and fascism, 17
Hansen, Miriam Bratu, 18, 107,
    156, 162
Hardness, 9–14, 16–18, 20–26, 32,
    53, 57, 67, 87, 88–90, 92, 97,
    107–108, 117, 122, 130–131,
    151, 153, 169–170, 172–173,
    178, 205, 209. See also coldness;
    manipulativeness; protofascist
    personality
Hauser, Kasper, 80, 82
Hearing, 64, 67–68, 70, 78, 88
  and commodity listening, 89–90
Heller–Roazen, Daniel, 180–181,
    185, 192, 198
History, 20, 27, 41, 46, 58–59,
    60–61, 63, 70, 76–79, 81, 92,
    93, 119, 121, 123, 125–127,
    130–131, 152, 185, 205, 209
  and radio, 71–72
  as catastrophe, 89
  as minor history, 80
Historicizability, 36
Hitler, Adolf, 6, 10, 14, 130, 149,
    177
Hoffmann, E.T.A., 78–79
Horkheimer, Max, 58, 60, 87,
    171–173, 177

Imagination, 21, 32, 44–45, 58,
    65–69, 72, 92, 104, 158,
    195–196. See also grotesque

Inheritance, 22, 32, 40–42, 45, 50,
    55, 58–61, 72, 74, 91
Inlay, 81–84, 89, 152
Innervation, 12, 18–19, 21, 23,
    25, 34, 98–99, 101–102, 104,
    106, 108–109, 137–138, 149,
    155–156, 162, 164, 167, 170,
    174, 176, 206, 209
Irrelevance, 78–79

Jameson, Fredric, 91, 181–182, 189

Kafka, Franz, 11, 25, 42, 46, 95,
    97–98, 100, 114
Kant, Immanuel, 12–13, 69,
    138–139
Knowability, 31, 34–39, 44, 46,
    48–49, 53, 56, 58, 60, 63, 68,
    70, 72, 114–115, 126–127,
    131, 137, 140, 147–148, 151,
    166–167, 171, 181, 184, 191,
    195, 205–206, 208
Kornmeier, Uta, 69
Kraus, Karl, 54

Laughter, 61, 155–156, 167–175,
    177
  in relation to breath and aura,
    175–176
  wrong laughter, 171–173, 177
Learning, 11, 20, 21, 25, 31–41,
    44–48, 52, 54–55, 58, 60, 64,
    66–67, 73, 79, 81, 90, 103–
    105, 114–116, 119, 125, 128,
    139, 144–147, 151, 153, 155,
    157, 181, 198, 206–209
  and cinema, 158, 160, 166
  and poverty, 47–48
  and riddles, 192–193
  and teaching, 37, 46
  in the city, 144–147, 151, 153,
    158, 160, 166, 192–193

Learning *(continued)*
  versus studying, 114–115
  See also awakening and swelling
Lacis, Asja, 93, 148
Lowenthal, Leo, 8, 56, 58, 61–62

Manipulativeness, 9–14, 16–17, 20–22, 24, 58, 131, 151, 209. *See also* coldness; hardness; protofascist personality
Marx, Karl, 98, 136, 181–185, 188–189, 191, 196–197
Masschelein, Jan, 168–169
Memory, 69–70, 72, 85–86, 120, 204–205
Mimesis, 17, 19, 23–24, 95–97, 99–102, 106–107, 155, 177
  and creativity, 100–102
Moscow, 81, 84, 98, 144, 147

Naples, 144, 148
Nazism, 1, 5–7, 55, 130–131, 149, 201–202, 204–205
  and cities, 149
  and collecting, 130–131
  and education, 58
  See also fascism; Goeddels; Hitler
Neumann, Franz, 5–7
Newman, Jane O., 26, 55, 94
Noncommunicability, 25, 186, 188, 191, 194–197
North, Paul, 46–47, 78, 116, 134, 139

Origin, 37–40, 47, 49, 59–60, 95, 124, 137, 183, 197, 209

Panlingenesis, 58–59
Paris, 60, 76, 82, 95, 113, 121, 136, 148, 150. *See also* arcades
Photography studio, 95–96, 103

Play, 134, 150, 156–157, 162–164, 172, 178, 188, 193, 195–196, 201–202, 204
Politeness, 48–49, 53
Potentiality, 4–5, 13, 17–27, 31, 34–36, 38, 40, 42–47, 49–51, 54, 57–58, 60, 63–64, 72–73, 77–79, 81–84, 92, 96, 102, 104, 108, 114, 130, 131, 135, 142–144, 147, 149, 152–153, 159, 164, 165, 167, 169–174, 176, 178–179, 185–186, 191, 193–196, 198, 204, 206–209
Protofascist personality, 5, 9, 11–12, 16, 17, 107–108, 131. *See also* coldness; hardness; manipulativeness

Richter, Gerhard, 32
Ross, Alison, 17

Salzani, Carlo, 83
Schiller-Lerg, Sabine, 63
"Sleeping Beauty," 50–52, 60, 68
Simons, Maarten, 168–169
Storytelling, 41, 73–75, 80, 85–86, 90
Studying, 20–21, 25, 38, 113–117, 119, 122, 125, 128–129, 131–133, 148–151, 153, 158, 161, 165, 169, 173, 178–179, 181, 187, 192, 198, 206, 208–209
  versus learning, 113–114, 125
Swelling, 4, 19–20, 23–25, 27, 31, 33–41, 43–47, 51–56, 60–61, 62, 64, 69–73, 77, 82, 88, 91, 93–95, 98–99, 101, 103–108, 114, 119, 122–123, 125–127, 130, 134, 138–140, 142–144, 148–149, 151–155, 161, 163–164, 166–170, 172, 174–176, 178–179, 182, 184,

186–187, 191, 194–195, 199, 204, 205–209
and allegory, 122
and dreaming, 34
as laughter, 169–170
and learning and teaching, 37–41
and riddles, 184, 186–187, 191, 194–195, 199
and sound, 69–72
and the city, 148, 151
in attention and distraction, 43–46

Teaching, 11, 20–21, 25, 31–32, 36–42, 44–49, 51–53, 55–56, 58–60, 64, 73, 105, 114–116, 130, 139, 151, 153, 184, 188, 206, 208–209
and poverty, 49
as agitational, 56, 58–60
Thought image, 35, 64, 68, 127, 152, 165, 193–194. *See also* thought sound
Thought sound, 64, 69, 72–73, 78, 86, 93, 152, 205. *See also* thought image
Touch, 64, 95, 97, 99–100, 106, 115–120, 124–126, 128–131, 141, 147, 149, 159, 164, 175, 207–208
and allegory, 131
versus possession, 118
See also mimesis

Toys, 55, 60, 83–86, 177, 201–206
Trace/traceability, 25, 36, 60–61, 84, 115, 117–120, 125–131, 174, 190, 203, 209
versus aura, 117
Transmissibility, 25, 31–32, 36–38, 40, 42, 47, 53, 58, 60–61, 70, 72, 105, 184, 188, 206, 208
Trauerspiel, 26, 50, 93–94, 179
Trump, Donald, 1, 4, 5, 14–15, 22, 55–62, 131, 149–150, 197–199. *See also* neofascism; teaching as agitational

Van Zuylen, Marina, 57, 138
Violence, 50, 52–55, 57–59, 61–62, 130, 170–173, 205, 208
divine, 53–55
mythic, 53, 130, 172, 205, 208
Vlieghe, Joris, 168–169

Yielding, 38, 46–49, 57, 60, 142, 147, 152, 164, 170, 175, 187, 203
Youth, 31, 35–36, 54–55, 63, 71–72, 80, 93, 140, 144, 153, 155, 193, 204, 206–207, 209
German Youth Movement, 31, 55
Radio Frankfurt Youth Hour, 63

Zipes, Jack, 26, 109

www.ingramcontent.com/pod-product-compliance
Lightning Source LLC
Chambersburg PA
CBHW030538230426
43665CB00010B/940